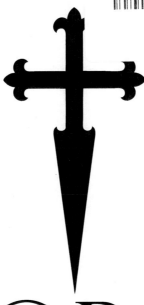

WORDS
OF
PASSAGE
HANS BURGMAN

Published by

MELROSE BOOKS

An Imprint of Melrose Press Limited
St Thomas Place, Ely
Cambridgeshire
CB7 4GG, UK
www.melrosebooks.com

FIRST EDITION

Cover designed by Jeremy Kay

ISBN 978 1 907040 46 7

Printed and bound in Great Britain by:
CPI Antony Rowe. Chippenham, Wiltshire

MIX
Paper from
responsible sources
FSC
www.fsc.org   FSC® C013604

ALSO BY THE AUTHOR

Losgelopen woorden

Losgelopen woorden: Voetnoten bij een kleine dood: een voetreis naar Santiago de Compostela

Paperback: 284 pages. Size: 149x226 mm. Language: Dutch. Publisher: Gooi & Sticht (2000)
ISBN-10: 9030409932 ISBN-13: 978-9030409939

CONTENTS

February

THE FIRST MONTH

FEBRUARY

2ND FEBRUARY.

The shivers I feel are not due to the cold weather. They are the shivers of one who knows that he is going to do an impossible thing. I am starting on a 6,000-kilometre walk. I want to walk to the shrine of St. James at Compostela, there and back. And not just from A to B to C: I plan to meander across Europe for nine months, visiting abnormal places I always wanted to see like Andorra and Lichtenstein, touching far away waters, crossing the Pyrenees twice, and the Alps lengthwise, spending four seasons on the road, and disregarding everybody's advice not to do it for God's sake, for I have a prosthesis in my right hip. I am not doing this rashly, for I had a 50-day trial walk in East Africa last year; and moreover, I have walked from Holland to Compostela before, albeit when I was 27 years younger. My starting point this morning is the same as the one 27 years ago: the porch of St. John's Church in the small town of Roosendaal in the south of Holland.

The farewell now is as simple as it was then: a couple of photographs taken, a few handshakes given to friends staying behind. After a dozen steps I calm down but deep inside my throat I have again the heavy feeling that what I am going to do is utterly nonsensical. Does it really help to have done it before? Things have changed beyond recognition. Already as I leave the town I lose my way on account of a new viaduct. Frozen rain is coming down; the slippery road makes the going difficult, for I am top-heavy with my rucksack.

This walk will give me plenty of time to reflect. On what? On matters of philosophy, my own profession. That means that I

1

will probably reflect on everything. Once you reflect deeply on anything at all, you will be thinking about everything in less than no time.

Another thing: we are living in a world where the cards of destiny are being shuffled again. I want to try to better understand what kind of game is being played. I want to look under the table as well to see if any cards have been dropped. I am looking forward to having 'deep thoughts'.

This morning deep thoughts are not coming on demand; the only things passing through my mind at this early stage are old stories. So, let me think about stories. The initial stage of everything, be it religion, philosophy, science, love, a human being, is a story. A memorable story is more than just a story. It is often a tentative answer to a vaguely felt question. An old story often proves to be the egg of future reality, the way a child is the parent of the future person. Woe betide those that belittle an ancient tale – or a young child. Stories and children have their own demands and their own restraints: they have to be taken seriously and their parts have to fit their totality.

I pass two allied war cemeteries, reminders of the bitter battles fought on the southern border of Holland in September 1944 for the sake of control over Antwerp harbour. Whenever I pass here I say a silent prayer for the fallen young soldiers. There is hardly a living soul around. A cyclist overtakes me, accompanied by his big galloping dog; the dog is scared of me, refuses to pass me by.

On entering the outskirts of the town of Bergen op Zoom I lose my way again. I wander on till I reach the banks of the Oosterscheldt estuary. I want to touch the North Sea waters; I can even walk on them as they are frozen solid. The next seawater to touch will be the Mediterranean; then, ages after that, hopefully, the water of the Baltic Sea. At 5.00 in the late afternoon, my first day ends with friends at Hoogerheide. It seems so unreal. I have not yet taken enough steps to turn this dream walk into something real.

My friends' hospitality opens the door to a certain feeling of discomfort. For months to come I shall have to appeal to people's hospitality. That is fine when you are with friends. But when you have to do that with strangers it becomes a form of begging. No doubt I will get a cold shoulder now and again. What am I to do then? Somehow I will have to cope.

* * *

3ᴿᴰ FEBRUARY.

Off to Antwerp in Belgium; the crystal morning air is sharp with frost. At the army barracks the early soldiers stare at me with unfeigned curiosity. The sergeant asks in a vapour-clouded voice where I am off to. "To Spain," I hear myself reply; I feel as if I am lying. Yet it is true. My head is not yet in step with my feet. Or is it the other way around: my feet are starting a new dialogue with my head? Truly, thoughts, too, run their course.

My feet fill my head with vapour-like thoughts. It is true: I am really on the way. I have started that most delightful of religious adventures called a big pilgrimage. A medieval pilgrimage is deliciously low-brow, a combination of holidays, sports and devotion, seasoned with a sauce of unavoidable penance. Often the penance part is a bit of a laugh, for there is so much fun. Serious church renewal rarely invests in pilgrimages. The Imitation of Christ (1400 AD) teaches: "Those that often go on pilgrimage rarely become holy". The Reformation dismissed the pilgrimage as being too much of a religious funfair. Yet, surprisingly, the bishops of the Second Vatican Council found inspiration in the idea of the church being a group of pilgrims on the way. That image recalled the Israelites struggling through the desert; the Jews going up to Jerusalem every year. The image is a horizon of liberation and joy. Even now I feel that way. I feel an indefinable happiness that refuses to go away. It is like a springtime euphoria. The Canterbury Tales come to my mind; when you pronounce the lines in a Dutch way – as they probably did in Chaucer's days – they get a lovely poetic cadence:

Wan that Aprille with her showers soote

Hath persed Marches droughte to the roote

Than langen folk to goan on pilgrimage.

This journey means so much to me: it is an exploration of new spaces, not only material spaces but spiritual ones as well. It means gazing at horizons of the landscape as well as of life itself. I am going to meet people under adventurous conditions, often with a whiff of nostalgia. The child in me is getting its way.

In the little village of Putten, astride the Belgian border, I come across a small chapel with the Latin legend: "Nec temere nec timide" (neither rashly nor timidly), wise words. As a gift in return, I put all my Dutch coins in the alms box on the door. One of the minuscule coins slips through my numb fingers. In a cautious balancing act, I go down on one knee to pick it up. People watching me from a nearby window imagine that they see an old man making a slow and reverent genuflection for the roadside sanctuary; but all I am doing in fact is picking up a tiny coin.

My entry into Antwerp is an untidy ramble over viaducts, over long flights of stairs, through cold slush from town plan to town plan. It is evident that you are not any longer supposed to enter the city on foot. In the city centre my two long walking sticks elicit much mirth and snide remarks such as: "Art thou looking for snow?" or "Hast thou forgotten thy skis?" From now on, whenever I walk in a town, I compress my sticks in telescopic fashion and hold them nonchalantly under my arm.

St. James' Church at Antwerp is an ancient gathering point for pilgrims from England and Scandinavia; I get a stamp for my pilgrim's passport. I sign the pilgrims' book; the previous entry goes back to September 1995, five months ago.

* * *

4TH FEBRUARY.

I keep a rest day already, so as not to make this walk into a mad rush. I spend time in a grandiose church built in the 'thirties; it has monumental confessionals made of marble and brass, mosaics that sparkle in the dim light, and on the walls precious murals by the renowned painter Joan Colet. The sacristan sighs deeply as he tells me that not even 10 years ago the church was too small; and now you will see 30 people on a Sunday morning. Still, it is a splendid space for quiet meditation.

Some people told me that I should never even have dreamt of making this journey on foot. I happen to have an artificial hip, and according to them the vibrations of the footsteps will cause the prosthesis to rattle loose. I have trained so thoroughly, however, that this does not worry me. There is something quite different that worries me. The vibrations of a long solitary walk can rattle awake old thoughts; thoughts that you have brought under control with considerable effort, or even suppressed. This I find a more disturbing prospect. Being a priest I have had to suppress a large number of dark thoughts in years gone by. Usually this happened in the context of the church renewal in which I was involved. Sometimes that was a bitter struggle. You found yourself sitting between two fires; from the one side the modern world was shooting at your religious positions with heavy calibre artillery; and from the other side you were being targeted by the very church members you were trying to defend. The latter did not recognise your motives. If you put on "civil dress" because you did not want to look like "men that wear long habits so as to be greeted reverently in the market places, that sit down in the front seats of the synagogue and take the places of honour at table", then it was suggested that you did this because you felt ashamed of your priesthood. In the same way you studied other philosophies because of "unhealthy curiosity", you pleaded for more dialogue because of "lack of humility". If you had a problem with your priestly identity, then that was a form of disloyalty. Fellow priests, who ventured too far into the danger zone, lost their way and left the priesthood were once compared to Judas Iscarioth. If you wanted to remain within the fold you had to swallow a lot. You did that with a laconic shrug, since you knew that around you many "broken reeds" were still leaning on you, many dead fires still had glowing embers, and young people still offered themselves to be inspired by you. Some old sores have remained buried under slabs of loyalty. Is this walk going to rattle lumps of buried rancour loose? Too many bitter thoughts would spoil my journey.

A Burundian refugee family has found shelter with friends of mine. Very cautiously they try to be like Belgians; the little girl points at my long walking sticks and says: "Skiing?" My gentle African jokes make them thaw; they also give me a little whiff of homesickness for Kisumu in Kenya where I ought to be right now, among our parishioners. Do they understand why I have run away to make this pilgrimage? Probably less than I do myself.

Why indeed? A sabbatical, my friends, a sabbatical year. It is a celebration as well: I celebrate that I am able to walk properly again with my prosthesis. Add to that another factor; the itch for the impossible: to walk 6,000 kilometres, to be a stranger for nine months on end, to be alone with my thoughts, to observe, to appraise, to align, to review. And yearning for the things that lie stored up in the arsenal of hours that have not been lived yet.

* * *

5ᵀᴴ FEBRUARY.

On to Malines. A pedestrian continually observes what is lying on his path; in Belgium, that is an extraordinary amount of dog manure. Nature is grey, cheerless and chilly. The landscape is boring, without distance, and just ugly, let us be honest. The vegetation is drab brown and thorny. Electricity poles and telephone cables are everywhere, together with box-like houses and gaudy advertising boards and paths made of black cinders. I turn my attention inwards and roam through my mental landscape.

I wanted to start this walk in wintertime. Winter is like death; and death is the opening story that has occupied people's minds from the very beginning.

In ancient Mesopotamia they celebrated winter with lamentations because the god of nature seemed to be dying: was he still slumbering in the subterranean regions of the dead? Are there any magic herbs that may restore life? Surely if nature herself dies we are all lost.

For the ancient Egyptians the pharaoh was the summary of human life. As long as he survives, we all survive. Surely his mummified body retained a tiny spark of life. The pharaoh's body was laid in the centre of the pyramid; it is said that on his body they erected a big wooden penis. Via a long shaft the penis stood aimed at a star in the Orion constellation that represented his dead queen. The pyramid was the launching pad of the royal divine seed.

Oh, the joy of arriving slowly! For one whole hour you see the small St. Rombouts' tower grow big and then you suddenly know that you are there. So many things tell you that you are a stranger: the very paint on the houses, here especially a rich cobalt blue. In a shop window I spot things on small dishes, some delicacies? No, they are different types of anthracite. (Do people still know that beautiful word for hard coal?) In a neon-lit tunnel, a small mouse runs ahead of me. It does not belong here at all: there is no place to hide, it will exhaust itself, it is bound to die. I find it endearing to see that animals, too, can make blunders.

On this walk, I shave every morning. I used to let my beard grow on previous pilgrimages. This time I don't, for a good reason. Firstly, I want to feel my normal self as much as possible. Secondly, day in day out I will have to find lodgings for myself; and I feel sure that a neatly shaven and groomed tramp has a better chance than a hairy and unkempt one.

In a 'pension' I get the bridal honeymoon bedroom. Everything is in style: the soft porn on the walls and the sexuological bookshelf next to the bed. One is never too old to learn. So I immerse myself in a book that is not just dealing with positions but with interior attitudes. 'Transcendental Sex' is its name. The book shows very clearly that our forbears were chained down with taboos and were awful bunglers, sexually; and also that people from other cultures are eviscerated by guilt complexes. So, how have we to go about it? Away with all restraints! Flow! Undo yourselves of everything; then sit opposite one another and sing-say together very slowly: "LOVE!" And then: "I LOVE YOU!" After that one of the two should say: "Of all the universe I have chosen this spot to linger, and you are the one I have chosen to be with. I am determined to share with you all the love I feel at this moment!" It was around 1980 that the lady wrote this; and she felt that truly modern readers would be happy to follow her advice. Marginal groups like Chinese, Indians, Africans and South Americans would follow once they were that far. A jarring dissonant is another book about Chinese erotic art, so naughty, fooling around with clothes and forbidden fun and peeping Toms. Shame!

The sweet hostess tells me about a couple that had recently fled from the house in panic because they sensed that the house was full of evil spirits. That was really ludicrous, for less than a year ago she had had all the rooms thoroughly cleansed with the exorcisms of a Surinam shaman.

* * *

6ᵀᴴ FEBRUARY.

Oh, the joy of travelling on foot: sniffing the tangy morning air, seeing the landscape glide past quickly, feeling the power in your legs, pondering with your head held high rather than with your head in your hands. Sensing that all visible things come with an invisible echo in their wake, that all lines run to a common point behind the horizon. What kind of point? A what or a whom? I must avoid making shortcuts to God.

To think about God or to talk about Him is absolutely risky. When people want to talk about God they become linguistic contortionists. Surely all our words are human words. If you really allow that statement to penetrate, you will see that "God does not exist" is just as problematic as saying that He does exist. This puts orthodoxy and theology into an interesting perspective.

In the past, God's stalwart defenders have always tried to protect Him where they felt an attack was endangering Him. Long ago the battle against polytheism raged: there is only one God, and ours is the one and all other gods are idols, impostors. For us this is not a real battle any more, unless you designate Money or Power or Sex as contemporary idols.

A much tougher battle rages over the dogma of atheism: God does not exist at all, He is merely an illusion. For Atheists there is no room for God in the universe. Systematic theology has invested much energy in this question and has come up with a number of arguments that can prove God's existence. According to the Church's teaching, valid arguments are available; but the ones that have been presented so far have not convinced many. Quite a number of people think that their validity stands or falls with a preliminary agreement: "And that is the one we all call God".

This makes me think about a silly joke about Adam. God had entrusted to Adam the task of giving all the animals their proper names. One evening when he came home Eve asked him what wonderful animals he had seen that day. Adam described an incredible beast he had treated: it was very, very huge, with enormous ears and a nose in the form of a long trunk and two oversized teeth protruding out of his mouth. Eve asked him what name he had given to that animal. Adam said: "Elephant". And Eve said: "Why did you call it an elephant?" "Because," Adam said, "it just looked like one."

What makes atheism attractive is that it relieves you of the impossible job of forming a reasonably correct image of God. What makes atheism unattractive is that it gives you the even more impossible job of forming an image of creation without a Creator. Only housebound professors can be content with the idea that everything just happened by itself.

You can still make another approach to God, through what is known as Pantheism: God is everything and everything is God. This is a pious position: it will make us all into part of the divine. Logically it is elegant. For, if you want to be really orthodox you have to maintain that there cannot be anything outside God. What about ourselves? Either you see yourself as outside God – but we have just said that there is no room outside God, no living space for us either; and so this point of view destroys your own existence. Or you see yourself as inside God, somehow or other. If you admit that you do in fact exist then you can only choose this second possibility. By doing so, you create a new problem: you infect God with everything evil and imperfect that is part of our being. This would seem a lethal infection. But Christianity encourages us to take this road all the same. The doctrine of the "Indwelling of the Divine Spirit" has pantheistic overtones. Or take the scriptural words "Deificati sumus", we are made into God. Summing up, it would seem better not to battle too fiercely against Pantheism; perhaps we could adjust the name and settle for Panentheism?

Personally, I am inclined to think that the important thing is to allow ourselves to be drawn into the divine circles without being able to define exactly what this entails; and that it is better not to treat God with the filleting knives of our reason. We should approach Him, rather, with a warm and loving heart and with a poetic spirit; if you stay close to honest love you will surface sooner or later in the divine, even without meaning to. "Lord, when did we see you hungry or sick or naked or in prison, and gave you help accordingly?" And if you really, really want to come to the point, I think that God is quite able to take care of Himself, even if we cannot find good arguments for defending Him: His life does not depend on us.

The windows of the sex club along the road are decorated with blue neon lights. Is that correct? I always presumed they had to be red. But blue is indeed appropriate too.

On entering Louvain I see a prayer written on a chapel: "Mother of Grace, protect us against war, sickness and expensive times".

For an arriving pilgrim, the town hall of Louvain is a miracle in white. The Grand Beguinage by lantern light is a time capsule carrying you back to the Middle Ages. I drink beer in an inn that has an underground connection directly with the brewery, like an umbilical cord. I stay in a hotel near the railway station. Hotels near railway stations often carry an aura of nostalgia, still echoing sounds of past glory. This is particularly so with hotels that go back to the days when the very rich made long journeys by train and returned with breathless tales and suitcases that triumphantly sported stickers of foreign hotels.

* * *

7TH FEBRUARY.

Houses here have notices displaying unusual occupations. I find, for instance, a carriage painter. But most have to do with healing: a 'kinetist', a 'magnetotherapist', a 'radiesthesist', an 'acupuncturist', a 'phytotherapist'; all of them people who think that they get a special message from nature. Only the shaman is not there.

There is not much to see on the way. I try to think about nature but you cannot force the direction of your thoughts. From time immemorial people have been thinking about nature but they always did that in a practical context. I don't think that there is such a thing as purely theoretical science, or that there are such things as unequivocal answers from the side of nature.

The way to examine nature is: to question her. There are rules about these questions and they resemble a kind of game we used to play as children. One child is separated and the others choose an object, and the separated child has to find out which one it is. The questioning child points at an object and asks: "Is it this one?" If that object is near the one chosen by the children, they say: "You are getting warm"; if it is far away the answer is: "Now you are getting cold". This is the way nature answers. "Is the world round?" "You are getting warm." "Is the sun turning round the earth?" "You are getting cold." I do not think that nature will ever answer our questions with an unconditional yes or no. That is because our words are straight and nature is curved.

The village supermarket is about to be opened when I take a short rest on its steps. I sit among the empty boxes piled on the stairs leading to the store. At the bottom end of my walking sticks, there are rubber disks to prevent the sticks from sinking into loose sand. That really makes them look like skiing sticks. I decide to cut the disks away with my sharp dagger. People look at me with suspicion.

The small town of Tienen has a special silhouette: not just one church tower but two: Our-Lady-at-the-Pool and Saint Germain. I arrive there quite early, at 11.30. I look around in the double town centre; it makes me think of an egg with two yolks.

A couple of kilometres outside Tienen I take a hotel room; there another book lies waiting for me. An enterprising Moroccan has written it for Belgians to give them a complete account of all types of alternative healthcare that are so popular among them; one in four Belgians uses alternative care, compared to one in 15 Dutchmen. The book continues the ancient Babylonian quest for magic life-giving herbs. What do you have to take for "the turning of the years"? An extract from agnus-cactus seed, milli-leaf, lavender blossoms and Mary's thistle. Herbalists come out with exciting things. Would they really work?

I am reminded of an article I once read in a medical periodical in Africa about a comparative study of clients going to Western psychologists on the one hand and clients going to an African witchdoctor. Of the psychologist's clients, 30 percent were cured, 30 percent were not and 30 percent felt a little better. Of the witchdoctor's clients, 30 percent were cured, 30 percent were not and 30 percent felt a little better. Finally, they also tested a group of patients who neither went to the psychologist nor to the witchdoctor. Of them, 30 percent were cured, 30 percent were not and 30 percent felt a little better.

Travelling on foot makes you meet unusual people. The innkeeper's daughter is utterly addicted to horseracing with sulkies and can tell you all about it. At 5.00 in the morning, I have breakfast with a scientific English guest labourer.

* * *

8TH FEBRUARY.

My appearance makes dogs very nervous. The rucksack makes my contours grotesque and my two walking sticks turn me into a quadruped. Do they take me for a nightmarish creature, something like Salvador Dali's elephants with the spidery long legs? The only dogs that do not go into a frenzy at seeing me are polar huskies: they just stare at me with ice-cold eyes.

The trees are without leaves so they cannot get any food from the air. Does that mean that they are now living on some fat-like provisions they had stored away in a hidden corner?

In wintertime you walk in the midst of tree skeletons. But it shows you the basic pattern of trees more clearly: a fan of branches up in the air, the counterpart of a fan of roots down in the soil, the two being connected by a solid stem. Underground, mother mole says to her children: "You know that all these roots together down here are called a tree; but you will be surprised to hear that there is as much of the tree above the ground as there is down here". Trees are most intriguing: they are like huge staples linking heaven and earth to one another. It is not surprising that in olden times trees were venerated as nodes in the divine nervous power-system that permeated all creation; and that they were seen as symbols of transcendence.

10 a.m. and I am already at the end of today's lap, the small town of St. Truiden. I enter a coffee shop to have a nice cup and some cheesecake. Smart serving girls are getting everything ready for the new day. My working day is over already; I enjoy the contrast. When it comes to contrasts, sitting in this civilised place is contrasting sharply with this morning's walk. For many hours I have been struggling in the nasty cold weather, splattered by monstrous articulated lorries, gingerly picking my way through withered thistles and discarded plastic lemonade bottles like a gloomy tramp; and here I sit between spick-and-span citizens in a warm cloud of coffee aroma under over-generous lights. Neat.

* * *

9TH FEBRUARY.

To the ancient city of Tongeren along an imperial Roman road, through a snow-covered countryside. This snow is in no way different from Roman snow. Time disappears.

All snow is eternal snow. Winter is winter; it passes right through us. All that is part and parcel of nature passes right through us. Everything has to do with everything. There are many separate items but they all belong to one big network. The thoughts about ONE AND MANY are primordial thoughts. There are many things but you can only call them many by virtue of the fact that they belong to an underlying unity. You can only count if you start with "one". But counting by itself presupposes a certain order. You cannot add just any odd things: you cannot add a human being and his head.

Adding and subdividing are next-door neighbours. People subdivide things into categories of good things/bad things. That gives rise to the next question: Goodness and Badness, are they really two fundamental and equivalent categories? Is it correct to say that there are good things and bad things? Or are bad things really good things that fail to make the grade?

If you want to talk about Good and Evil as being on the same line, then you choose Dualism. The ancient Persian thinker Zarathustra (700 BC) was such a person. He believed in two divine principles: Ormazd (Good) and Ahriman (Evil). These two have created contrasts or opposites. Even before their birth, human beings have to opt for one of the two; they can do that, because they still retain a view of the eternal landscape from which they have just come. The contest between the two is carried on into earthly life. Good tries to oust Evil with purifying fire. The ultimate victory of Good over Evil will be the start of God's Kingdom on earth.

The Greeks were more rational; they preferred to postulate a fundamental unity that is good. Pythagoras (530 BC) saw this unity in the harmony and order that is to be found everywhere in nature by those that know how to look. This order is hidden rather than obvious and can be detected through esoteric formulas. In your deepest essence you are soul and as such you are a short summary of God. Small wonder if you bring about order around you: you yourself are order. Your soul is the order of your body; anima est ordo corporis. You detect the harmony of the world and having detected it you can control it. Numbers and proportions are part of this divine harmony. Mathematics has to be considered part of the divine mysteries.

The ancient Greek Cosmologians made matter the starting point of their reflections. Thales (580 BC) proposed that water was deep down responsible for the fundamental unity of all beings: all things are water in one or other form. (If you think of the hydrogen atom, you have to admit that Thales was quite warm.)

Parmenides (500 BC) taught that the multiplicity you seem to see everywhere is really nothing but deception; truth remains what it always was: one and the same. Look at your own identity: basically you have remained one and the same person. The great all-embracing cosmic reality is eternal and unchangeable; it is reflected in us, it thinks in us. Many things do not change at all. All snow is eternal snow.

Weighing it all up, one is forced to admit that all these contrasting thinkers were quite warm.

Halfway through today's distance, I come across a small chapel where hermits have been living up until recently; the last one was Brother Gielen from Sittard who died in 1908. In the drawer of a cupboard I find a packet of biscuits, untouched as a sign that this is a holy place with nothing but honest people.

I always felt bad about knowing so little about Belgium. That is the reason why I wanted to cross it diagonally at the beginning of my course. It gives me great satisfaction to fill in the blank areas in my internal atlas.

A colourful youth hostel offers me hospitality. In its dining room I find a recent copy of Cosmopolitan; it carries a seducing banner: 'Sex-lessons For The Advanced'. Since my studies in the bridal chamber of Malines I think I qualify and so I take the bait. Aha, you see how you have to keep yourself up to date. For things have to be done in a different way now. You have to go and sit in front of a mirror all by yourself, you finger yourself here and there and note that this is nice; and all those feelings you should write down on a piece of paper, you see. Note down, also, the various sexual fantasies that come into your head. Do this for three days on end. And then you call your friend and let him read the lot. And then incredible things will begin to happen. Mmm. It sounds a little dotty: like a desperate effort to make sex exciting again. It seems to have gone a bit slack.

* * *

10TH FEBRUARY.

Liège, a city made up seemingly of nothing else but viaducts, flyovers and roundabouts, is the city of Saint Lambert. He was born and bred at Maastricht and murdered there in 705 AD. He became the favourite patron of itinerant hawkers; thus his fame went from Liège to Cologne in Germany, then via the 'Koelnische Strasse' northwards to Munster, and from there again westwards, around 1500 AD, to my own hometown Hengelo in Twente, the Netherlands.

On this pilgrimage, I want to visit many sacred places: St. Willibrord's grave at Echternach, the old pilgrims' sanctuary at Conques, the healing sanctuary at Lourdes, St. James's grave at Compostela, St. Boniface's tomb at Fulda. Among the sacred places I also count some where unimaginable and impossible events took place, such as Verdun where 600,000 young men were slaughtered; Vézelay, where not only pilgrims gathered but also crusaders to serve God by the sword; the Carcasonne region of the merciless Inquisition; Avignon of the ambitious popes; furthermore Alpine summits like the oldest passes and an artistic summit like van Gogh's Arles. I have now arrived at my first sacred spot: the tomb of St. Lambert, patron saint of my home parish and my home town.

The old Liège church of St. Lambert, once the largest church of Western Europe after St. Peter's, was demolished by the French Revolution; its reliquary with the Saint's bones is now kept in St. John's Cathedral. It is noon and the church has to be closed for the lunchtime meal; the church guardian lets me in on condition that I will pray really briefly.

Pilgrims' time is miracles' time, I am ready for them now. Unable to pray in the church, I withdraw to the next best place for prayer – a pub. I start the Rosary but at the third mystery, the Birth at Bethlehem, I doze off. St. Joseph nudges me to accept a traditional birthday drink, a glass of Bethlehem raisins in brandy and cinnamon... but no, it is not St. Joseph, it is the waiter with a cool glass of Hoegaarden wheat beer, a gift from an anonymous drinker.

There is a St. James' church as well; there I attend the Saturday evening Mass. It is a wedding at the same time, complete with the well-known wedding march, the floppy hats and the jovial priest; pastorally rather worn and flat.

The Church has become like a mother of pearl shell where, like a snail, the faithful withdraw at serious times to cherish the moment. That is something good but also marginal in respect of the Gospel. If this is all you do, it is hard to be the salt of the earth: salt and snails don't go together very well.

In the church, my pilgrim's passport is being stamped by a Walloon priest who speaks Flemish: another minor miracle? Standing before the statue of St. James – always recognisable by the cockleshell on his hat or his jacket – I plead with him to look after me well. As I turn around to go, a man bars my way. Pointing at the cockleshell on my breast, he says: "I see that you are a pilgrim of St. James; may I invite you to come to my house for a meal? And would you not like to have a shower? Where is your luggage? I can give you a bed." As far as the bed is concerned, I have already booked one with a lady in the Street of the Bat; but for the other things I am delighted to accept his offer. I am moved by the fact that he asks me who I am only after we have arrived at his table. When at 9.00, I lie stretched out on my mattress in my tiny pension, my friend pushes a letter under the door to let me know that he has already arranged for my lodgings with tomorrow's parish priest.

* * *

11TH FEBRUARY.

Nothing is more quiet than a big city on a Sunday morning at 7.00 a.m. Near the railway station the window wenches languish in fluorescent underwear staring at a gazette. They wave at me. Sorry, I really have no time now to explain to them the finesses of the Malines lessons in transcendental sex. The time has come for me to ascend the Ardennes, sharply climbing roads and villages hiding in small but deep ravines.

At Aywalle I eat a new French word: a 'dinde'. From the dimensions I can guess that I have to do with a turkey.

The French called the bird a 'Coq d'Inde' because they presumed it came from India; the Dutch called it a 'kalkoen', thinking it came from Calcutta; the English were sure it came from Turkey and thought 'turkey' would be a good name. It came from America, of course.

Hour after hour, I walk alongside a river that streams on placidly as if nothing ever happened; then again, I am in landscapes that appear threatening and cruel.

Landscapes do reflect several emotional situations but not all. Feelings of evaporated hope and angry resentment do not easily find equivalents in the landscape. Would that be a sign that these are emotions that we should not take too seriously? These are emotions that have not been strangers to me as a church minister over the last decades. Fortunately, they did not upset my peace of mind completely. When we sat together as a group of colleagues, we would praise one another as ardent defenders of lost causes. That was not meant to be cynical. Sometimes I think I am best at rearguard actions. I swear in all honesty that my first concern always was the worry about sheep getting lost.

It was my job in the 'sixties to inspire young people to opt for the priesthood, notwithstanding the difficult climate. This was the image I gave them of the task of a priest. A priest had to allow himself to be infected by the current religious crisis in order that he might produce in the inner recesses of his soul some kind of religious vaccine. He had to offer himself to be really disturbed by arising dilemmas, so that out of his disturbance a spiritual antidote might be distilled. By the time his friends began to come under attack from the same bacteria he would have his vaccine ready to help them. Quite clearly some might well consider this to be an unsuitable approach, too risky; but it had an epic side to it and young people went for it. What really frustrated us was something much more unpleasant.

There appeared to be a painful misunderstanding between the worried renewers of church life and the faithful defenders of the church's traditions. The bottom line for those who fought for renewal was the conviction that the church would lose its sheep if certain measures were not taken. We thought that this argument was incontestable and ultimate, even for conservative church members. But that did not appear to be the common ground. Slowly we woke up to the disconcerting idea that several of our leading church members had reconciled themselves to the notion that large numbers of sheep had to be written off in order that the flock itself might be saved. To us this looked like a methodical abandonment of lost sheep. I have often asked myself: what are we shepherds going to say to Jesus Christ when we appear before his throne and he asks us: "Where are my sheep?" Would we really dare to shrug our shoulders sadly and say: "We have shouted loud enough but they did not want to come. Moreover, maybe we lost the sheep, but at least we saved the flock"? To me this is like a nightmare. These are brooding thoughts, doing me no good. I notice that the wounds in my heart have not been healed at all yet.

At Harzé, the parish priest entrusts me to an elderly couple exuding hospitality. The man was born in Katanga (Congo) whilst his father was busy building Elisabethville and designing the copper mines there; he himself grew up to be District Commissioner. Stories about old-time Africa fill the evening. By way of "extra" I get a lesson about the region of Liège, Maastricht, Aix la Chapelle, as far as Tongeren and Trier. The people of those areas are the inheritors of the royal Franks, the Merovingians. Their land is the cradle of proto-Europe of 800 AD, the home of Charlemain. Dutch, Belgians, French, Germans, they are all Johnnies-come-lately.

* * *

12TH FEBRUARY.

The magic chain is working: one parish priest securing hospitality for me with the next one.

Bent over forwards, I bore myself a passage through the solid squalls of stinging hail that have overwhelmed the hills. Exactly for a situation like this have I provided myself with long 'thermal' underpants, the latest item for survival in arctic climes. But they are in my rucksack, so how on earth do I get them on? In the shelter of a lonely bus stop, I strip down like a nudist at the North Pole.

I reach the area of the German Ardennes offensive in December 1944. Exactly where it ground to a halt is a café. It is closed, since it is Monday, but the proprietress opens the door for me because the weather is so bad and gives me cup of coffee. Her daughter has to interrupt her petting bout with her boyfriend and can't wait for me to finish my coffee.

After the war, the damaged villages were thoroughly reconstructed and made boring. In all the windows the portraits of two small girls are staring at me, Julie and Melissa; they have been kidnapped. Later on it will appear that at this moment, not all that far from where I pass, the two children are immured under the ground and dying, writhing with hunger and despair to supply entertainment for lovers of child porno. Above ground level, there is fairness and Christmas card-like peace, and all problems are attended to. But not those of Melissa and Julie, for quite a number of influential persons find child pornography too much fun and reasonably innocent.

At Lierneux, the priest proudly shows me the parish church; the parish goes back to the year 692 AD. He sees to it that I will get a place tomorrow evening.

* * *

13TH FEBRUARY.

During the night everything has been glazed over with frost and after that covered with snow; it is the most slippery set-up you can have. Sure enough, on a cambered road at the top of a hill I crash down in a flash. The first part of my body to hit the ground is my right shoulder. A small torch in my breast pocket causes a rib to be badly bruised but the prosthesis in my hip has not been affected.

> When you walk through nature, anything may lead to philosophical flights of fancy. The Greek thinker Anaximenes (550 BC) considered his breathing. He noticed that breath turns cold when you press your lips together and warm when you open your mouth wide. That gave him the idea that compression makes things cold and expansion makes things warm; he found confirmation for this in the three stages of water: ice, water, steam.

In the tiny church of Montleban there is a memorial plaque on the wall with the names of the prisoners of war that returned on 7th September 1919. It is adorned with a curious text saying: "Vivat Christus Qui Diligit Francos":

Long live Christ who loves the French. Or did the parish priest take Francos to mean "Free People"?

A testy old man refuses to give me a drink of water. A little farther on I come upon a café, closed because it is Tuesday. But the lady allows me in and gives me two glasses of beer free, in honour of St. James.

At Tavigny it is a young widow that puts me up. She has a young daughter. They spoil me: my clothes have to be washed, telephone calls should be made, a fine meal must be prepared; it makes me feel as if I were a long lost favourite uncle. Yesterday's parish priest spoke a true word when he said: "Compostela is one large mysterious family".

* * *

14TH FEBRUARY.

After one hour's walk I enter a new country: Luxemburg. No more dog manure. The frosty cold bites more and more; there is no place anywhere to sit. The bus stops have no benches. My half of the road seems to be covered with grimy snow all the time. And because it is Wednesday everything is closed. But God is merciful: at 1.00 p.m. I reach an inn where they serve huge beefsteaks made of horse meat.

My path leads to the abbey of Clervaux, a place where there is no time.

That abbey is a spiritual Hubble telescope that tries to catch glimpses of God from high above the hurly-burly of the earth. What am I going to say to the monks? Should I start this way: "Reverend Fathers, forgive me for I think that I have gone crazy. For I am a 20th century European, and as such one of those who are willing to reduce the whole of creation to rubble in order to satisfy our avaricious cravings; we are willing to jettison all the cultural insights we ever inherited, for the sake of spreading our own superior superstitions. That we have made ourselves into God is bad enough but the worst is that we have preferred to take on God's bad qualities: self-centeredness, stubbornness, jealousy and meddlesomeness"?

The doors of the abbey swing open by themselves; the widow manipulated them by telephone. The monks feel disappointed that I stay for one night only;

most visitors remain there for a week at least. They pamper me somewhat
ruggedly. Everything is different but recognisable.

People might think of an abbey as a spiritual Asterix-and-Obelix village. It is not. I enter the abbey but the abbey enters me just as much. The monks are, unlike ourselves, not welded to the present: uninhibitedly they talk about our future and our past. They preserve spiritual chromosomes, that had gone lost long ago, for future use.

There is one question that stirs strongly within me. Long ago, there were hundreds of these abbeys: what is really the idea that gave birth to them? Not the Gospel. I think that this is what took place. People had a picturesque idea about heaven: everybody was sitting on thrones in a big circle around God; they sang His praises, together with the choirs of angels and seraphim; the eternal song in the eternal light. People also felt the challenge to anticipate heaven on earth a bit. The proper songs of praise were available: the Psalms. God could be given regular solo-time through the Scripture readings. People started doing that in a setting that was – and still is – otherworldly in many respects: the ritualised gestures, the big heavy chairs, the ample space; nothing finicky, nothing tawdry, no trashy gimmicks; everything must be grand and pure. This same style determines the lives of the monks: with them, too, things are grand and pure: the buildings, the fabric, the estate, the beer. They have tried to create a little bit of heaven on earth, to establish among us a bridgehead of the kingdom of heaven. It seems that heaven and earth take delight in joining the play: the apples become king-sized, fruit-juice becomes liqueur and impossible tasks become feasible. God is clearly present, with miracles and peace.

* * *

15TH FEBRUARY.

Delayed on account of the Lauds and burdened with an oversized luncheon-packet thanks to the monks' generosity, I gingerly descend the snow-covered steep slope into the small town. Now I really appreciate my long walking sticks – with shock absorbers. But here, too, when you use these sticks, half the people that smile at you laugh at you.

After an hour I cross a kind of snow-line; it is very strange the way you step from a totally white world into a greyish-green one.

For the time being, very practical questions keep me occupied. Such as: why is one's nose running every 50 yards? Has any candidate for a Ph.D. degree taken this as a topic for his thesis? I have plenty of information available for him.

When I am having a nice cup of soup in a restaurant the place is suddenly filled with dressed up children; they sing a tune and receive their reward in the form of sweets or coins. It is a custom that you find in many different places, and so it must very old, and with the same tune everywhere. I have read somewhere that it is an ancient Germanic melody; and that is why Ring-a-ring-a-rosy, Oranje-boven for the Dutch royal family and Silent Night Holy Night are truly indestructible.

At Vianden, practically all hotels are closed, since it is wintertime. Fortunately, the 'Hof van Holland' is open for loud Dutchmen and witty Belgians ("Hast thou come on roller-skates perhaps?"). It is lovely to be able to speak Dutch for a change. "Waiter, this fish has a mouldy taste." "That is probably because it is dead, sir."

* * *

16TH FEBRUARY.

Today I will reach my next sacred pilgrims' place, the city of Echternach where the body of St. Willibrord is resting. My path runs along the river Our. The river itself is the border between Luxemburg and Germany. It twists and turns; at one place I take the inside bend through Germany. Mean and sneakily hidden old casemates protect the German Empire against assaults from the Luxemburgers. From porous rock, gigantic candelabras have grown made of countless icicles, a process that has been the same for thousands of years.

Anybody can tell you that a quiet walk is the ideal entourage for mulling over problems and solving them. So why is it that I cannot think of any problems; I just walk, and that is all? I hear my footsteps, the clicking of my sticks. I look at the landscape closely; I am determined that no beautiful thing shall escape my attention. But no problem, neither about religion nor about anything else, presents itself. This is the way a doctor must feel when he has just opened a new surgery and no patients appear in the waiting room. Deep in my heart I know that it is right this way: problems are not things to be called up, they ought to take you by surprise.

Under the abbey church, so grandiose and dignified, he rests: Willibrord, the first Archbishop of the Friesians, in a world of white light, titanic stones and splashing water. Yes, a well bubbles up in the crypt. The water tastes cool and pure. The dean tells me that the tourist season tends to contaminate the water: people throw coins into it. A strange and universal custom: why do people like to throw coins into wells and waterholes?

In Willibrord's time, around 750 AD, missionaries did not found dioceses with cathedrals but rather abbeys full of monks. The abbot was the big boss (abbas, father) and one of the monks was ordained bishop so that there would be somebody who could ordain priests.

It is granted unto me to establish peace in a noisy café where old-age pensioners full of 'Gluehwein' dash their cards on the table; a great commotion arises when one of them refuses to follow the suit of trumps. They appeal to me, being a neutral stranger. As a one-man UN delegation, I solemnly declare that the world over the suit of trumps is always followed, and that is that.

Why is the Dukedom of Luxemburg an independent country? I must have learned it at some stage; there is only one reason I can think of now. At the Congress of Vienna, somewhere around 1815 AD, the Netherlands, Belgium and Luxemburg were joined together as a bulwark against France. After that, France succeeded in antagonising the French-speaking Walloons and Catholic Flemings against the Dutch-speaking Protestant king and that resulted in the breaking away of Belgium in 1839 AD. Luxemburg remained joined to the Netherlands. But when King William III died around 1890 AD there arose a problem over the succession, because his successor was his daughter Wilhelmina. The legal system of Luxemburg did not allow for a female successor whereas the Netherlands system did. So Luxemburg went its own way after having traced the nearest male Nassau prince.

All major hotels are closed because of the winter season. I find a cosy room at 'Le Petit Poète', where the Portuguese owners use the drinking parlour as the sitting room for the whole family; all the members sit round the TV to watch the football with piercing screams.

In my room I find a magazine offering me the sad tale of a Playboy-Mate who, when she discovered that she was a lesbian, had already been infected with AIDS because once in a fit of recklessness she had failed to make her sex safe. Even though I commiserate with her, I appear to be a lout all the same because I do not know what a little licking rag is; and the tetchy lesbo adds that if I cannot imagine how two women can have sex I am guilty of outright anti-feminine discrimination.

Letzeburg German is quite something but it just misses the status of being a serious language. The greeting is simple: "Moin". That is what we say in my Twente home area as well.

* * *

17ᵀᴴ FEBRUARY.

Travellers on foot come in all sorts. Some loathe tarmac and will walk on nothing else but grass or rough soil. Others will opt for a scenic route, however far it takes them off course. I belong to the type that tries to find the shortest distance from A to B; if possible, I will choose small roads but otherwise I will take a big road just as well. Like today when I have to get from Echternach to Luxemburg. There are ways of making walking on a big road bearable. Start long before the crack of dawn, so that for hours on end the road is all yours. Enjoy the villages and towns you pass through: often they are pleasant intermezzos where so many human things draw your attention. And if you have enough exciting things in your head to think about, a day without a scenic landscape will not kill you.

When you walk by yourself you are very much preoccupied with yourself, or with your leaking nose. How I envy those people that can blow their noses without a handkerchief, just with one finger on one side. Where do you learn such a thing? I never manage. I always cover myself with snot, even now.

On entering the city, I pass a sky-high viaduct. The legs of the arches end in a point; is that a better way?

23

The Redemptorist priests are giving me hospitality. They have a parish for the international community; and the priest who serves us from the kitchen has a job in the European Parliament at Strasbourg.

* * *

18TH FEBRUARY.

Snow and squalls cannot spoil my festive mood: today I will enter France. Just a few kilometres this side of the border I celebrate Sunday in a well-appointed restaurant in the midst of smartly dressed people whilst the water is slushing in my boots.

Is spring coming at last? Promising signs are there: I have seen a group of lapwings, a twittering lark, a fat earthworm on the pavement and a Chinese restaurant called 'Springtime Is Starting'. Day by day, the sun climbs a little higher.

That imperceptible climbing of the sun has never escaped peoples' notice. At the same time, it proved very hard to find an explanation for it. Perhaps most people said it was something so small it could not be of any serious consequence and so it was not worthwhile to rack your brains over it.

Tiny exceptions in natural phenomena often lead to big upheavals. In nature, there are no exceptions. In nature, there are only rules. People say that the exception confirms the rule; well, in nature the exception proves that the rule is wrong. Another thing with nature is: you usually start with the exception and then you try to find the rule that confirms the exception.

Many laws that we presumed to be obviously right were shown to be in need of correction by the exceptions: obvious fundamentals like the fact that the sun turns round the earth; that by their very nature things stand still rather than move. Progress in science ran via the exceptions.

Whosoever lives in the land of the obvious and points at exceptions will not be very popular for he disturbs the peace. He will be stigmatised as a fool or a villain intent on ruining everything, or as an irritating fusspot. The fact remains that the obvious often turns out to be wrong because it is not tested critically. Truth is served better by criticism than by self-evidence. Endorsing the obvious is the initial phase of knowledge, the "dogmatic dream" as some philosophers called it. The awkward question makes a crack in the self-evident, through which a better truth can come to the surface. Who forbids awkward questions chokes the human spirit.

In relation to the obvious the exception is an impossibility. Progress is hidden under the so-called impossible. That is why people are intrigued by impossible deeds and ideas.

French custom officers are on their qui vive with Dutch wayfarers, even when it rains. In a matter of metres a car stops next to me; they check if my name occurs in the computer list of international drugs dealers. I say to the officers: "Sirs, does this mean that from now on my name is included in the book of the criminals?" To my astonishment, I say this in fluent French. This gives me confidence: if I can say this in French, I can say anything in French. After that I entrust myself again to my own interior thoughts.

As long ago as 500 years before Christ, Pythagoras and his cronies toyed with the impossible idea that the earth was not flat but spherical. This clashed with everyday experience. A thousand years later Copernicus toyed with the impossible idea that the earth turned around the sun. This clashed with everyday observation and with the Bible. Some 500 years before Christ, Heraclitus toyed with the impossible idea that everything was in motion ("Panta rhei kai ouden menei"). Surely that would be a fatal blow for cognition: certainty rested on immutable truth. Hegel only (around 1800 AD) managed to integrate movement into philosophy by giving the movement a regular pattern. Today, we all hold that even the sun and the stars move, that standing still is really equal movement, and that motion is even more fundamental to reality than Heraclitus or Hegel could ever have imagined.

The landscape of the French Borinage suffers from utter decay. A hundred years ago it was a ruthless industrial area; now all industry has been allowed to collapse. The government authorities try to cheer it up a bit with new tarmac roads and playgrounds.

Even a landscape lives and dies, it is in continual movement. Immobility in nature means that the change is so slow that you do not perceive it. And even if they say today that standing still means equal movement, that is not quite correct, for there are no two objects in nature that move absolutely equally.

Movement is part and parcel of our very bodies. At certain intervals all our bodily material is replaced by other material, whilst our identity remains the same. New matter is taken on board by us, stays with us for some years and is then jettisoned again.

This makes me think of the little whirlwind that goes through the dead leaves on the ground. One by one the leaves are lifted up, turn around in the air a couple of times and then drop back on the ground. This creates the illusion that something passes by. In Uganda, they call such a whirlwind a soul; in English, we call it a dust devil. This process of taking up matter and dropping it again leads to a new idea of our body.

To let that penetrate into your mind you can do a thought-experiment. First of all, take a very big long hall in which you can store a lot of things. Then get hold of a newborn baby and put it at the very beginning of the hall. Now you must calculate exactly what kind of materials this baby needs to put into his body during his whole lifetime: via his alimentary canal, via his lungs, and any other way of absorption, and how much. All these materials, you put in the hall stacked in long rows: carbon, hydrogen, oxygen, phosphor, iron, etc. Assistants have to feed all these materials into the baby. But at the same time they also have to collect all the materials that leave the baby's body by breathing out, defecation, urinating, sweating, evaporation, everything. And all these collected used materials should be broken down into their chemical components, so that they can be stacked nicely again in the hall but on the other side of the baby. If you come back after 10 years you will see that the child has moved up through the materials and quite a long way already. Whatever matter lies ahead of him still has to go into him; whatever lies behind him has been inside already. After 40 years, you will find him halfway. After 80 years, you will find him at the other end of the hall. All the items are there again, neatly stacked: carbon, hydrogen, oxygen, phosphor, iron... perhaps a little less in quantity because a certain amount has been changed into energy; but all the building materials of the body are there again, this time at the other side. The person has gone through them all like a small whirlwind; so what is his body then really?

Today's final stop is Longwy (Haut). The town is cheered up a bit by fortifications laid out by the famous Vauban; they go back to the time before the industrial revolution.

* * *

19ᵀᴴ FEBRUARY.

One of the most useful things I carry with me is a square piece of foam plastic with a thickness of about 1 cm; it enables me to sit down anywhere without discomfort and without getting a cold bottom. My prosthesis makes it difficult for me to sit on the ground; I have to sit on something higher. On these lonely snow-covered French roads the plastic kilometre-markers are a good support.

I reminisce about my hosts at Longwy; they were a group of enthusiastic Redemptorist priests who dedicated themselves to a kind of urban apostolate, something similar to what our group is doing in Kenya. It occurs to me that their outreach is rather restricted and they have to console themselves with the thought that they are practising the "apostolate of being present". They deserve something better. It should be made possible for them to crack open old structures with a crowbar and liberate people from whatever keeps them fettered. But what exactly does that mean in practical terms?

What is it that frustrates ordinary people? Do we, church people, know anything about that? During the last centuries, church champions have locked themselves up inside impregnable bastions. Today, those bastions and citadels are not anywhere near the present frontline. That is the reason why, when we started our work in the slums of Kisumu, we took up a different position: we moved out of the church buildings to start living among the very people of the slums. That gave us some idea of what bothered the people, because it bothered us as well: insecurity, garbage, vermin, threats, bad hygiene, powerlessness not only in deed but already in word. We tasted problems for which we had no solution. And at the same time we enjoyed the presence of the common people, frustrated and jolly at the same time. Before you can get a glimpse of what the meaning of "redemption" might be, you have to feel at home with your brothers and sisters in distress. The theological term for that is: "Incarnation".

The weather today is inclement: blizzards of snow and gusts of cold wind. I halt in the last village before Verdun, called Mangiennes. In the village restaurant, they serve me with the same food the family has cooked for itself today, albeit with a few more frills. I like it that way. But there is no hotel. There is a presbytery near the church, but the priest is not there. The village has a 'Madame la Maire'; she has a farm a few kilometres outside the village but she too is not there. Monsieur Lecler, a friendly parishioner, opens the parish hall for me and I start installing myself at a table there, when in the nick of time the parish priest turns up. I find it quite fascinating to compare pastoral notes with him; he has to serve 12 sub-parishes and he has no pastoral workers.

My rib is hurting; it is broken, in fact, but I will not find that out for a long time to come.

The French language is not only sounds, it is also gestures. One example: you open your eyes wide, lift your shoulders and blow your breath out through pouted lips; that means: you don't know. Another gesture is: wiping your plate with a piece of bread; that means thank you for the food. One of the most awkward forms of discomfort is a crack in the toilet-seat: when you sit down your skin moves into the opening crack and when you get up the skin gets caught mercilessly.

* * *

20TH FEBRUARY.

The snow is deep and as I lift my feet high, the parish priest says grinning: "Not like Kenya, is it?"

I now get near to where on 21st February 1916 the great German attack on Verdun broke loose.

It was based on an entirely new concept of warfare, much better than anything seen so far.

The artillery – the Queen of the Battlefield – was to pulverise the enemy trenches with an incredibly concentrated fire-power; all the infantry had to do after that was occupy them at leisure. It would force the French to bring up new troops to block the gap and the process was repeated. Inexorably, this would draw the whole French army piecemeal into an inferno of destruction until it was bled white. And then the war was won. It did not work out. The French had a lot of artillery, too, and their foot soldiers had hidden themselves so deeply under the ground that they could surface after the barrage to tackle the German infantry. The mutual slaughter ceased only when both sides had lost more than 300,000 men each.

Eighty years later now, one walks through this demonic domain shivering with abhorrence, past the German cemeteries (two corpses per one black cross) and the French ones (one corpse per one white cross). All of them were young men, carefully ripped to pieces. People took that: it was acceptable. Those that found it normal have gone and now the loathing at this nauseating episode is overwhelming. In order to tone down the elated feelings of triumphant national pride the French are restoring German fortifications. Arrows have arrived: here was a German trench; here a barricade of barbed wire; here a shell hole. Mother Nature is a great healer; only the names remain sick: Douaumont, Fort de Vaux, le Mort-Homme, Verdun itself.

I work my way through the Bois des Caures (nobody can tell me what Caures are) where Colonel Driant held his ground with his chasseurs for two endless days, like men in an oversized turning cement-mixer. I wondered why those soldiers liked to entrench themselves in forests. An old photograph of Driant in his position shows why: all the trees have been sawn off to supply timber for the underground bunkers.

The deep snow prevents me from visiting the various parts of the battlefield. From far away I see the big monument: a long building with a high tower in the middle, sprouting up in an immense field of crosses. According to some you should see this as a sword, thrust into the ground up to the hilt. It makes me think of the pharaoh's mummy, its huge phallus aimed at a life-giving constellation in a desperate last effort to make the wasted seed of all those disembowelled young men be fruitful in some corner in the heavens.

The friendly bishop of Verdun invites me to stay in his house.

* * *

21ST FEBRUARY.

Day of rest. Today is Ash Wednesday, the beginning of the Lenten fast. The bishop has moved out of the real Episcopal Palace and gone into a smaller – but still quite respectable – residence. The old palace is being changed into an international conference centre for peace. Verdun wants to get rid of its warlike triumphant overtones. The name Verdun should become a synonym of dearly-bought peace.

The bishop with his simple ways contrasts sharply with the lifestyle of his predecessors whose portraits adorn the walls of his house. Their game is over, the cards have been shuffled and Monseigneur Herriot has to lead. He has a difficult hand. In all his nine years of being a bishop he has ordained two new priests. He is prepared to go to extremes to establish a link with the contemporary world, if you go by the crashing colours that decorate his chapel: egg-yellow and drab violet.

I have deep cracks in the skin of my hands due to the cold. The wintry season will soon come to an end but all the same I buy myself a set of expensive goretex gloves: on a trip like this you must not try to save money on your outfit.

What counts above all is weight: what you have to carry should be as light as possible. Neither must you take things along that are merely useful; stick to the things that are really necessary. As the funny man says: "whatever you lose, you gain". I carry no sleeping mat, not even a blanket or a sleeping bag. I have a weightless thermal foil and a sleeping sheet made of pure silk weighing a few grams. I trust I will be able to get hold of or improvise some kind of blanket anywhere. I carry no food either, except for two fruits, some sweets and two cups of water. Maps are important; I have reduced them to long laminated strips. Every afternoon I wash my clothes on arrival, so that I need only one extra of each item. My rucksack weighs no more than 14 kilograms. In a few weeks' time I shall have lost some 14 kilos, so from then on I will really walk without luggage. For years on end, I have trained myself to walk in many different types of weather wearing the same kind of light clothes, just a shirt in fact for my top half. That has activated a thermostat in my skin making sure that I always feel comfortable walking outside without having to put on extra clothes; except for really rough conditions.

I have arranged my route in such a way that every day I end up in a decent place where you can find a place to stay and other things you need. Once a day I eat in a restaurant. I have money: I saved up my old age pension for two years.

* * *

22ND FEBRUARY.

Snow is everywhere, mist hangs low and a silver sun tries to shine through it; it is like walking through a world of luminous candyfloss. Abbé Guéry, a man exuding joy and adventure, accompanies me for a while to make sure I find the road. How big is the contrast between the warm poetic personalities among the church ministers and the doctrine that has been made harsh and drab and legalistic.

Hooray, another little problem. The church needs magnetic personalities. How do you get those? Not through training. They have to be ignited by other magnetic personalities. Church training is training in sacred structures, sacred dogmas, sacred laws, sacred texts, sacred traditions and sacred actions. Through a thorough training, a church leader becomes an authority in sacred matters. But how do you become magnetic? You have to be charged; sparks will have to fly. A strange kind of electrification has to become noticeable. May we think here of the Holy Spirit? Can you just switch that Holy Spirit on? Or does he have to be jump-started by some kind of short circuit?

How can it be that only the bottom halves of the trees are covered with snow and not the top? I saw it but I can't understand it. Once again, I am struck by the fact that walking gives you a real sense of speed. You see a church spire in the distance; after an hour you stand next to it; another hour and you see it far away behind you.

All things shift their positions, move along with me. Is it possible to think movement? It is not by accident that another phrase for solid thinking is: "dwelling on something". We think in images but these images seem to stand still, like in a film. We think in contrasts; but contrasts also are pretty stable. All this has led to remarkable points of view. Take the following.

In antiquity people found life to be the basic fact; they even considered the whole cosmos to be a living being. But it was a static kind of life: it was eternal and immutable, highly elevated above the boring bustle of ordinary things. Immovable life therefore! Nevertheless, that led to fruitful ideas.

According to the ideas of Xenophanes (540 BC), God is the permanent inside of everything and what we call nature is the outside of everything. Later thinkers will call creative divinity

31

"natura naturans" and created nature "natura naturata". God is the singer and nature is His song.

Today it happens again: a dog wants to join me. With a determined look in his eye, he walks next to me but just a bit ahead, so that I cannot chase him back. He is very alert, sniffs right, left and centre and intercepts imaginary enemies, just to sell himself. I feel a cad but I have to let him know with clods and sticks that I have no room for him. If you do not do that immediately, you can't get rid of him anymore.

Thoughts about the inside and the outside of things and how they relate to each other are another set of primeval thoughts. We experience that our inside and our outside do not always agree with each other. You can be scared on the inside but pull a brave face on the outside; you can be angry and yet look friendly. A woman can look like a lovely darling and yet be a fiend inside. In all this, primacy belongs to the inside; the outside is something like a presented appearance. In many cases, you can force the outside into line by an act of the will.

This could lead to the conclusion that there is no necessary link between the outside and the inside. That you can do with the outside whatever you want provided you have enough power to do so; or even manipulate your outward body totally, through magic powers, so that it could look like a tree or a bird.

Once you are of this opinion, you will be on the verge of creating a really big problem if you add the idea that the soul is the inside of the person and the body only the outside. This will make you say that the word belongs to the outside of knowledge and truth to the inside, and finally that "doing" belongs to the outside and "being" to the inside. In my conviction, however, you have to maintain through thick and through thin that doing and being are inseparably welded together. I get hot under the collar when I hear people say: "What matters, is not so much what you DO but what you ARE". At such a moment I wholeheartedly throw in my lot with Aristotle who teaches that for those who walk, "walking" is "being": ambulare ambulantibus est esse. Hence, for the active person to act is to be. There is no such thing as to be AND to do. The two coincide. What you do is what you are. How on earth can you say: "John is a very good fellow but he always does bad things"? It sounds like rubbish to me.

32

So also: you ARE your body. Human existence takes place on various levels: on the bodily level, on the spiritual level, on the outside level, on the inside level; and whatever a person is or does penetrates all levels. The levels are connected by identity. But it is an identity we have to call "analogous", an identity that includes some kind of otherness. Being is analogous, not univocous. The humanity of all people is in essence identical in life and in death; yet every person lives his own life, dies his own death. And truth IS word.

My expensive gloves give me much satisfaction. But they make it a little more difficult for me to handle my spectacles or blow my nose.

Here are some hints for the fellow who is graduating on a leaky nose. The more you blow your nose, the more it leaks. Blowing the nose seems to push the liquid back into the nose, nothing more; trimming the little hairs inside your nose is of no use.

Benoite Vaux, the Blessed Valley, is the name of the place to which the bishop of Verdun has directed me. It is run by a religious community whose members are all German-speaking French Alsatians. Half the ice-cold church is taken up by confessionals, cupboard-like wooden structures where people can confess their sins and receive absolution. A memorial on the wall announces that in the First World War, 12 seminarians were killed as soldiers and eight priests.

* * *

23RD FEBRUARY.

Footprints of deer in the unriven snow show that big animals are walking round in a landscape that seems to be empty.

The things you see and the things that are there differ a lot at times. Once I was fishing in Lake Victoria in Africa when suddenly a hippo came up under my float; it looked at me, flapped its small ears and sank slowly down again. From that moment, I always look at the surface of the water with a different state of mind.

My path takes me along the Voie Sacrée, the sacred road, between Verdun and Bar-le-Duc. Via this road an endless stream of men, horses and things were pumped to Verdun in 1916, through an umbilical chord of death as it were. Each kilometre-post carries the word Voie Sacrée and a soldier's helmet on the top.

The sisters at Bar-le-Duc think that my command of French is quite good. That is due to a trick on my part. I only talk about things for which I have words; I do not verbalise facts, I factualise words.

I like these sisters because they don't care about symmetry in their house.

Symmetry puts me off because it leaves so little room for life. Symmetry is utter balance, the last stage before death. Nets are invisible to birds and fishes because they are so symmetrical. If you enter a perfectly symmetrical church then you, being an intruder, spoil the symmetry: there is no room for you. In many convents, I notice how sisters arrange their rooms symmetrically: six chairs here, six chairs there, small table here, small table there. I think this has something to do with their ingrained aversion for disorder. Their very societies are called orders. Once I saw written on a convent wall: "Where there is order, there is God". No, no, no; please give me an untidy God, a God of surprises. These sisters in Bar-le-Duc are on my wavelength too. May God bless them.

* * *

24TH FEBRUARY.

My average daily distance is not very big: it is about 24 kilometres, like today's lap to Saint-Dizier. Since I hit the road at a very early hour I often arrive around midday. Nevertheless, I find my programme a little hurried. The afternoons are too full. When I arrive, I have to look for a place to stay; then I have to rest a little, wash my things, look for tomorrow morning's route, see something of the town, buy some provisions for the evening meal and for breakfast or otherwise talk to my hosts, then write my diary, work on some articles for newspapers, study philosophy, study the Gospel, and keep in mind all the time that I have to depart the next morning at a very early hour. I really should make my programme more relaxed.

Once again, I stay with a family, friends of yesterday's sisters. We all pile into a car to go to the Saturday evening Mass. I am introduced and several people press money into my hand. I meet a worn-out priest who has been tortured by fanatics in Morocco; I notice that one knuckle-bone of a finger is missing. The parish priest is invited for the evening meal: that will be nice for both of us, for he comes "from near my place", from Dunkirk. Everybody likes to hear about the work I am doing in Kenya; the parish community is lively. I feel at home; it is a pity that I cannot stay for some days.

Even if I have some sore spots on my soul, they fortunately lie buried under 20 years of exciting pastoral work in Kenya. The priorities are different there, the solutions you have to look for, the obstacles you have to overcome, the frames of reference, the background situations, and they are all so different from those in Europe. Pastoral work in Holland differs from pastoral work in Kenya the way chess differs from football. If you are successful with your work in Kenya, it takes on epic proportions. That has occupied me all those years; I lived like in a dream. Wonderful years they were: living in a slum with dust and stench and noise, sleeping on the ground, bothered by lice and rats, hoping that the robbers would not visit me and being called after by the children because I was a white stranger: Mzungu! Mzungu! But more: being in the constant company of lowly people who are happy with themselves the way they are. Am I boasting of my experiences? I speak like one less wise. But I do think that it gives me the right to finally open my mouth about things that really nagged me. It could also be that we have been silent too long for the sake of peace. Are our ecclesiastical superiors really aware of the havoc wrought in the lower regions? I do not think so. Silence is not always golden. Kierkegaard says that silence makes corrections impossible.

My friends here think that the pope is too old: "Why does he not appoint a number of under-popes to rule over the various continents?" Among the family members there are the prejudices of all normal French families: English food is inedible, in Sweden they eat sugared fish, Dutch cheese is boiled and not fermented like proper French cheese.

* * *

25TH FEBRUARY.

The sky is now really full of lapwings, cranes and larks, the fields are full of daisies and alder-catkins; but there is no fragrance in the air yet. One searches for small signs that betray the presence of big happenings like the changing of the seasons.

Gathering impressions, sorting them, comparing, assessing… that is now our way of reflecting. But when our Western philosophy started 25 centuries ago they did things differently. People started with the presumption that all creation was one big living being, divine. Divine Logos was stalking through the universe with giant strides. A spark of that cosmic divine fire was imprisoned in our interior like in a lump of clay: deep inside ourselves the heart of the universe was throbbing. If you wanted to know the true aspects of reality, you had to go and look for them inside your own self. Knowledge was anchored in the fact that there was identity between your most private and immobile personality and the all-encompassing immobile outer spheres of the universe. Between these two poles there was the immense grey area of the misleading multiplicity of things.

Even the old Cosmological philosophers stuck to the primacy of that identity. There is water and fire inside us as well as outside us; because we know the water and the fire inside us, we know the water and the fire outside us. Whatever happens with the earth on a big scale, happens inside us on a small scale. Just as the world is a huge ball of earth with fire inside, so we are small balls of clay with fire inside. Knowledge is a question of identity: you can only know what you are. Could anything be more obvious?

At Montier-en-Der I refresh myself in Café de Paris. It is bulging with pupils dressed in black; the boys' mopeds are lined up on the pavement. They smoke and are bored; and when they do something odd, they look to see if the lady at the bar and myself approve.

The village has an abbey dating back to 690 AD. In that same year the founder was murdered by a monk from another abbey. Soon the latter sensed that he had done something that was not quite all right; after that, he led a life of exemplary holiness. The French Revolution turned the abbey into a stable for elitist racehorses.

* * *

26TH FEBRUARY.

How agreeable it is to walk through undulating Champagne with its ochre-coloured soil and houses of cream-coloured stones and dark red roofs.

Here are some more notes for the graduand of the leaking nose. The purpose of the leaking cannot be cooling, a kind of sweating in the nose: the warmer the weather, the less the nose leaks. The simplest therapy is: just let it leak. But then you walk with a permanently wet upper lip. Further experiments reveal to me that if you pull down your upper lip as far as you can, and then you give a mighty sniff outwards, much of the liquid flies out and away. What is left you blow into the palm of your hand and wipe it on a handkerchief tied somewhere.

Napoleon is all over Brienne-le-Château; he studied there as a boy at the military academy. In Hotel Les Voyageurs I work out a new scheme for my whole journey. I have discovered that God was right when He decreed that man had to rest on Sundays. According to my original plan, I was to go across Germany from south to north, from the Lake of Constanz to the Baltic Sea near Luebeck, and from there go back in a south-westerly direction to arrive at my home town of Hengelo. I would have walked then from the Mediterranean to the Baltic, a nice thing to be able to say. Now I decide to drop the northern circuit to the Baltic: let me go from Fulda in a north-westerly direction to Munster and then home. In that way I save enough days to be able to have a rest every Sunday. The total distance will come to 6,000 kilometres and the time needed nine months. I rewrite the whole scheme meticulously on sheets of paper to send it to my mother so that she may know where I will be from day to day.

My fear is always to leave something behind by oversight. To prevent this, I never put anything away from the other things and I make sure that every item has its proper place; your rucksack becomes your house, you have to find your way in it blindfolded.

* * *

27ᵀᴴ FEBRUARY.

Walking in the rain is not really bad; why would being wet be such an awful thing? It is not, as long as you keep warm. A child in the womb is wet all the time.

How can you blame nature for rain? Rain is part of the big chain of natural events and we have to fit ourselves in. Living Nature, embracing us all, that was a theme of the oldest schools of Western philosophy. The grand total was given, the individual was the question, just the other way round from what we feel today. We say: "I am here but what are all the other things over there?" Formerly, they felt that we all belonged to the one living divine and therefore creative reality that stretched out far beyond us and into which we would fit if we behaved properly. The next question was: where does all the fragmentation come from? What makes things be different? But then again, even in the multiplicity, there is some form of harmony; is that harmony a secret formula that creates order in multiplicity?

Five centuries before Christ they thought: let us call that grand totality that penetrates all things with its unshakeable truth and its universal energy 'divine'; and the kaleidoscopic fragmentation of the world 'a phantom reality'.

Later Greek philosophers toyed with the big question: how does that big one, good and true World-Spirit, the Pneuma, the Nous, the Logos, influence the myriad creatures?

Much later, in 17ᵗʰ century Europe, the human individual was given complete autonomy; by that manoeuvre the human person ascended God's throne in fact. People in our day and age are a bit tired of having to play God all the time; the ancient yearning for being allowed to fit into the penetrating grand total is on the increase again.

Also in this respect the cards are being shuffled.

In this part of France, the farms are not near the fields; they rather keep each other company in the villages. That makes the fields deadly empty. Today it is worse, for it is misty too. Now and again, a small cemetery looms up in the mist as an indication that one is returning to the land of the living.

The motel of Magnant is situated right on the motorway. In the dark, that is a fascinating sight: an endlessly streaming river of red and white lights marking tinned tiny humans speeding through the dark at full tilt.

* * *

28TH FEBRUARY.

Two metres away from me a lark presses itself flat against the earth hoping that I will not see it. I am amazed at the amount of rubbish the French throw into the ditches: empty beer bottles and plastic water bottles in countless numbers but also mattresses and refrigerators.

My search for simple but good hotels leads me to the hamlet of Maisons-les-Chaources. Everything in the village inn is simple and attractive, and the food is very tasty indeed. That should not come as a surprise, for the establishment has a Michelin star; on the wall a parchment charter is displayed to prove that the owners have made a solemn vow to Bocuse to promote the glory of the French kitchen.

If you think soberly, you must admit that taste is a most questionable thing: cheese reminds one of sewage, white wine of silage and Hoegaarden beer of iodine.

Every evening I faithfully fill my diary with interesting sights I saw and memorable thoughts that occurred to me.

My diary is becoming a hotchpotch of observations and reflections that are at first sight entirely unrelated to each other. But there is one binding element: that is myself. They are all thoughts of one and the same person. So there is bound to be a coherence somewhere. You could say that this is analogous to the landscape; there too you have a potpourri of seemingly unrelated items: ants, bus stops, weeds, clouds, cement-mixers and church towers. Looking at it from that angle, I could call my diary an interior landscape.

* * *

29TH FEBRUARY.

Despite the warm weather, I still see snow in the ditches here and there. I pass through villages where absolutely nothing happens.

Counting up the day's events I must say that I saw nothing happening except for two things. First of all there was the small poodle; it had to produce a little dung and bark at me at the same time whilst it was being dragged along by a grumbling old lady. Secondly, there were three playing children; a small boy jumped on a flat stone, slipped and fell on the bottom of his spine, and shrivelled up with pain; the other children collapsed with laughter and started imitating him. In 50 years' time the boy will get complaints in his lower spine and the medical diagnose will be: stress.

A war monument in a village proclaims that its sons have fallen "for the end of all wars"; dated: 1918.

In the same village, soldiers are holding manoeuvres; these have to do, apparently, with establishing communications. One of the soldiers uses a telephone booth. I don't think that is fair; that way I also can carry on a war.

The proprietress of Hotel Du Centre at Tonnerre gives me a special pilgrim's discount.

The parish church is nice and clean but a bit gaudy; maybe that is what the people like.

It is not always easy to adjust inherited popular devotions to the words and the tastes of today's people. I read somewhere that on the island of New Guinea they got really stuck when they wanted to translate the Hail Mary into a local language. The problem had to do with the phrase "full of grace". In that language the only word available for grace or happiness was the word for orgasm.

THE SECOND MONTH

MARCH

1ˢᵀ MARCH.

The first month is gone; I have completed 700 kilometres; I am well below Paris. In the first light of dawn I pass a main artery of the French Railways; every few minutes a TGV train glides through the landscape, like a living TL-tube. Today I must do the penultimate stretch before Vézelay; that is where I will join an ancient high-road to Compostela. The hamlet of Nitry gives me a choice between two lodging places. The one is slightly seedy; the barkeeper tries to cheat me with the old trick of doing as if I had given him a banknote of 100 francs instead of 200. So I go to the other one, Axis.

There I meet a man who had made a solemn vow before having an operation for cancer of the nose: he had vowed to go to Jerusalem on foot if the operation was successful. The operation had been successful and so he is in trouble. After weighing up the case from all sides, I advise him to go to his bishop and ask his permission to change the vow from Jerusalem to Compostela. "Bishops can do that," I assure him.

* * *

2ᴺᴰ MARCH.

Vézelay is not just a place where you arrive: Vézelay presents itself. It lifts itself up above the things of daily life, the average grace of towns, normal historical interest and sea level. The way there has nothing special. I pass bus stops with tasteless graffiti, such as "Fuck the Religion", swastikas and "Vive le Hard". Fortunately, the sun is shining and some graffiti are even funny, like "Your Mother is a Beach".

Useless thoughts are floating along with me. Are there still other graduands looking for useful subjects for a thesis? How about this one: the pebble in your shoe. Why do I always get a pebble in my left boot and never in my right boot? The thesis should have appendices with graphs and experiments.

Slowly the high contours of Vézelay descend to the level of the normal horizon and with great dignity. Another bend, a narrow winding street at the end of which the coquettish cathedral of Mary Magdalen reveals itself bit by tantalising bit.

Vézelay is renowned for being the "concours français", the traditional gathering point for the Compostela pilgrims coming from the north-eastern part of France, northern Germany and the Netherlands. Here my runway ends. Here I get airborne.

On reaching Vézelay 27 years ago, I met an artistic French lady. I think she was called Edith de la Heronnière; she too had caught the Compostela infection and she was going to write a book about it. She told me that in former days the pilgrimage was so difficult that the medieval pilgrims called it "la petite mort". In some lands condemned criminals got the option of making the pilgrimage instead of going to the gallows. The terrifying dangers are not there any longer. But there are still very dramatic sides to it. When you step into the road on the very first morning, you have a faint feeling of going to the scaffold. One takes leave of one's normal life and everything becomes unusual. During the walk, something in you dies and something may be born in you. They say that on your deathbed you will see a lightning-fast review of your whole life. I don't know if that is really so; but if you make this walk by yourself it does happen, though not lightning-fast. It takes the form of an endless chain of associations loosely connected to what one experiences from moment to moment. These thoughts relate to the walk the way footnotes relate to a book. They are often of fundamental importance, for in the footnotes a narration touches the solid ground.

I ask about the lady, to see if she has written the book. I find no trace of either.

* * *

3ʳᵈ MARCH.

Day of rest. Day of dreams. It is lovely to sit in a sacred medieval space, so beautiful that you become a stranger to any fixed time, a time-tramp, a dreamer.

Yes, a pilgrim is a dreamer: he follows a star shown him by an angel and he refuses to wake up from his quest; he is prepared for the best. The Three Magi are his cronies.

The services in the cathedral have been entrusted to monks who call themselves 'Monks of Jerusalem'. Jerusalem really stands for today's big cities. They want to put the heavenly bridgehead of prayer within the reach of urban dwellers.

Vézelay is also well known because it was the place where, in the 13ᵗʰ century, Saint Bernard preached the Second Crusade by orders of the pope. And he did so with overwhelming success, making the hills ring with the cry "Dieu le Veult!" Apart from the question of whether you can use the word "success" in the context of a Crusade, this Holy War eventually turned out a dismal failure. Crusades should never have been allowed. But non-violence is a difficult enterprise: it is not in our nature, it requires a thorough conversion.

Whoever wants to be part of the New Testament has to convert himself. God Himself has given us the good example. He is the first convert. In the Old Testament, He was advertised as the champion heavyweight. He asserted His majesty with nuclear force and destroyed his enemies by fire and sword. In the New Testament, He presents Himself as being powerless, a lamb, a baby, living in solidarity with the rejects and the oppressed. He hands Himself over to us, He allows us to describe Him, He would not know what to do without us. Rilke has written an amazing poem about this.

43

What will you do, God, when I perish?
I am your cup, when I get shattered?
I am your drink, when I get putrid?
I am your cloak, your daily toil,
When you lose me you lose your sense.

With me you lose your house in which
You relished greetings, close and warm.
You feel the sandals that I am
Fall slowly from your tired feet.

Down falls your big and heavy cloak.
Your gaze to which I gave my cheek
To rest on like a cushion soft,
Will start, will look for me in vain,
Will put, after the sun has set,
Some senseless pebbles in his lap.

How will you cope, God? I am scared.

(Rainer Maria Rilke, *Das Stundenbuch*: 'Was wirst du tun Gott, wenn ich sterbe')

People abuse you when you are not violent. When some time ago the television programme 'Spitting Image' made a persiflage on Jesus Christ, they had nothing to fear: Christians are not supposed to hit back. But then the Muslims got into the act, for Jesus is also their prophet. Quickly and cowardly, the programme was scrapped.

* * *

4TH MARCH.

The steely cold dawn crackles with frost. I now walk along the same way as I did in 1969. To my amazement, I recognise nothing any more. The surroundings have changed but probably my memory as well.

My memory plays games with me. The memory as such is a mysterious link in the chain of perception. Plato (375 BC) took the memory to be the very anchor of knowledge. Through the memory of what we have seen during our pre-existence in the divine heaven of light we carry within us a large collection of priceless ideas. These reminiscences are stirred awake by our daily contact with our surroundings. Knowledge is remembering. For Plato the memory is more reliable than observation. Our living experience seems to confirm that. You can only know a person well if you remember much about him. That is why a mother is in the best position to know her child well: she still sees in him or her, the helpless baby, the toddler out on discovery, the child, the teenager, the young person. God's knowledge would be similar in character.

Plato is the first philosopher in Greek antiquity to construct a great synthesis. He embraces Pythagoras and the mysteries of Orpheus with their stories about the fire-soul locked up inside the prison of the body, about the body being the tombstone of a soul (sooma sèma); about the irresistible urge (eroos) inside the soul to climb up again back to the light. Plato joins this up with the idea of Heraclitus, the man who saw everything in constant change; he establishes a link with Parmenides, too, the man who rejected all change. The result is: there is a core reality that is unchangeable, primarily spiritual and made up of ideas, but that has a kind of companion world of matter, a changeable world of the senses.

Plato founded his Akademeia in Athens, a scientific institute that would last for 900 years. It is said that all Western philosophies have run via Plato ever since, either by way of imitation or by way of reaction.

The first dead animals of spring appear on the road: a squirrel, a mouse, a hedgehog.

I have been on the road for a long time: one whole month already, enough to qualify for being a tramp. Have I learnt anything so far?

When I test myself about this, I can think of nothing else but trivialities, like the way you have to peel an apple without touching it with your fingers, using knife and fork only. I saw father abbot do it. Put your fork into the bottom of the apple, and divide it into four parts, each one of them falling on its back. Next, you stick your fork into the belly of that part, you lift it up, and now you can peel the skin from its back. Long ago, I watched the BBC interviewing a prominent politician at breakfast; I do not recall his political message but he did teach me how you can safely decapitate a soft-boiled egg. That is a very useful skill: if you hit the egg too high, then the opening will be too small for the egg-spoon to enter; if you hit it too low, then the yolk comes running through your fingers. Well then, with the side of your spoon, you gently crack the egg-shell at exactly the right height and continue doing that on all sides whilst turning the egg round and round; after that you can easily push the spoon through the crack. It is so simple that you can even give a political discourse in the meantime. Trivialities, quite honestly. Trivialities keep on coming. How does a zip work? When will they develop the kind of zip that does not get pieces if cloth or skin caught in it? And how do press-studs work? Formerly we had studs we called pick-pack buttons: you put a small piece of cloth over the top, squeezed it together until it said "pack" and then it was fixed forever; do they still exist? Those I understood.

I find this landscape not all that different from Holland. Formerly, this was really "abroad" for me; but since I have spent so many years in Africa, it has now become "homeland".

Six or seven hours I have to fill with thoughts every day. This is not as simple as it seems; I remember that this gave me a lot of trouble back in 1969. This time I prepared a thought-menu for myself. These are the main courses: prayerful meditation, reflecting on the history of philosophy and reciting St. Mark's gospel by heart. My walk starts every morning with three hours of prayer, a meditation on the mysteries of the Rosary. When you pray for a long time during a walk, your footsteps become a mantra. The philosophical reflection I prepare the evening before by selecting some topics to think about.

"You are early," the proprietress of Hotel Europe at Corbigny says. "Pilgrims come by the end of March only." It is a cosy place, with two civilised little cockroaches; not the frog-sized whoppers we have in Kenya.

* * *

5TH MARCH.

Today's distance is somewhat long: 34 kilometres. It forces me to stick to the main road. Cars roar past; memories rush past; the undulating landscape makes you quiet and gives scope for quietly undulating thoughts.

Not many people see the connection between walking and thinking. Thinking is something people do sitting on their backsides rather than walking on their feet. Nevertheless, one of the most ancient and venerable schools of thought of Western philosophy, the one of Aristotle, was called the "peripatetic" or "walkabout" school. That was because the classes were given to the students as they were walking round. Students had to absorb the subject in their heads, not in their notebooks. When you talked philosophy and at the same time walked about, the walking represented the ever slightly varying contact with practical human reality. Not many people will deny that truly important thoughts have to be tied up with ordinary daily life.

I find it amusing to know that the oldest universities were institutes of philosophy and that they were to be found in huge gardens. Plato founded his institute of science in the garden of Akademos, a mythical Greek hero. On that account, Platonists are sometimes called "academics". Our word "academy" is derived from Plato's school. Apart from philosophy, the students were taught mathematics, astronomy and physics.

Aristotle founded his own study-garden near the temple of Apollo Lukeios, so that the garden got the name of Lukeion, or Lyceum as we would say. There the "courses" (from the Latin word currere, to walk!) were: logic, physics, philosophy or meta-physics (after-physics), psychology, ethics and politics.

The philosopher Epicure had his school in a place simply called The Garden. He promoted a sober appreciation of science leading to peace of mind, mental balance, aversion to doing extraordinary things and a preference for civilised enjoyment.

Another famous place of learning in Athens was the Stoa Poikilè, the gaudy colonnade. It was the headquarters of a group of thinkers who became known as the Stoics.

The garden institutes indicate the ancestry of philosophy: it started with debates in the market or chats in a quiet spot behind somebody's house. Something similar is indicated by the fact that our word "school" is derived from the Greek "scholion", meaning free time. How far are these terms removed from our stuffy lecture rooms full of nodding students and the – partly fictitious – isolation of the laboratory.

The only hotel at Châtillon-en-Bazois had let me know that their cheapest room was 180 francs. I took it but when I got there, I had to go on my knees to beg for it.

* * *

6TH MARCH.

Another long distance of 34 kilometres today, over endless stretches of tarmac.

The word "techniquing" bounces round in my head; I don't think it really exists. I got it once from a skating colleague and it was supposed to mean: to skate around the track slowly and deliberately checking all the aspects of your skating technique until the movement is absolutely perfect. I often do something like that during my walk. Am I stretching my back in the right way? Do I bend my knees properly? Do I give my feet a rolling movement? Do I give a good push with my toes? Do I use the two walking sticks in the right way? Do I catch my weight on my arms? Do I push the sticks away backwards? By conscientious "techniquing", you begin to walk like a lightweight within a few minutes.

That skating priestly colleague was a story by itself. He was a fine athlete; to invest in a healthy old age he decided to go in for skating. To go skating everyday he had to travel to the neighbouring town of Eindhoven where there was a good 400-metre track made of artificial ice. He would ride a bicycle from his home to the railway station, take the train to Eindhoven – in the railway carriage he could nicely fit in the prayers of his breviary – get to the ice-rink, do his "techniquing" for an hour and then come back the same way. In those days, the Russian super-champions Grishin and Matusevich were training on the same track; my friend rode in their wake, copied them and became a veritable crack himself. One morning when he was on the way to the railway station a motor car hit him so badly that he was confined to a wheelchair for the rest of his life. This may sound like a cynical and cruel falling of the curtain. But it was not. He started "techniquing" in his wheelchair until he became a crack at moving around with a wheelchair; he even managed to drive a car again. Alas, one bad day he was involved in heavy car crash; from then on he was bed-bound. But above the bed there was a bar with a handle that we call a "parrot" in Dutch. Soon my friend was "techniquing" with the "parrot" and before long, he could stunt around like no one else. This endeared him so much to the haptological kinesitherapist lady who treated him that they fell in love, married and "techniqued" happily for ever after. That last bit is nonsense of course but as far as the "parrot", it is true. When he died, he must even have been able to make something of his death.

At Décize I am given hospitality by the parish priest, and yes, the magic chain begins to work again. Tomorrow I will be welcome in a house of spiritual retreats at Moulin.

* * *

7ᵀᴴ MARCH.

There are quite a few beautiful animals that don't even make the spring. Today I recorded the following road casualties: an owl with feathers yellow like honey and a spotted woodpecker; yesterday there was a knocked down roe. Crows are cawing in pairs and fight over twigs in the air. Ewes stare at me and summon their lambs; I never knew that a sheep trots like a horse. Since the invention of plastic flowers French cemeteries have improved a lot; they look more cheerful even than the village churches. Has Nietzsche's word come true, that the churches are the tombs of God?

During a long and slow descent, the pilgrim is allowed to enjoy the panorama of Moulin with its twin cathedral towers. The winding road makes the two towers shift quickly under a heavy pack of white clouds. What do they remind me of? It is as if a colossal feather-bed is being supported with a huge pitchfork. Or it could also be a huge tuning fork inviting us to get the right pitch for our spiritual music.

The inside of the cathedral is full of the fragrance of age-old wood marinated in hundreds of years of incense and hundreds of kilograms of beeswax.

Why has nobody ever thought of making a museum of historical smells?

The church contains a number of breathtaking pieces of art from the late Middle Ages. Has there ever been another period like that, when so many astonishing pieces of art were made for the common people, who evidently loved them? One looks at the triptychs in the style of Van Eyck and one loses all awareness of time. The same is true of the almost life-size wooden statues representing the burial of Jesus in a most touching manner. The devotion to the dead Jesus has always been a very popular devotion, as is proved by the statues at the back of so many ancient churches and glass coffins with the dead body of Jesus in side chapels.

Everywhere by the roadside and in churches I see images of the crucified Jesus. People try to make them beautiful; but there is a contradiction in a "beautiful" crucifixion. If it is really beautiful, it is not a crucifixion; if it is really a crucifixion, it is not beautiful. Putting Jesus on the cross in an aesthetic way is so untruthful. Aesthetics has its limits. You cannot make a chorus of Sudanese children dying of hunger or a church full of Rwandese being burnt to death. It is not right to make a painting of Algerian women who have their throats slit in an aesthetic fashion. If you really know about the ancient evil urges and the ancient sorrows, you will find it impossible to sing hymns about them.

Maison Saint-Paul has an agreeable atmosphere. It is a diocesan centre where people from different walks of life feel at home. Everybody is friendly and helpful; nobody ignores you. I feel a family spirit that comes from a common inspiration of fraternité.

It is a whiff of an ancient and authentic inspiration that you find in all corners of the world, and in the stages of history. I feel it runs back to the people that composed the gospel of Mark.

Something is happening to me as I learn the gospel by heart. To carry the gospel of Mark inside you gives you the feeling of being pregnant. What was formerly no more than a collection of separate texts takes on a coherent and structured life of its own. An overall unity begins to establish its important contours. It begins to hurt too, now and then. The pain that slowly gets worse in me finds its origin in the sad contrast between the exercise of authority in the church and the rules Jesus lays down about that in Mark 10:42–43a: "You know that among the gentiles those they call their rulers lord it over them, and their great men make their authority felt. Among you this is not to happen." It is not often that Jesus forbids anything in uncompromising terms but here we have a case. Should that not make us, leaders in the church, pause for serious thought? I think I have perused all the documents of the Second Vatican Council but I cannot remember having found this text anywhere. Surely, they will not have left it out on purpose? In these Council documents, I do find the admonition that the boss has to be the servant but nowhere this stone-hard, straightforward and courageous prohibition. Meanwhile, look what happened to the word servant: it became an honorary title in human society: His Excellency the Minister.

* * *

8TH MARCH.

Because the distance to Saint-Pourçain along the big straight road is 31 kilometres, I am afraid that smaller country roads might be very much longer. So let's have another day of cautiously braving the heavy traffic on the very edge of the road. The road goes up and down; that is a relief of sorts. On the left side of the road, there is a slowly changing panorama of the meandering river Allier: a pale sun low in the sky turns all the water into silver. I have to be content with a monotonous road and a nice but static scene next to it and so my thoughts wander far away.

I wonder if there ever was a time in my life when I was as free as I am now. Nobody tells me to do anything whatsoever, for months on end. I think of all the people that feel they are imprisoned in their own world. Could that also be due to themselves? Is freedom a state of mind? But surely, not all the time?

On this journey my thoughts go back often to the prisoners of the big Kisumu prison where I have been chaplain since 1980. Two thousand persons, caged, dressed in white clothes, leading a phantom life, many of them in a state of decomposition. They eagerly listen to my sermons when I tell them that they are like people buried alive: nobody takes them into account any more. At home, people rob their property, steal their land and perhaps even their wives. They have discovered that they have no rights anymore: the laws stop at the prison gate. They can be killed without any bother; they can be tortured and raped by their very fellow prisoners.

The only thing normal, the only thing that still reminds them of their world outside, is the Mass that has followed them into prison and is being celebrated in the same way it is at home. During the Mass, they sing from the bottom of their hearts, their bodies swaying in common movement like seaweed moving under the waves. They feel: God is still the only one who sees them, from afar.

Long ago, I proclaimed a Eucharistic amnesty: anyone who likes is allowed to come to Holy Communion. I am often moved to tears; sometimes on account of the scurvy-ravaged hands on which I am allowed to put the Body of the Lord. Then again because I see their bodies decomposing with AIDS, then again because I see some who have received Holy Communion go to the back to give their shirt to somebody else who has none, in order to receive Him "who descended into hell, and on the third day rose from the dead". And I assure them that for them, too, the third day will come. They are full of resignation: they know that they have no more credit with God: otherwise, He would not have allowed them to be caught. Some of the officers treat them with respect and can do a lot of good; but once the officers are corrupt, their evil keeps bouncing round like in a closed grotto.

The prisoners are so vulnerable; only a little thing has to go wrong and they are lost. Many of them die because of injustices committed against them by prison officers, offences that would count for little outside the prison but that become diabolical inside. Like stealing the prisoners' food.

Prison is a holy place; I am convinced that Jesus dwells there. "I was in prison, and you visited me." I try to explain this to our normal parishioners and tell them that therefore they should genuflect when they pass the prison. It amuses them: "The parish priest always makes us laugh with funny statements."

In modern European life you never stumble across prisons; they are out of sight. All the same, it is good to realise that a prison is never far from our door – and that there are prisons of many different kinds.

Quite a few people carefully construct their own prison to live in, especially a mental prison. Even when we make a choice, we lock ourselves up inside that choice. Rigid convictions can become a permanent prison. Thus we can create for ourselves a ghetto in the wide land of what Rilke calls "the unlived things". You find that idea in a nice poem of his.

And when at night I try to have a break,
and leave my garden where I strained my back,
then I am sure, all paths lead to the same:
the arsenal of un-lived things ;
there is no tree, the land is flattened out,
and all around there is a jail-like wall,
without a window and in seven rings;
its gates made strong with solid iron plates
to frustrate those that want to go inside,
its barriers are made with human hands.

(Rainer Maria Rilke, *Das Stundenbuch*: 'Ich bin nur einer deiner Ganzgeringen')

Even language can become a prison. Language is built up from solidified experience. Sometimes there are no words available anymore for new experiences; in that case, you have to make new words. That is the way language develops. Whoever nails his mind down on formulas with a fixed meaning will not be able to make progress in thought: he too is in prison, locked up inside formulas.

Sometimes the French cuisine disappoints me, probably because of its high reputation. I think French soup is often tasteless; the afters often ordinary, like the eternal caramel mousse.

Ah, there I see again the minuscule church of Chãtel-de-Neuve. I remember noting in my diary in 1969 that the church was so small that you could only get inside if you left your sins outside. At last, I find something that I have seen before.

The town of Saint Pourçain goes back to the year 300 and something. I come across a member of a very rare species; a young French priest, ordained one and a half year ago. He is one of those that are determined to start a new game with a newly-shuffled hand. But, at the end of the day, he too will have to address the ancient questions to which we have never given proper answers.

When you consider the breadth and the width of Western philosophy, you notice that there were three questions that challenged people; all the time. The first one is: what are the right things we have to do so as to avoid catastrophes on earth? The second one is: what is this reality all around us and can we influence it? The third one is: is our knowledge any use in grappling with these questions? The attempted answers to these three questions are to be found in the three classic tracts of philosophy: Ethics (On how to behave correctly), Metaphysics (The study of reality in its deepest being) and Logic (On how to build up true knowledge).These three questions overlap each other entirely and cannot be taken separately. And they are very, very difficult questions, all three of them.

One can illustrate the difficulty of these questions with a small example. Imagine that somebody is born in an aeroplane and continues to fly up there all his life. His first concern should be not to make a wrong move that would cause the plane to crash. Secondly, it will dawn on him sooner or later that he is sitting in an aeroplane and what that entails. Thirdly, he will wonder if he can ever understand his true condition if he remains locked up inside his aeroplane.

If ever I write a serious book on philosophy, I want to start with this image. I see it before me already.

'Slowly the passengers in the plane wake up. The little gong sounds to warn them that an announcement is coming: ping ping. Good morning Ladies and Gentlemen, this is your captain speaking. We seem to be cruising at the usual speed; but I have one urgent request to the passengers. Is there perhaps anyone among you who knows what is going on? Are we really flying, or do we stand on the ground with the landscape moving quickly underneath us? Is there anything at all outside? Or are the windows merely glass screens showing moving pictures?' And so on and so forth.

* * *

9TH MARCH.

The weather is warm and sunny but no speck of green is yet to be seen anywhere. Another 12 days and the plants will transgress the rules of nature en masse. My condition is tip-top; steep, mean little hillsides that used to make me huff and puff as I clawed my way up are a piece of cake now. I pass impoverished noble estates, monuments to past arrogance. Feudal arrogance has not been exterminated; it has just been shoved aside as being irrelevant. Is that very same process now taking place in the Church?

Do we, church leaders, realise how feudal ecclesiastical authority appears to many ordinary people? According to contemporary standards, the church's form of rule gets low marks. For people of our generation it is unimaginable that all management should be gathered into the hands of one person. The pope himself appoints all the bishops and by the time he has ruled for 15 years, most bishops are people who he himself has selected according to his personal preference, including the college of cardinals, the ones that have to choose his successor. That is an unheard of concentration of power. That has come about over the last few centuries. It has not always been like that and it does not have to be like that. And however humbly the supreme ruler keeps saying "I am but the servant of the servants", and however devoutly we may assure ourselves that this system is a charisma and a gift from God, to many ordinary people it just looks like plain corruption of power. To make matters worse, our claim of divine illumination gives people outside the church the feeling that our leaders think they can claim a monopoly on wisdom. This global concentration of power certainly needs an immeasurably large bureaucracy. Within the confines of such an extensive and vulnerable bureaucratic apparatus, human rights can be damaged.

Within that set-up it will not be difficult for lesser masters to create small independent territories for themselves where they escape controls and checks; the perceived hubris trickles down from the higher echelons to the lower regions; it is the very structure itself that is reputed to be arrogant. I personally know many bishops who are friendliness and kindness incarnate, who are completely unpretentious and "common" and humble; but that does not seem to make any difference to the reputation of the institute as a whole.

On the left I see blue mountains far away; I ask some ladies what mountains they are but they have no idea. The town of Gannat shows its southern character; the shutters in the windows have small wooden louvers; the houses become more cubist and pastel-coloured; in the market squares you see jeu-de-boules courts and on the walls you find announcements about pelota tournaments. The transition from north to south is very gradual.

The landscape knows no quantum leaps. The Pyrenees Mountains will evolve quietly from the simple farmland I am in now.

* * *

10TH MARCH.

Sunday – day of rest. The priests who are my hosts swarm out in several directions to do Eucharistic services in outlying places. They leave me the whole day to my own devices, lovely. In the evening one of them, a crippled old man, returns. He makes coffee and talks in endless monologues, sometimes for 20 minutes on end, with a small piece of bread in his hand. About his family in Limoges who worked in the porcelain industry; about his wartime adventures as prisoner of war in a factory in Bohemia; about French arrogance in former days. At the end he thanks me for listening so patiently; otherwise he would have been sitting there all by himself, he said.

Church renewal is not a very hot item here. Renewal? The church just seems to have disappeared. And it seems that very few want her back, because for the common people the word 'church' stands for empty pomp and glory. Very radical things would have to happen to bring about a change here.

There have been moments when the church authorities felt uncomfortable. The tiara, the papal Triple Crown, has been stored away, together with the big papal carrying chair and the fans made of ostrich feathers. In a way, that palanquin of the big chieftain was quite entertaining, like the main float in a liturgical cortege. When I studied in Rome in the 1950s, I used to see how the visitors in St. Peter's made a sport of getting the white skullcap of Pius XII. The pope was quite willing to exchange his own for another one offered to him. But high on his Sedes Gestatoria he was out of reach. Enterprising spirits did the following. They made a skullcap and attached to the top a long thin stem bending downwards; thus, they could reach the pope on high with it. He took it then, held it on his head for a moment the way you snuff out a candle with an extinguisher, and returned it to the supporter below. There must be a large number of skullcaps of Pius XII lying around.

There was of course a little adder in the devotional grass, the adder of imperial veneration. To combat this, there used to be another custom in the same St. Peter's ages ago. Now and then, a barefoot monk would bar the way of the papal cortege with a bunch of burning straw, shouting: "Thus passeth earthly glory!" Has the time not come for us to revive a custom like that for all processions with ecclesiastical dignitaries? Behind the last and therefore most eminent dignitary an old woman should walk representing Mother Church; and every ten steps she should give the highest boss an almighty kick in his backside with the words: "Remember what Christ said".

* * *

11TH MARCH.

Today I have enough courage to gamble with the paths a bit. Whenever I reach the top of a hill, I view the assortment of available paths and chose the most likely one. I know the general direction. And I ask for the road if necessary, for I do not want to stray too far.

I am as free as a bird and I have a lot of free time; but free time is fun only when you do something nice with it; otherwise, you are just bored or irritated.

Other worlds come floating by and mix in with my present day in a restful rhythm of marching feet, tapping sticks, shifting vista and passing cars.

Even though I walk in Europe, my insides are full of Africa. In 1957, I went to Uganda for the first time; since 1977, I have been living and working in the grimy shanty-town areas of Kisumu, the third largest town of Kenya.

In such places, you have to allow yourself to be re-educated by your local friends. In the course of the years, I gained more and more insight into the local culture. That culture founded itself firmly on nature, where every living being has a bigger or smaller amount of power, and all of them together form a pyramid of power. People, too, form such a pyramid of bigger and smaller powers among themselves. Everything derives from power: honour, money, justice, happiness. Now, how can a less powerful person hold his own against a more powerful one? The answer is through wisdom; and this wisdom includes cleverness and craftiness. In the Luganda language they use the same word for wisdom and for clever fraud: Amagezi.

When it is a question of misleading, Whites are no match at all for my friends if the latter really try. My friends themselves take no great delight in cheating Whites; it is too easy, it is like shooting tame pigs. "Wuondo Muzungu ok tek" (Cheating a White man is too easy) the Jo-Padhola used to sing. Traditional local heroes look a bit like Till Eulenspiegel of European literature, the foxy cunning survivor. As a result, several Kenyan banks are headed by Till Eulenspiegels; and government departments as well; and enterprises; and reform committees. Things go wrong time and time again but there is never a dull moment. A corrupt official is envied rather than ostracised. And if you do not want to be ground to bits, you have to sway with the mighty. The only spot where you are free and autonomous is your deepest secret interior. The only effective defence of that private spot is an outward appearance that can mislead the more powerful, an appearance that gives the powerful the illusion that they are in firm control. Europeans often mistake this duplicity for hypocrisy but it isn't, as long as you stick to the rules. The main rule is that you should mislead the more powerful. You should not mislead somebody who is weaker than yourself; towards such a person you have to show mercy. Deception is the weapon of the powerless; you cannot just take that weapon from them.

Unity is very important: it should create greater power. Often, however, co-operation does not work; everybody wants to keep his power to himself; power-sharing is often felt to be a loss of personal power.

Truth is established when many people agree about a certain point; truth can be created.

Mutual love often has the character of: not being afraid of one another.

All this highlights the importance of the outward appearance. One is inclined to say: whatever you do not see is not there. For the car, the wash is more important than mechanical maintenance; clothes have to be smart first of all; a uniform bestows an identity on you. To make an impression is a source of great satisfaction. My friends love acting and are superb at it. On the debit side, they show a liking for putting their heads in the sand, a preference to wait for possible disaster to strike rather than try to prevent it, for maybe the thing you are trying to prevent will never happen and then you have been exerting yourself for nothing. One has the feeling that even carpenters and builders are showing too little concern for structural soundness. I do think indeed that my friends detach the outside too much from the inside of things, so that there is not enough scope left for logic and even for symbolism but all the more for magic; little poetry but many anecdotes. And I also think that this accounts for the considerable layer of fear that you notice in many relationships.

My friends are not slow to criticise the Whites; they often find us nervous and "not free" and unnatural. They find it amazing that European mothers may well refuse to breastfeed their babies in order to keep their figure beautiful (something like: not going to the toilet in order to save your backside).

They do not know the Western obsession with the female breast; they think that our perfectly spherical breast is rather unpractical: it is better for the breast to be a bit more manoeuvrable so that baby can shift around a bit and mother can lift her breast more easily over the edge of her clothing. With my African lady friends the erotic magnetism has concentrated itself more in their thighs and their buttocks; for that reason they tend to find the Western female fashion of baring the upper legs offensive and tasteless. Nor are they able to imagine that a mother would not want to carry her baby but rather put it in a small cart; that the tiny child is not cuddled in mother's bed but is exiled to a separate lonely room. They also think that we allow our children to behave without social manners. What they impress on their children from the tenderest age is that company is the nicest thing there is; they have no word for "privacy" to pass on to their children.

The parish house of Riom is manned by friendly and elegant ladies who think of ways to help you. They are a pleasant alternative to the normal parish priest who eyes you wondering whether you come for confession or to beg. The ladies are volunteers from the parish, taking up this job for want of priests but not for want of better. They insist that I should refresh myself with beer, bread and cheese.

* * *

12TH MARCH.

A pleasant little country road enables me to avoid the big traffic artery to Clermont-Ferrand. There is a lot to do at Clermont-Ferrand: collecting the Poste Restante, fetching money from the bank, eating, reading letters, listening to somebody who has had an apparition of the Blessed Trinity and admiring the cathedral. The many columns in the cathedral remind you of a strip-code, just like the tree trunks in a wintry forest.

When I knock on the door of what seems to be my clerical hostel, I am rudely chased away. I discover that I am supposed to be at the building next door. I had been knocking on the door of a fortress belonging to the ultra-conservative Lefêbvrists who sized me up pugnaciously and suspiciously: I must be an enemy or perhaps a friend all the same?

In our own ranks, too, there has been a lot of pugnacity in the past with calls to join battle, to stand in battle array, to raise the battle cry loudly, to decide a holy question with fiery combat. That is surely the human side of Christianity, from the crosses on the shields of Constantine's soldiers to the pictures of O. Lady on the automatic rifles of Lebanese soldiers. But it is not the proper Gospel way and it may well lead to horrible consequences.

A favourite image of the Church is that of a ship. Does the Church also have a certificate of unsinkability, like the Titanic?

Recently I was struck by another comparison. Centuries ago during a naval battle in the Baltic, the new and capital Swedish flagship suddenly capsized. They had put so many cannons on the decks that it had become top-heavy and they had perforated the bulwarks with shutters in order to be able to aim their cannons better at the enemy. The ship made a sharp turn; the shutters were still open and the water entered through them; the ship overturned and the men were crushed by their own falling cannons. Is it possible that something similar could happen through the Second Vatican Council? There is no doubt that in the course of the ages St. Peter's fishing boat has been rebuilt into a man-of-war. If we want to be able to manoeuvre the old boat, we will first have to dismantle all these heavy cannons and not insist on having the bulwarks pierced in order to keep our guns trained on the enemy.

* * *

13TH MARCH.

Climbing up and away from a big city is a remarkable experience; only a few hours ago you were in a thunderous metropolis, now it is just a picturesque panorama in the distant valley behind you. At this time of the year, the light is unreal: it has the intensity of summer light but it is flat. That is caused by the fact that there are no leaves on the trees yet: the sun shines through the vegetation without producing shadows.

Once you have arrived on high ground you can see how badly diseased the landscape is: the valleys are being clotted up with housing schemes that have sprouted out of Clermont-Ferrand like metastases. Forests and wild animals are on the run.

At Saint-Amant I find simple lodgings in a house adorned with the licence for 'tabac' on the façade I like the small town, just the right size for a pleasant afternoon stroll; parts of the town remind me of sections of Old Mombasa.

* * *

14TH MARCH.

The higher I climb into the Auvergne Mountains, the more I go back to winter: ditches full of snow, squalls of stinging icy rain. At long last, I come to a point I remember, the place where I made a sketch of Saint-Nectaire's church in the valley below me, in 1969. But that was in the month of July. It takes a lot of imagination to believe that this chilly, cheerless, wet, grey empty village buzzes with flashy holidaymakers in summer time. The church is hermetically closed, for there are no tourists. There are no other signs of life either.

In the hotel, there is one other guest, a Frenchman. "France is a good country all things considered." "Do you know of any bad countries?" "Well, take Spain or England; you can't eat there, can you? Be honest, all the big chef-cooks are French." "Do you think French breakfasts are so good?" "Come on, breakfast is not a meal!"

Africa, Kenya, they are inside me terminally. So many funny little things come to my mind all the time. There is humour in the language. For "forgetting", they say in dhoLuo "spraining your head"; the plural of "woman", dhako, is mon or "pestering"; the plural of "homestead", dala, is mier, which really means "to quarrel".

By Western standards, you would call the Kenyan women a bit prudish. They do not enjoy giving others a peek at their underwear. Even when clothing consisted of little more than beads and decorative patches, the ladies would take good care that nothing serious was revealed. Now they are very happy with voluminous skirts and they always sit down cautiously. From very early on, girls are taught to sit down "properly"; and sure enough, in all the 20 years that I have been around I have never seen girls sitting improperly. I have heard women who visited Europe come back with shocking tales about the uncivilised way many girls and women sit down there, another sign that Western mores are unseemly. Sometimes they would add acidly: "And people coming from there want to tell us how to educate our children".

* * *

15TH MARCH.

I go higher and higher into the dripping cold. Surely I don't have to go to those snow-covered ridges that I saw towering high above me these last two days? Oh yes, oh yes. Through ragged holes in the grey clouds, I can see the big castle of Murol on the next mountaintop, frozen solid. How could people formerly survive in such a building in this kind of weather? Cars with skis tied to the roof squeeze past me between walls of snow.

Admittedly, I deeply enjoy the battle against time and inclement conditions. Battle is an intimate form of engagement. Our deep unity with living nature, and especially with nature's ingenuity, is a tricky topic for us Westerners. Nature's ingenuity was always linked up with God's presence. When the traditional God had to be dismissed from active service because He stood in the way of science and of our own autonomy, the question arose where exactly the amputation had to be made. To make quite sure, we amputated ingenuity in nature as well. We were not any longer allowed to discern "purpose" in nature, we had to stop short with "chance occurrences".

In the time of Romanticism, the "Weltgeist" became popular but it was not much more than a philosophical Father Christmas, decorating the romantic season.

Teilhard de Chardin, in the 'fifties, proposed a new vision of a grand living cosmos; but many philosophical pundits thought that it was too much like pseudo-religion. The only item you are allowed to be sure of without losing your reputation is yourself. But then you are on a track the final station of which is Solipsism: I am the only form of reality and all other beings are no more than patterns on the wallpaper with which I have decorated the walls of my soul. Admittedly, there are not many thinkers that will push their conclusions that far. Many are prepared to admit to some atomic or biological consanguinity with nature; but an intellectual consanguinity, no, never. Then we prefer to stay solitary.

The ancient Greeks would describe somebody who held such an opinion as an 'idiotès', a singular freak, an invalid who had carefully erased his own horizon.

Who is going to cure us? Speaking with Nietzsche's Zarathoustra, our healers will be "the poets, the riddle-solvers and those that can redeem chance". Poets, because they can give us new images; riddle-solvers, because they are not obsessed with logical certainties; and redeemers of chance, because they make chance respectable. Until that time comes, we are and we remain cosmic idiots. Our cosmonauts are not quite sure where they are going and have to be content with crawling over our spatial wallpaper like cosmic flies.

The streets of Besse-en-Chandesse are covered in smudgy old snow. The kindly parish priest puts me up in Hotel Providence but listening to my talk makes him yawn.

* * *

16TH MARCH.

The more I think about the nearby mountain passes, the more my worries grow: are they passable? The route which I have chosen will lead me across one of the highest passes of the Auvergne, the Pas de Peyrol, 1,589 metres, over the Puy Marie. It could well be that it is still closed because of deep snow.

I am familiar with the landscape I am passing through; I know it from those childhood pictures where you saw a Guardian Angel keeping two children away from the edge of an abyss. The children were lucky in that their weather was not nearly as rough as what we are having now. The primeval struggle with the inhospitable weather leaves little room for mental excursions.

In my small hotel at Condat I find two Dutch guests from Barneveld; they are installing machinery for the mechanisation of the local cheese industry.

* * *

17TH MARCH.

Sunday – day of rest. The people of Condat are long-suffering: at 7.00 in the morning, the parish priest shatters everybody's slumbers by clanging his massive church bells but there is no angry revolt. I receive my reward for attending Sunday Mass. I am told by the parish priest that the road over the Puy Marie is indeed closed: the snow is two metres deep. Now I need the rest of the free day to work out an alternative route for the next three days. I am a stickler for details; I want to be reasonably sure that I can find a hotel or a pension in the afternoon. It seems to work; after much searching, I have a route that is only a little longer than the original one: 81 kilometres instead of 80.

* * *

18TH MARCH.

At noon, I reach a nice little rural bistro, run by an amiable couple who are farmers at the same time. Coffee? Certainement. And a little bread with it? With cheese and meat-cuts straight from the farm? The French know how to say this in such a way that your mouth begins to water instantly. In a short time the table is filled with sausages, rolled-up bacon and Cantal cheese, one of the French cheeses that mature. The man tells me about his cows, 20 of them. For months on end, they have to stay inside because of the long winters. He knows Dutch cows too, prodigious producers of milk. But his own Auvergne cattle are xenophobic: as soon as a cow of another race is made to join them, they refuse to give milk. "But France is a really good land, isn't it?" he says. He has probably never seen another country and he is not likely to do so: you can't eat there, can you?

At Laveissière, after 36 kilometres, I am so tired that I sit on a bench next to the hotel till nightfall without ever moving a limb, staring at the high mountains around me. The shapes of these mountains emit a strange radiation. They are like abstract statuary. Adolf Hitler used to sit on his Berchtesgaden balcony in the evening till deep in the night staring at the titanic Alpine massif; he became entangled in demoniac dreams.

When I rise up from the bench, a fairytale feeling floods through me: you are out in the dark wilderness, and you reach a house, and through the window you see a beautifully lit room with warmth and cosiness and tables full of delicious food and sparkling glasses. I am allowed in.

* * *

19TH MARCH.

Yesterday's fatigue still drains my legs. After a couple of kilometres, I reach a tunnel which is closed for pedestrians. "Pedestrians have to pass over the mountain," people tell me with pity in their voice. Ha, let me show them. It takes an extra hour but so what. I climb to the spectacular winter sports circus of Super-Lioran; skiers swish by overhead, over a viaduct. The sun is shining bright, as it ought to in a place like this. The balconies of the expensive maisonettes are filled with bronzed sunbathers. At my right I see the massive Puy Marie, glittering like a mountainous wedding cake. Back on earth, I visit Saint-Jacques-des-Blats, one of "our" ancient pilgrims' staging posts. I present St. James with a big candle of one pound but for the sake of a nice round number, I put five pounds in the box. During a short pause, I observe how two blue tits are inspecting some hollows to see if they are good for a nest. I wonder what they are looking for. One puts his little head inside and then out again to see if there is danger. Maybe that is all. The second titmouse joins the first. How do they come to an agreement? You never see them quarrelling over a house.

I really miss the Kenyan animals and the stories that go with them. Take the chameleon. Like a tiny lion he crawls on, clutching a branch with feet of four toes, two of them this way and two of them the other way; his little eyes are encased in small cones on the side of his head, they turn like turrets independently of each other in all directions. The people are scared of them but they do no harm. I often put them on my hand, to people's utter consternation. Everybody says that they are poisonous. And when they bite they cannot let go until there is a thunderclap. And when the pregnant female wants to bring forth she sings a prayer: "Oh God, why did you make me so strange?" When she has finished her prayer, she bursts open, the little ones come out and the mother dies.

I suffer the kind of thirst that can not be cured by drinking; against my better judgement I try all the same, a few kilometres away from Vic-sur-Cère, with a whole litre of cider. It is a mistake.

* * *

20ᵀᴴ MARCH.

The Family Hotel costs more than my budget allows, so I have to get the maximum benefit from it, in this case a gargantuan breakfast. After that I have to speed up in order to reach Aurillac at 12 noon exactly. I am expected in a house for retired priests and they usually stick to the clock. It is raining and I drop all short breaks. In all of nature, there is no spot of new green to be seen yet. I always thought that the more southerly you came, the earlier the trees would start budding; but now I begin to think that they are all doing it at the same time. When I knock on the door at 12.00 exactly, the old gentlemen are standing around the table already. It is good fun to be with old people now and then.

If you want to register progress or even change, you need old people. You always have to make a comparison with how it was before and old people know all about "before". Another interesting thing is that you notice change only when you do not look for some time. I noticed that as a young boy. We used to have a big clock on the mantelpiece; when you put your nose closely to the dial you could clearly see that the hands were not moving but if you looked away for a while, you could see that the hands had moved. This can lead to strange conclusions, like this one. In order to know something really well you have to take notice of its changes; but you can see the changes only by not looking at the thing for some time. So, in order to get to know something really well, you should stop looking at it from time to time. It must be so.

* * *

21ˢᵀ MARCH.

When I entered Aurillac yesterday after a quick march, I looked on it from on high, it was raining, and it seemed to me to be a really huge place. Now I leave it, I have rested well, the sun is shining, the day is still young, and now it looks just like a normal provincial town. The road undulates a little; every time I reach a top, the snowy mountains behind me are farther away.

Now and then, I have to face the big question: am I still enjoying it? The answer is never a wholehearted "yes". Often, very often, I am deeply moved by the kaleidoscopic beauty of the scenery and the colourful multitude of humans, all of them the same and all of them different. But sometimes you have to grit your teeth a bit; but that is the same with other nice activities such as cycling, skating, and mountaineering. And whatever it is you have decided to do, you always have to push yourself a little now and then.

In the small hotel of Lafeuillade they do not serve supper; that is no disaster, for my stomach is still trying to recover from the litre of cider.

* * *

22ND MARCH.

The weather is pleasantly warm, the small roads wind and twist in all directions along the deep gorges, cut out as with a knife; the pink prune trees and the yellow forsythia are in bloom. It was a fantastic idea to decide to make this pilgrimage. My departure today was late, at 8.30, because it was going to be a short trip: 17 kilometres. Then I see that Conques, tomorrow's destination, is only 35 kilometres away. In my present state of euphoria I should be able to make that; it would give me a little more space to manoeuvre in the coming days when many distances are a bit too big. So I do it.

The Norbertine monks of the old abbey of Conques make me welcome as if they had been waiting for me. The whole abbey complex is different from what I remember it to have been on my visit in 1969 but in the old pilgrims' book my Latin inscription is traced by the same monk who made me write it then – he actually remembers me. A lady from Strasbourg arrives together with me; she started nine days ago from Le Puy. She is surprised that I follow a wild route, not one of the four official ones.

* * *

23RD MARCH.

Day of rest in honour of Conques, the old pilgrims' abbey of Sainte-Foy. The monks of Conques stole the sacred remains of this 3rd century martyr from her original resting place at Agen; and by countless miracles, the saint made it quite clear that she had a much better time at Conques than she had ever had at Agen. Her famous statue – La Majesté de Sainte-Foy – stares at you with large hypnotising eyes. The town of Conques is the opposite of the miniature town of Madurodam at the Hague; the latter is the normal world reduced to the size of a dolls' house; but Conques is a Medieval dolls' house enlarged to normal proportions.

A kind metalworker puts two emergency metal tips on my sticks: they have worn away.

Conques is a magic name conjuring up medieval Europe; with all the surprising aspects of monastic life, venerations of holy relics, evangelising compulsion and doctrinal tournaments: a very typical and time-bound inculturation of the Gospel. In our infancy, many of us were given that medieval edition of Christianity to digest and assimilate as if it was all very normal. Since then the question of Gospel inculturation has become topical again. It is incontestable that you cannot squeeze 20th century persons into a medieval European mental harness, certainly not if they come from Asia or Africa.

Inculturation has always been a risky undertaking. Once Christianity had become the official state religion, it eagerly took on government airs. The contests with the emperors and the first dogmatic conflicts began to run along political dividing lines: the areas of Byzantium, Egypt, Syria, and Rome. Islam brought the great catastrophe: the Church lost control over large tracts of territory and did not manage to assimilate Islam from within. From then on all efforts were aimed at regaining control and not losing still more. To regain lost territory the obvious method seemed to be the Holy War, the Crusades. Later on, to retain control over orthodoxy, the thought police of the Holy Inquisition was created. After the Renaissance, the Church lost a lot more territory. From then on all major developments took place outside and in spite of the Church. Almost the entire body of philosophical literature after the Reformation ended up on the list of prohibited books, not to be read by the faithful, declared to be a forbidden and an inaccessible area. After three centuries of this, we finally woke up to the fact that the Church herself had become foreign territory.

Among our missionary confraternity, there is a lot of talk about the need to "inculturate" the Gospel in other cultures; but the sad fact is that over the last three centuries we have failed to inculturate the Gospel into our own Western culture.

It is amazing how much has changed in the pilgrims' world since 1969. In those days, I had heard little about Compostela. The major resource book 'Les Chemins De Saint-Jacques' of Yves Bottineau had appeared a little earlier, in 1966; but I never knew that. The idea of making a pilgrim's walk to Compostela occurred to me by chance in the year 1968 and not because I had heard of others doing it. That there were four established old routes running through France was something I learnt only when I reached Vézelay. I had simply charted a route from north to south through regions that seemed attractive: Brussels, Reims, Vézelay, the Auvergne, Conques, Lourdes, Roncevaux, Burgos, Leon, Compostela. The old way from the Pyrenees to Compostela was known to the local people, I noticed, and they would tell you if you asked them; the parallel road for cars was marked by the cockle-shell of St. James. Today, the 840-kilometre-long footpath across the north of Spain, called the Camino Francés, has been marked with yellow arrows. It has been chosen to be a European cultural monument; as a result very nice sleeping places have been built every 15 kilometres or so. The four French routes are developing in the same direction. Today's pilgrims would be well advised to chose one of the four traditional routes in

France; they have been described in daily stages in an ever growing number of publications.

* * *

24TH MARCH.

You cannot leave Conques very early, for the monks want to give you the pilgrim's blessing after they have finished Lauds; and these start at 7.45 only. If you are a tough customer, you begin by going down into the valley, crossing the Roman bridge, and then follow the path of Charlemain after having made a steep detour to the old chapel of Sainte-Foy.

It is Sunday; in the café of Noailhac I stop for a cup of coffee in the midst of impeccably dressed farmers who have just come out of church; the room is full of fragrance of coffee and liqueur. It makes me think of long ago, when after the Sunday Mass we would visit our grandparents to find all the uncles and aunts gathered there in a fragrance of coffee and cigars and sweetbreads.

My midday meal I eat at Firmi – strange, such an Italian name – in the company of well-to-do citizens; they eat slowly, to fill the Sunday, but I eat quickly to fill my stomach and push on, for the road is long. At 6.00 in the evening, I find one hotel at Montbazens closed because of the season and the other one closed because it is Sunday. I have to take a taxi to a hotel well off the route.

* * *

25TH MARCH.

As I start again at Montbazens, I am still quite tired on account of yesterday's long march. I pass through small villages; the only food I can get are two apples, an orange and a Mars bar. On my previous walk, I went from Conques to Villefranche in one day, 62 kilometres; and then I had to rest for two days to recover in a home for retired priests. Nobody remembers that home now at Villefranche. I get a place in a youth hostel. All through the night, I hear the loud murmur of the river; in Holland, they would have long ago built a silence-barrier there.

* * *

26TH MARCH.

The region through which I pass now is a region of sharply rising roads and sharp historical conflicts. Charlemain fought many battles here. The Counts of Toulouse tried to defend their autonomy against the encroachments of the French king. The English carried on the Hundred Years' War here. The Protestants held out in numerous strongholds. The Royalists carried on desperate campaigns against the Revolution. It is a region for stiff walks, not as a form of torture for the body but rather as amends for years of abuse. The old battlefields are now hidden under blossoming vegetation and gentle villages. Things have improved. Except that all towns and villages still have monuments with the names of numerous fallen sons; the wars have not gone, they have just moved farther away from home.

In my mind, I keep dwelling on the matter of inculturation. When you think about the inculturation of Revelation, you have to realise that there are a number of models that you can take.

First, there is the classic model. Its starting point is that Revelation is a collection of religious truths that have been made clear to the faithful by God, especially through Jesus Christ. This collection has been delivered as a complete and fully elaborated body of knowledge. This precious treasure has been entrusted to the teaching authorities of the Church; they have to guard it and see to it that it is handed on in full and undamaged, and that it is translated and inserted into all existing cultures. All cultures have to be examined carefully. Cultural truths and values that are in agreement with Revelation have to be encouraged; cultural truths and values that do not fit in with Revelation have to be suppressed as being false. The final word about this lies with the teaching authority of the Church.

But there is another model available as well. Revelation is the Word of God communicated to us. That Word is like a seed that contains everything within itself but has to be sown. Once that Word is sown, it becomes incarnate: the Word becomes flesh. The Word was sown, first of all, in the Blessed Mother Mary and after that in all the disciples that accepted the Word and kept it in their hearts. The Word of God must become incarnate in all cultures. Through the Word the culture grows and through the culture the Word becomes more and more explicit. The culture grows because the Word makes all the valuable aspects of that culture come into their own, making explicit what was only implicit so far; it cleans the imperfect cultural elements, not abolishing them but bringing them to their full implementation, every iota and every title. The

Word grows, too, because the culture awakens in believers insights that were indeed contained in the original revelation but which they had not really noticed yet. So nothing is added to the message; it is just being understood better through the working of the Holy Spirit who is active in all human cultures. Thus all cultures can come to their completion through God's Word. God's people recognise and accept this incarnation as an ever more profound unfolding of Revelation. The Church learns and is being enriched by its much needed contact with cultures and religions that are still in their Advent stage.

The second model requires a special kind of courage: the Church must not be afraid of contamination. Here, too, a word of Christ seems applicable: sullying does not take place through what enters the body but through what comes out of the body. So also with the Church. We should be confident that the Holy Spirit knows how to assimilate all incoming newness with his own kind of holy stomach-acid. That newness will not contaminate the church. What does contaminate her is selfishness, discrimination, arrogance, cruelty, servile flattery and fear.

Najac is an old Celtic fortress from before Roman times. I have learnt to recognise those on this journey: oblong towns on high ridges with steep slopes on all sides.

It takes a big effort to get permission to stay in a bungalow on a campsite that is not open yet. I don't feel comfortable. My lonely light betrays my presence to all robbery-prone drug addicts and psychopathic serial killers for miles around, an irresistible invitation. To be prepared for all eventualities I put a chair against the door.

* * *

27TH MARCH.

Many villages and towns in this region have been thoroughly renovated, so that they look a lot older now. This makes the area an ideal place for tourists. But outside the season things are all the more dead: practically everything is closed. It rains almost the whole way, which makes the area even more cheerless. What would cheer the people up here? Money? Sports? If that is so, then their lives have lost most contact with nature. Although when the religious wars were being fought, conditions were not much better. And one must admit that there are still people who think it is a meaningful thing to kill their brother or sister for the sake of the true religion, or to be killed for the sake of the true religion.

I think you sow the seeds of failure when you start an argument about "the true religion". You make a very bad start by saying: "Christ revealed the true religion, namely the Christian Faith as we know it now". I think you put yourself on the wrong foot when you start off by saying that Christianity is one of the many religions but the true one in fact. That is a terrible shortcut. Christ's redeeming message is not just one of the many religions. That message became incarnate in a number of existing religions; first and foremost in the Jewish religion, then also in several Greek and eastern cults through a process by which those religions, too, were themselves redeemed and brought to fulfilment. As soon as you reduce Christianity to one of the many religions, you have put yourself into a hopeless position and evangelising dialogue becomes impossible. Because then you have to state explicitly that your own Christian religion is the best of all. Mind you, if you do not take up this flawed position you will get into trouble with the church authorities who will – unjustly – accuse you of indifferentism and relativism.

No. It is my firm hope that in the end, all those who now call themselves Christians, Muslims, Hindus, Brahmins and Shamans; and all those that have been touched by God, will learn so much from one another that they will come closely together and nourish themselves with the Word of God as it was revealed above all in Jesus Christ. And that all people of good will discover that He can hold them all in his embrace without demanding that they should throw away their own precious inherited values.

It is a myth that the whole of France is a gastronomic paradise. True, if a restaurant is good, it is very good. But there are lots of sub-standard eating places; almost everywhere I was disappointed with the omelettes and the pancakes. In unknown places the pedestrian should eat where he can. At lunchtime, I find myself in a village called Montricoux: no food in sight except for a tobacco kiosk; so I have a coffee with Twixes and Bounties. But as I leave the village I hit upon a splendid restaurant, good for a top quality beefsteak. I don't let that chance slip by. But the chips are soggy.

When I hear the name Saint-Antonin-Noble-Valle, my memory serves me with unpleasant vibes. It was here that I found all hotels and guesthouses chock-a-block full; and then the parish priest categorically refused to let me put a foot inside his presbytery: I could not even sleep on the bare floor of his veranda. Fortunately, there were merciful sisters around. This time there is the Hotel du Commerce.

* * *

28TH MARCH.

During my walk, I rely heavily on my map. Before starting on my pilgrimage, I had selected my route in minute detail and bought the relevant Michelin maps, on a scale of 1:50 000. I spread out the maps on the floor of a big hall and pasted them together. Then I marked the route with a pencil, making sure that the route was as straight as could be. I cut out the route on a strip of 20 centimetres wide and folded five centimetres back on each side, so that I got a long ribbon of 10 centimetres wide. That strip I laminated with thin plastic. It happened very rarely that I had to diverge so far from my planned route that I got off the map completely. But today I did.

In the Yellow Pages, I found a small hotel in a place called Vaissac. From there it is only 20 kilometres to Montauban, my stop for tomorrow. From my room I can spot in the far away distance places that are found on my map. In the morning, I always depart at such an early hour that often there are no people around; so tonight I have to explore tomorrow's path with extra care. These are logistics that can take a lot of time. There are moments when I am a really busy little fellow. But I just manage it all nicely.

* * *

29TH MARCH.

The mimosa and the peach trees are blossoming, and I pass about 200 excited swallows sitting on a telephone cable, all of them nattering at the same time at the top of their voices.

In Kenya, animals are never far away. When there are ten ants walking on a kitchen table in Holland, some call for the fire brigade to cope with the plague. In my house at Kisumu you can tell that the rains are coming when hundreds of thousands of tiny black ants crawl across the wall together like a king-size pancake, carrying their brood. Cockroaches can be the size of frogs. Rats and mice! I once grabbed a rat that had

hidden itself inside a packet of oats. Another time I slept in
the house of one of our parishioners. I found out that there
were many rats, so I put a big iron trap near the feet-end of
my papyrus mat. The bang woke me up at 2.00 in the night.
With my flashlight, I could see a whopper of a rat in the trap.
But it still moved. And more and more. It even stood up, and
jumping up and down it tried to wrench the trap off its neck
with its front paws. It came nearer and nearer. With one of
my boots I bludgeoned it to death whilst in the rafters scores
of other rats squealed their alarm signals. Then what? Here I
was with the body of a dead rat next to me; and I knew that
the germs of bubonic plague are spread by fleas that leave the
bodies of dead rats. It was a job and a half to get rid of the
corpse: put on your clothes with your flashlight in your mouth,
then clear away the barricades from the bolted door, then open
it gingerly to see if there are any thugs around, then go outside,
then fling the dead rat far away and reverse the whole process.

Once, one of our American sisters was given the bed of the
mother of the house to sleep in. In the middle of the night,
she woke up because a kitten had installed itself on her warm
tummy. The Sister caressed it gently until she reached the
kitten's bottom end where she felt a long hard scaly tail.

*To celebrate the safe arrival of a whole bunch of letters at Montauban, I start
off by eating a nice pizza; then I install myself in a trendy tavern to peruse the
letters, drinking a lot of cool beer. Yes, I have switched to beer. It has been
made clear to me that wine is not the drink that can quench the type of thirst
that I have. Through some conscientious experiments, I have found out that
beer has a better effect on me when I take it in a sufficient quantity.*

*The best bed that the diocese of Montauban can offer me is six kilometres
further on. That is good in a way, for it reduces tomorrow's long route to a
manageable 30 kilometres. But it goes very much against the grain to pick up
the rucksack at 5.00 in the afternoon to hit the road again.*

*On the outside, the buildings of the Missions Etrangères at Montbeton look
like an outdated missionary bastion but on the inside, I find it quite vibrant as
I sit at table together with Vietnamese and Indian priests.*

* * *

30TH MARCH.

The walk goes through flat countryside, monotonous and slow. For hours on end, I am "techniquing", quietly pushing the tarmac away from under me. It reminds me of running on a children's treadmill in a playground.

A friend of mine – not quite normal – maintained that the earth rotates like that treadmill because all people push it away with their feet. I objected that this could happen only if all people walked in the same direction. But no, according to him it works even now because during the day's 24 hours all the people of a certain section of the earth sleep and therefore don't push at all, whilst on the opposite part everybody is pushing. Still, he has not convinced me yet.

Marching for hours. Thinking for hours. Thoughts float along with me like clouds. There is one that has been floating along with me for some weeks and it keeps on irritating me. It has to do with a photograph I saw in a magazine. It is a picture of a small boy, having a holiday on a farm. He polishes his teeth next to a moss-covered old water-well and he spits the water back into the well with a big arch. The accompanying text tells us about the quality and the price of his cotton shirt. Why does this photograph bother me so much? Because in a way it is quite obscene. It is a little as if you publish a picture of someone on the electric chair to advertise his outfit. The fashion magazine evidently did not know that the boy did something all cultures find revolting. The Chinese have a saying: "Do not spit into the well from which you have drunk". Wells have always been sacred, symbols of pure life. That is now a thing of the past. Nowadays water comes, like all good things, out of the wall: together with electricity, money, food, information. And over the last few decennia in our Western culture we have been encouraged to spit and vomit into our water wells; for everything that has been handed over to us by previous generations constitutes a threat to our own spontaneity. We think we can make progress by looking at previous generations with disdain. To be out of fashion is the ultimate nightmare; even to be old is a pitiable handicap without more ado. I am sure we are going to have to pay a price for presuming to think that way. He who disowns his past robs himself of his future.

At Beaumont I stay with sisters who manage to combine old religious values with the present time in an inspiring fashion; I find them beautifully relaxed.

* * *

31ˢᵀ MARCH.

A short trip, no more than 20 kilometres. It is Palm Sunday. We hear the story of the dead son.

I come across a dead fox and a dead badger: after a short life of hot excitement, they lie here quietly, decomposing gently but coldly.

The decomposition taking place in death gave some Greek thinkers of around 400 BC the idea that then birth would have to be the reverse process: the linking up of existing elements. Death being "cold" had already made people think that then the soul had to be a tiny lump of hot fire. Is it nonsense? But how many people are there who can tell me exactly what it is that makes my body warm from the inside? I cannot remember that I have ever been taught this. We get buried under an avalanche of new questions even before we have answered the old ones.

Cross-country cyclists in flamboyant outfits carry their bicycles like crosses on their backs in order to climb over fences and then rush on through the fields.

No more than 20 kilometres and still on my arrival in Au Cheval Noir at Mauvezin I am so tired that I sleep through the whole afternoon. It seems that when you shorten the walking distance, you merely cut off a piece from the beginning, never from the tired back-end.

THE THIRD MONTH

APRIL

1ST APRIL.

If something happens really slowly it is as if it does not happen at all. Very slowly I have reached the south of France; and it is as if it is not so. I have to pinch my arm to make it real. I have also become a morning person; I do not want to miss the rising sun and the pungent morning air and the supple moving of limbs that have rested for a whole night. Early in the morning, there is still space for non-human forms of life. By way of irrefutable evidence of this, three big deer suddenly skip through the fields and meadows to my right, throwing their white backsides up in the air: strange intruders in a strictly-controlled world of grain quota, milk quota and manure quota. Or would they have a deer quota as well? At noon, the curtain of clouds on the southern horizon is suddenly pull up; and there all of a sudden the Pyrenees mountains present themselves, high as heaven, white as hail and sharply focused, like a theatrical backdrop hardly in line with the landscape.

Auch is really a small town that pretends to be big by monumental manners and airs: flights of stairs that Paris would be jealous of and statues that irritate the bourgeois. The people of the youth hostel are good to me; the place is really "complet", but they manage to find a corner for me since I am a Compostela pilgrim. Being 67 years of age, I still fit in reasonably well with youth.

Have French children been spoiled more than ours? Twice I saw that a small child was allowed to eat a whole packetful of biscuits, not just one or two. But what truly horrifies me is the way the French youth are addicted to smoking cigarettes.

In the newspapers they talk about pollution of the air and possible face masks to protect the population; in France such a mask will only be acceptable if it has a small hole in it for a cigarette.

* * *

2ND APRIL.

On huge billboards along the road, jolly geese and ducks advertise their livers and their "confit", boiled meat preserved in molten fat.

Marching along a big tarmac road has its advantages. You don't have to agonise about the route, you make quick progress, and because you do not have to inspect every inch of ground to see where to put your feet, you can do a lot of mental spadework.

Philosophical spadework is fun. It means digging for something that lies deeply hidden under the obvious, like a lost aerial bomb under the town square or a submarine under the quiet waves, by sending out soundings from different angles.

A topic that intrigues me at the moment is: "cheating". What do we have to think of "fraud"? We get different signals. We have been educated to think that it is wrong. Is that really so? In nature, all living beings try to mislead each other. Then, when a baby kids his mother, we think he is so cute. Furthermore, it would seem that for lying you need more ingenuity than for telling the truth: a lie you have to create, truth you just reproduce. Often, I suspect that our friends in Africa hold that telling the truth is for those that do not have enough intelligence to construct an interesting lie. What you need most of all for telling the truth is courage; but courage and dimwittedness go together quite easily. I sense that underneath those different signals there is something big that we have not yet got hold of.

In Mirande I search for the sights of the town that I have stored away in my memory since 1969 with utmost clarity; nothing of that can be found any more.

* * *

3RD APRIL.

Some pieces of road are extremely straight and long. I know now how to tackle those. First, study the map properly so that you are prepared for them and know how long they are; that helps a little. Once you start on the long stretch, you can play games with it: "look at that tree far away, I will never get there... hey, I am there already; I wonder what that white spot over there is... well now, it is a white gate; that bend in the road... I can't believe that that is the end already... my goodness, it is!"

A nine-month walk is really the acme of luxury. You just drop all your normal work and leave it to others. You grab down in a reservoir of saved-up cash. You don't have to take anybody else's ideas into account. Day in, day out, you can just do what suits you best and at the end of it, you can cheat yourself into thinking that you have done a big thing.

My condition is first class. As I arrive at Rabastens I am still as fit as a fiddle. Twenty years ago, it was a different story by the time I had got as far as this. Then I really was at the end of my tether. I was bargaining with myself: just a few more days and then in Lourdes I will call it a day. Once I had made Lourdes and had had a two days' rest I decided to add at least another five days to reach Spain. Having arrived in Spain I threw in the towel and took the bus; but after two days I got out to walk the last five days. Nothing like that bothers me now, even though I am 30 years older. I think it has something to do with my tight mental programme for every day.

* * *

4TH APRIL.

Several of the traffic victims are quite big animals. Today there is a giant otter first and after that a really big badger; lying on its back it displays its bear-like flat feet.

Walking has built-in asceticism. You see many delicious and useful articles but you know that whatever you buy, you either have to eat it or carry it with you; that leads to wonderful detachment. Another point is this. Once you are on the road you cannot blot out nagging thoughts with a distraction.

You have to grant all the thoughts that knock on your door hospitality, whether you like them or not.

Today is Maundy Thursday. I join the ceremonies in the cathedral of Tarbes, presided over by the bishop himself. He introduces me to the congregation. Afterwards, a family invites me to a festive supper, together with the bishop. He sends a telephone message to a house at Lourdes to help me to get accommodation. When I tell him about a diocese in the Sudan where a bishop has to work with two priests only and 275 catechists, he says: "Wonderful". His reaction sets me thinking; would he have trouble with his priests or is he putting so much hope in catechists?

* * *

5TH APRIL.

Good Friday will never become an ordinary day for me. The name carries too many overtones of disappointment, unimaginable catastrophe, treachery, pain, failure and smashed hopes.

Lourdes, the Virgin Mary's famous sanctuary where I will arrive today, will be one of the major stops and highlights on my walk. I hope to stay there till Easter Monday. Even the horizon supplies high points: the majestic peaks of the Pyrenees before me reach right into the radiant firmament. At times it looks as if the silk blue heavens rip themselves open on the ragged peaks so that the white downy fluff of the clouds comes popping out through the tears.

It may sound odd but on entering the town, I have a problem finding the basilica. I am too close and then you can't see the big buildings any more. All devotion concentrates itself around the grotto where Mary appeared to the peasant girl called Bernadette more than a hundred years ago; and where she put to her the not unusual request of building a church there. In the end, there were four big churches.

The centre of attention in this place of pilgrimage is the sick person; a lot of healing has taken place here. Friends had requested me to pray for their sick relatives and to burn a devotional candle for them. That will be the first thing for me to do; I am almost embarrassed over my good health between so many patients. I thought I was putting a jolly good-sized candle in the candle-stand until I discovered the stands of the really big ones. A newly-married couple in their Sunday-best – are they gypsies really? – come in a solemn slow march, the one behind the other, carrying a beam of a candle on their shoulders together, surrounded by family members who take pictures. But the absolute champion candle has been put there by an Irish social club: almost

80

the size of a ship's mast. The next day I will discover a bigger one still, the size of a factory chimney with a broad reinforced foot to prevent it from collapsing under its own weight: the mammoth under the candles, reaching the organic physical limit.

The Veneration of the Cross and the reading of Christ's Passion take place in the new underground basilica; the interior has been arranged in such a way that it seems as if the altar-dais rises up from a sea of sick people. Because they come from everywhere, the ceremonies are done in six languages, even Dutch. And because sick people may well have more difficulty in concentrating, there are spectacular stage tableaux, set up by young people (ex-drug addicts I am told), and lovely musical intermezzos. Thus it becomes a most appealing celebration for the sick and hence for the healthy as well.

Radio Lourdes is calling me in for an interview. They are interested in my view on the French church. I make an awful hash of it. I try to say that the French church comes across to me like an old lady who got a wooden leg 30 years ago when the church renewals started and who has now got so used to it that she does not realise any more that she has a wooden leg. Looking back on it afterwards, I am not so sure that I understand what that is supposed to mean; and my use of the French language was nothing if not intrepid.

I eat a pizza in a big restaurant; they serve vegetarian ones only, in deference to Good Friday.

* * *

6ᵀᴴ APRIL.

Near the basilicas, everybody seems to be leaning on everybody else. So many people keep their heads at a funny angle, many spectacles are impossibly thick, many persons walk with short irregular steps, now and then there is a sudden loud cry. I don't think that the sick people came here to be cured in a miraculous way; I think they came here because they are made to feel well. They are the guests of honour; the healthy visitors are invited to adjust themselves to the sick.

In one of the churches, a priest conducts a penitential service. He does it very well; people that wander into the church stay on to listen, the crowd grows.

When in the 'seventies individual Confessions began to disappear rapidly, many pastors began to offer common penitential celebrations as an alternative. High church leaders feared, however, that the popularity of the common penitential

81

services might deliver a death blow to the individual confessions and so they adopted a policy of not encouraging common penitential services, rather discouraging them. Now it seems they have lost them both. Would those church leaders never notice the damaging results of their policy? If they do, how would they cope with them? Would they be tempted to put their miscalculations on the account of the Holy Spirit among the mysteries of faith?

The Vigil of the Resurrection takes place in the underground basilica, in the presence of 10,000 faithful, that could be called celebrants. It is very well arranged, with moments of light and darkness, projections on giant screens, splendid music and 10,000 burning candles that go up and down with every "I believe". The sick, lying in immense rows of beds, absorb it all with their whole being. You can see how much they enjoy it; so do the children and so do all of us. Everybody is getting new spiritual energy.

Knowing St. Mark's Gospel by heart affects me deeply. Certain texts begin to vibrate, like this one: "The Sabbath is made for man, not man for the Sabbath" (2:27). It seems to imply that the Sunday service is, in the first place, not meant to be an act of giving honour to God but rather an opportunity to get spiritual energy for the coming week.

Another vibrating one: "The son of man has power to forgive sins on earth"; this saying should be linked up with the admonition that we all should forgive each other's sins (2:10 and 11:25). And then it begins to mean that we should not leave the forgiving of sins to God. Jesus tells us that God is giving us that task and that He will back us up all the way. And indeed, the most harrowing conflicts in the world all have to do with evil that we do not forgive one another for. If we would put the whole world into a state of forgiveness the world would be in a state of grace and be healed.

* * *

7TH APRIL.

Easter Sunday. At dinner in our home for old priests and sisters – that is by itself already a healing combination – we are given a festive aperitif of sweet wine and after the meal we get a glass of champagne and a chocolate egg to take away. It is my first egg-free Easter in living memory. It is also my last day at Lourdes; I try to make an evaluation of the sacred spot.

The place where Mary appeared was a patch of rubbish, where a bend in the river caused a lot of driftwood to be washed ashore. There are several famous sanctuaries that were originally built on places where they discarded rubbish and old bones: Saint Peter's in Rome; the Church on Mount Calvary; and Compostela (even its name refers to it). Some people consider Lourdes to be the Roman Catholic equivalent of the Benares River. Most renewal champions have nothing serious to say about Lourdes. That is a mistake, for Lourdes has a big place in the heart of many ordinary people.

Some Christians are disturbed by a kind of faith that lies so close to superstition. Yet Lourdes is quite scriptural. Everyday as I prayerfully recite St. Mark's Gospel it strikes me that I find a typical Lourdes atmosphere hanging in that Gospel. Sick people are irresistibly drawn to Jesus and want to touch the hem of His garments; patients are put on stretchers along the route where Jesus is going to pass, so that they may be allowed to touch His garments. "And everyone who touched Him was healed" (6:56). The power that emanated from Jesus was directed against the debilitating spirits of evil. Could it be that we have not paid enough attention to healing in the church? So maybe it was after all a good idea of Mary to rub that in in her own way.

She took a very long run, a hundred years ago, via a rubbish heap and via people that counted for nothing like this asthmatic peasant girl and via unintelligible terms like "Immaculate Conception" and via heaps of sugary artistic trash. By the way, is trash really reprehensible? For scores of people, art starts with trash. If that artistic trash is really genuine, it will clear itself up: even now the most saccharine mosaics in Lourdes are falling down from the walls by the shovel-full. The children and the sick are moving around with eyes big with astonishment. Perhaps something like Lourdes should rise from the dead in each one of us.

Compared with Rome, Lourdes has a big advantage: Rome has been made into the place of Christ Triumphant, whereas Lourdes is the place of the Suffering Christ.

* * *

8TH APRIL.

Easter Monday. Departing from Lourdes gives rise to a strange feeling: a place of pilgrimage is a place you ought to walk to, not away from.

I depart from the world of leukaemia and cancer, of handicapped children, drug-addicts and HIV sufferers. I step back into the ordinary world where, if I may believe the suggestions of the media, the biggest causes for suffering are cellulitis, dandruff and acne; the biggest worry is what kind of new car to get, and the summit of female beatitude is to be seductive.

At Nay, I knock on the door of an old monastery; it has been taken over by a "Communauté des Béatitudes". It is a new type of monastic community; it embraces a number of lay people (male and female, married and unmarried), a few religious sisters and a priest. They all live and work here at home like one big family; the couples have small flats, the other men and women live in separate wings. They are contemplatives, that means: focused entirely on prayer both communal and individual; prayer fills a large part of their day. The local population has a standing invitation to join in the prayer – it looks as if very few take it up – and strangers are encouraged to join them at table, an invitation many a tramp accepts gratefully. Today I do as well. They lead an extremely simple life, just from what friends give them. The Nay community is big and fascinating: some 30 persons, young, international, enthusiastic and charismatic.

It does fascinate me truly. It is a courageous effort to give modern persons a chance to take part in pure monastic life in a heroic observance of the Three Counsels of Perfection: the Counsels of Poverty, Chastity and Obedience. Yet, this is not what I am looking for. The life of poverty that this monastic rule pursues is not so much poverty but rather simplicity. Poverty means something else than simplicity. In a monastery there is space, health and quietude. But space, too, is riches; health is riches as well; quietude is riches. Real poverty means: too closely together, too rowdy, nagging neighbours, slippery dirt and pain that does not go away. We should not rob the poor of their "poverty". It could well be that we have robbed the sexually frustrated and the oppressed of their misery by sublimating it to "purity" and "obedience". Should we make amends and turn the Counsel of Poverty into one of real poverty? And rename the Counsel of Chastity and the Counsel of Obedience: a vow of voluntary sexual frustration and a vow of accepting oppression for the sake of the Kingdom?

What I am looking for is not just renewal. I want to find something for the disappointed, those that have cut the connection with God in anger, the traumatised faithful, those that say: "How they have cheated us formerly with the whole church caboodle". I feel that this touches me personally, for as a priest, I belong to the accused and I owe these people something. That is also why I walk here, searching.

In this region, church life has wilted even if you compare it with 1969: there is hardly a village where you can still find a person in religious dress. Traditional religious life: is that still in any way relevant to people's ordinary life? And again, does it really rest on a simple straightforward acceptance of the words of the gospel? Do we take up the hints given by Jesus with spirited imagination? Do we agree that the texts of the gospel should comment critically on our religious structures, the way these latter have been allowed to grow? Will Jesus back us up in everything we do? Sometimes I really do wonder. A simple example occurs to me.

In St. Mark, I read that the religious Jews were given an escape clause to avoid looking after their families, simply by making the vow of "Korban". Whoever said "Whatever possessions I have I now give to the temple of God" would not be supposed to support his parents any more. Jesus loathed that. Is there any truth in the frightening suspicion that religions are saying a similar thing with their vow of poverty? This question is urgent and particularly difficult for Africa, where large numbers of talented young women enter religious Sisterhood.

* * *

9TH APRIL.

Spring is shaking the whole countryside loose. The grass in the meadows has become woolly and three-dimensional; the flowers are waving to the bees.

How could all this fresh young life come out of the insides of dead wood? What is nature that it could hit upon a magic trick like this? The landscape is related to me. Nature inventing something like that is the same nature as the one thinking in me.

From a high pass I look down on an ocean of green hills; on the top of each hill you see a freshly washed white house. The cows have a friendly look in their eyes. But I notice that no cow can move her head smoothly along with my movement; they all do so with short jerks. They would be poor cineasts; they cannot pan through nicely.

* * *

10TH APRIL.

Sitting on the top of a hill I zero in on a group of galloping sheep on the opposite side of the valley; at such a far distance they look more like a group of wriggling maggots. The fluttering tune of a bagpipe-playing shepherd floats towards me but much of the music has evaporated on the way.

As soon as fresh new life bursts forth, all beings resume their robbery forays and raids. Robbery is in order, for every living being has to procure in one way or another the materials it needs to install into its body. Pure and formless matter is not available: it is all being used already by other creatures. You will therefore have to take it from those other creatures. The most efficient way of doing that is: eat them. The matter that you have secured thus can now be rearranged around you according to your needs and be inserted into the system.

Aristotle worked this out profoundly. His starting point was the word of Pythagoras that the soul is the order of the body; so he made the formula: the soul is the form of the body, anima est forma corporis. By saying that, you imply that all living beings have soul. When you devour another living being, you break down the form of that other being until you are left with a number of useful sub-forms, and those you assimilate; thus you install that matter into your own structures. The Aristotelians call this process "Hylomorphism", from hylè (matter) and morphè (form).

The soul is the energy source that will arrange all acquired matter in ever widening rings of identity around its centre; but the wider the circle becomes, the weaker the identity will be.

Your body is the first ring; your clothes are the second ring; your house is the third circle; they are all circles or rings that enclose the previous ones the way an onion is made up of tight concentric layers. If you peel an onion in an effort to reach its deepest reality, you will be left with a table full of layers; the onion is gone and you yourself are weeping.

According to Aristotle, the human being is like an onion. For Plato, the image of an apple is more appropriate: if you want to have the finest reality of an apple, you must peel it and then you have the delicious apple left. That is one reason why Aristotle's philosophy appeals more to me: it ties in better with the cannibalistic character of creation.

You can go beyond the image of the onion. For just as there are rings or layers of identity that grow weaker as you go further outward, there are also successive rings that go further and further inward, and grow progressively weaker. If you enter your body, under the layer of the skin you come to a layer of muscles, organs and blood where your identity is already considerably less. Underlying those you find a layer of cells that do not pay much homage to your supremacy any more. Go deeper still and you will reach a layer of molecules that have no respect for you at all; and below those you have basic elements that go their own way completely. From this, you may conclude that the human person is most fully himself somewhere halfway between his outer limit and his inner limit, somewhere between his skin and his clothes; that is the area of most sensitive contact with other persons.

I am sure most people are Platonists all the same: they like to think that their true honest self is hidden deep in their interior recesses and that their outward appearance is but a poor reflection of their true inner self, and is more like a mask that hinders them. I cannot work with that construction at all; the way I feel it, we are not hidden behind our mask, we <u>are</u> our own mask. And my mask enables me to make real contact with others.

In Hotel Bidegain at Mauleon, a classy little pension, I get an expensive room for the price of the cheapest one because I am pilgrim. The landlady invites me to share a beer with her. She is like so many ordinary people who, when they meet me, want to chat about something religious, a topic they do not so often talk about. They like to be confirmed about their pictures of Our Lady, their quarrel with the parish priest, their secret prayers, the little crucifix around their neck and the fact that they have stopped going to church because they were bored to tears. Sometimes I get the strong suspicion that this is the kind of public that flocked around Jesus in Galilee.

* * *

11TH APRIL.

When I sit down for my breakfast I find next to my plate a small collection of gifts from the hostess: a special medal of Our Lady, a big piece of chocolate, some crackers, a chunk of Basque cake, a chocolate Easter egg and two mini-bottles of brandy. Walking through the sleeping town, I see that on each front door a cloth bag is hanging, for the baker to put his bread in without waking up the whole house. Some of these bags have been beautifully embroidered, often with Eucharistic symbols. I am in the lower Pyrenees; the contours of the hills begin to dance.

In the Scriptures, the hills are often said to dance on joyful occasions. I wonder if that would be a poetic reference to dancing women who are, like in East Africa, shaking their breasts? This landscape is a feast of shapes.

I am happy that I have learnt to think in an Aristotelian fashion. Plato cannot think about matter very well but Aristotle can. He describes matter as the quarry of all forms: forma educitur e materia, all form comes out of matter. Pure matter does not exist; it always has some form already. Matter is the dark womb of all forms; give matter the chance to release a form, invite matter, encourage matter. I like that. I prefer it to Plato who places the world of forms in the eternal divine light. For Plato, everything that is good comes falling down from heaven. Small wonder that the medieval Christians considered him as a blood relative; Aristotle was no more than an in-law. And even today, Plato cannot complain about failing popularity; the New Age apostles are certainly disciples of him. They put their hope in heavenly or celestial promises.

Since yesterday I have been walking in Basqueland; the end of France is in sight. My feet are getting wings.

Walking has become normal, the normal posture. Walking is no longer a punishment for those people who do not have a car. Some time ago, I heard a little joke about that. This lady was pushing her five-year-old boy along in a pram. Another lady asks her: "Oh dear, can the boy not walk yet?" To which the mother answers: "Oh yes, he can all right, but thank God he does not have to".

Often, pilgrims have acquired a beautiful stride: you can tell that their bodies enjoy walking. They are well-sprung. Women tend to develop a graceful suppleness which they lack entirely when they walk on high heels. You wonder why women would want to walk on high heels. I can think of one obvious explanation. On account of these high heels their steps become more shaky, less firm, more helpless indeed. That gratifies men: they love to see women helpless. Apart from that, women on high heels turn their backsides in a more pronounced way, they wobble their breasts a little more and thus they draw the attention to their sex. But that is OK; we all do that in one way or another.

Steep descents stir up new pains in my joints. From my hotel room at Lancevaux I have a clear view of the pelote court. Something is written there in blobbed Basque script: Huna zer emaiten ahal duen herrian batasumak. None of the young men down in the lounge can translate it for me.

When you approach borders, you feel invited to make résumés. What did I see? What have I learnt?

One thing I have seen is that in the regions where I passed it is clear that the Church is not at all a people's church any more. Did I discover any cards that have fallen under the church's table? I learn in Saint Mark's gospel that Jesus came to install a new Spirit of power; the kind of power that drives out the spirit of evil but at the same time firmly rejects compulsion and human subjugation. It seems to me that the Christians have not been able to follow Him in this. Every time when they had to shuffle the cards, already in the first centuries, they dropped ever more hearts and handed out ever more clubs. They dropped the queens, too, by opting firmly for the patriarchate. In the course of time, they did not remember that there was something called trumps, whereby a small card could defeat a big one. The game went on but it was hardly the game that Jesus had taught. And now, many find the game so boring that they have stopped playing.

* * *

12ᵀᴴ APRIL.

With winged feet, I go to the frontier town of Saint-Jean-Pied-de-Port. This is my fourth time and so it must bring memories. It is a short stretch, no more than 15 kilometres. I treat myself to a sleep-in; I go on the way at 8.00 only.

The thinkers of the "Gaudy Colonnade", the Stoics, constitute a very important trend in philosophy, starting at about 300 BC and remaining popular for about five centuries. It was in fact the common view on life at the beginning of our common era. Many of the ideas of the Stoics ended up inside Christianity.

First of all the people of the Stoa reacted against Plato and his world of ideas. They had no time for in-born ideas: they hold that all ideas have arisen inside us as the fruits of our concrete experiences and observations. In that respect they were closer to Aristotle and what would later on be called Empiricism. Cognition, they say, starts with a new page, a clean slate, a tabula rasa. Concepts are only stickers to mark collections of experiences. This was a new starting point.

As for God, God is enclosed in creation: God is the inside, the soul of nature. He regulates everything with the care of His providence; He is the interior cosmic fire, from which our spark has been derived. That again sounds like Plato and Pythagoras.

Whosoever wants to be happy should fit himself nicely into the totality of things; without passion, for passion makes you blind and dizzy. To be virtuous means the same as to be reasonable; it means discovering the rules that govern the whole of creation; knowing these rules will enable us to speak of natural law, of civil law and even of international law. This is an early brand of Humanism but a religious one to be sure. A sense of duty, detachment and willingness to forgive: these were the ingredients of the Stoic view on life, for people like Seneca, Epictetus and Marcus Aurelius.

Mother Nature has put on her first foliage; it strikes me that for a number of trees their spring-colours are the same as their autumn colours: golden brown. Thus, also, newborn babies can resemble very old people.

Here we gathered, 35 of us, shivering with excitement because we were going to walk 840 kilometres – and could that be done? That was in 1971. We were from different backgrounds: Dutchmen, Tyrolians and English, men and women, believers and atheists. The eldest, my mother, was 69; the youngest girl was 18. My authority as leader rested on the fact that I knew everybody and above all, I knew very much about the journey. Knowledge is power. Here already the first complications had to be solved: for some stupid reason, five of our group had lost all their money. It turned out to be a wonderful and truly unforgettable journey, giving rise to many other ones.

Saint-Jean-Pied-de-Port is the starting point of the Camino Francés, the French Way, the official pilgrims' route through the north of Spain; it is sometimes referred to as the 'Milky Way'.

Our female Jacobean guru of 1969 and 1971, Jeanne Debril, is still doing her job of getting the nervous pilgrims into their starting positions. But she has grown old and tired and irritated by her own fame. She is worried that there might be snow on the ground tomorrow; that untrustworthy rabble is mixing itself with the genuine pilgrims; that the Spanish refugios will not have enough blankets; and if only somebody else could take over this job from her.

* * *

13TH APRIL.

It seems a bit too risky for me to take the road across the mountain to Roncevaux; I would rather go through the valley of Valcarlos. First of all, there is just a little too much snow on the mountain, so that the arrows may not be visible everywhere. Secondly, a solitary walker with an artificial hip should be aware of his vulnerability. I have done the mountain route before, one and a half time to be exact.

In 1971, we set off for our first day's walk. There was thick fog on the mountain; we got lost, walked in a circle and at 4.00 in the afternoon, we were back at our starting point in Saint-Jean-Pied-de-Port. Our luggage cars had gone up through the valley into Spain, carrying our passports, to put up camp in Roncesvalles. It was impossible to send messages by telephone to the meadows where our tents were being pitched at this moment; there was just Saint James. And he took care that at exactly 6.00 we were all ambling around our tents carrying hot tea and fried eggs in our hands.

A few kilometres across the border the yellow arrows make me turn away from the big road and follow a forest path, sometimes very steep. Sometimes vistas in ravines can be as spectacular as a mountaintop vista. I am all by myself for miles around, it seems. Lizards rustle in the dead leaves; a long grey snake sees me with a sudden shock and quickly glides off the path. On the pass of Ibaneta there is the monument for Roland, Roldan in Spanish. It was here that the rearguard of Charlemain's army that had destroyed the Basque town of Pamplona was annihilated by the Basques. It was here that the commanding duke, Roland, blew his horn Olifant to warn far-away Charlemain about his desperate plight. It was here that in mist and death an epos was born. And from this epos the huge abbey was born, a monument with human sides.

At the abbey, I try to communicate with invisible humans through the small speaking grid on the front door. Tinglingling. "Yes," the tiny robot in the grid crackles, "what do you want?" "I am a priest from Holland. I have come walking all the way and…" "Yes, just wait please." After waiting for a full 50 minutes, I try again. Tinglingling. "Yes, what do you want?" "I am that priest from Holland who…" "But did I not tell you to wait?"

Roncesvalles – Valley of the Brambles – is an abbey that worries about its identity. What is its task? Looking after pilgrims? But a refugio can do that too; so is it a job for clerics? An inspirational holiday camp for families? That is an awful lot of bother. A monument to history and culture? Are the monks part of a monument? The evening liturgy in which I participate is of unearthly beauty but no doubt elitist as well. The literal meaning of "liturgy" is "people's work". Now cognoscenti and aesthetes only are touched by it, not the big mass of people.

Sometimes I think that we were formerly given an overdose of liturgical beauty. The vestments, the movements, the ornaments and also the underlying thoughts; they were sublime without any doubt but at the same time they were routine, impersonal, in a foreign language that did not awaken any thoughts, and caught in a frame of rustproof steel dogma. You were not supposed to play with it. The only ones in the church that could play were the musicians. I am very grateful that the liturgy in our church at Hengelo has introduced me to composers like Bruckner, Diepenbrock, Sweelinck, Palestrina, Lassus, Josquin des Prés and Dufay and to Gregorian Chant. But the church services themselves, they rarely excited me; I found them rather dull. The uncomfortable hanging in the benches, the pious waffle and the slow happenings far away, it always lasted too long. I went to church because it was a good thing, not because it was pleasant. The only time when something interesting happened was when something went wrong: when the acolyte dropped the thurible catastrophically, when there was a stray dog or bird in the church, or when a money collector stumbled with his full money plate. Babies did not belong in the church: they did not know how to be reverent and protested too unashamedly against the boredom. Fortunately, the Second Vatican Council has brought some improvements: the faithful are participating more in the ceremonies; many people put their heart and soul into a proper preparation; and many a celebrant honestly tries to inspire the people. So it is a lot more pleasant to go to church now. But still I do not go for the pleasure. I go because I think it is good: one hour of recollection, with ancient stories of wisdom, poetic texts, mysterious actions and prayers said in union with persons who are miles and ages away. Yes, that I find worthwhile. I have to add that Africa has spoiled me: there, church services can sparkle with joy. We, Whites, we are a thoroughly boring lot in comparison.

It must be in this abbey that the expression "ice cold" has found its origin: the stones have absorbed a thousand years of frost and turn the building into a super-refrigerator.

Opposite me in the dormitory, two Dutch girls lie groaning softly. The mountain has broken them. Their luggage is hugely overweight by kilos; they even carry cuddling bears. Their dream journey is going to be a torture march because they did not think with enough discipline beforehand.

* * *

14TH APRIL.

Sunday. Rain comes down in squalls. Clouds touch the road. I am thinking of pilgrims that are even now departing from Saint-Jean-Pied-de-Port to start their journey with fresh but fearful courage. James, look after your pilgrims as they struggle over the merciless mountain. I slowly overtake two black flapping figures. They are a young French couple, students. They have decided to make the pilgrimage without any significant amount of money, surviving on bread and sardines and sleeping rough in sleeping bags. It is only 9.00, and already they are desperate, for they cannot find a bakery anywhere with French bread. I give them advice on passing: "Make sure you drink a lot of water." At my next stop they overtake me. They are a friendly pair, rather

Franciscan. She studies philosophy and wants to concentrate on the body of thought known as neo-platonism.

Most new movements in philosophy are combinations of previous visions. Plato made a synthesis of Heraclitos (the world around us is in constant motion), Parmenides (true reality cannot change) and Pythagoras (the human person is a mini-cosmos, a spark in a lump of clay). Neoplatonism, a movement that arose around 200 BC, is a synthesis of platonic theories and Stoic insights. Once again, a double world becomes popular: a pure eternal divine world and a deceptive material world; the divine world guarantees the good quality and the veracity of the life of all those that are locked up in the misery of the material world. God is active through a kind of illumination, a communication by light. This is Plato. The contribution of Stoicism lies in this that the material world, though inferior, is not considered radically evil: it is also part of creation. Neoplatonism gives a new impulse to the old urge to retain the ancient well-tried religious devotions and thus obtain eternal happiness. There was no compulsion to renew everything thoroughly. The idea that you can build up the earth was not a theme of Neoplatonism.

It seems unlikely to me that the two young French students will make Compostela. They give each other mutual support but to already suffer from lack of food on the second day is an ominous sign. I pity them and give them some bars of chocolate, my own provisions for today; somehow, I will manage. At my next stop a Spaniard with two young sons sits down next to me; he opens his rucksack and insists that I should accept two colossal ham sandwiches from him. Am I getting my reward for helping the two French youngsters? If you make room for reward, should you then also make room for punishment? The French will not make it: are they being punished?

"Punishment" is an awkward concept for emancipated modern man. And instead of "rewards" we prefer "rights". If you admit rewards, are you not reintroducing God by the backdoor? It is good to realise that you do not need God for giving out punishment: nature itself is very good at that. Originally, nature put the death penalty on all wrong behaviour, as you still see in the animal and the plant world. What is good behaviour? That is what you learn – gratefully – from the survivors. When people learnt to dodge capital punishment through craftiness and deceit, and when it became clear that the biggest frauds had most success in life, other punishments had to be invented.

I have to be on my qui vive so as not to miss any of the yellow arrows; I like to be right spot-on and keep the description of the route ready. That is not always easy when you walk with two sticks.

The camino is a very special monument by itself. It is a path of 840 kilometres, clearly marked. All those that walk there have one thing in common: they all have trained their sights on the cathedral of Santiago, even from hundreds of miles away, as if it were a space shot. And they all are doing something which they have been dreaming of for a long time. Even though they walk in an endless line, that started a thousand years ago, they are all solitary walkers: you cannot share your feet with anybody else; we shake hands, not feet. All this creates a mysterious bond. I think that ancient pilgrims' paths have a magical quality. If hundreds of thousands of persons full of irresistible dreams have moved across this path, surely the stones will have absorbed something of their radiation. Would this radiation have to do with the fact that many pilgrims feel themselves to be transfigured into medieval personalities? They are not just lucky. No, Saint James helps them with miracles. It was exactly in this region that we learnt this in 1971. Unfamiliar with the ancient camino we were sticking to the tarmac road until some farmers in a bar explained to us that we should take the old path a few kilometres farther on. Their indications were rather vague for us. When we reached the spot in question, one of our girls went down the possible path to reconnoitre it. She came to a split in the road and she did not know which side to take; then she spotted a piece of paper on one of the two paths; written on it was: "the Road to Santiago". We took that path until we reached a barrier blocking our way with the information that the meadows were full of "toros bravos". But then somebody remembered that this was exactly the day on which the bulls were made to run through the streets of Pamplona, so we had a free passage. This time the barrier just said: "Close please".

It is Sunday, it is still early, the sun has begun to shine, there are reasons for a celebration. I do that at Zubiri with three pork cutlets, two fried eggs with chips, three lemonades and one coffee with anisette: my first Spanish meal. At Larrasoana, I come across the renowned refugio for the first time. This one here has been erected by the European Community, which has adopted the whole way of Saint James as a cultural monument. It looks excellent; the burgomaster himself looks after it. He bubbles over with enthusiastic advice and makes everybody promise to send a postcard afterwards. In the restaurant next door, I have another meal: pieces of chicken with garlic. Quite a relief after all that French food.

* * *

15ᵀᴴ APRIL.

They have marked the path with concrete posts decorated with an artistic ceramic cockleshell; people with guns love to use them for target practice. The authorities claim that the marked path is also fit for horses and mountain bikes. If I were a horse, I would not try certain sections. It is fit for people over 65 even if they have a hip prosthesis; but certain stretches might be risky when the weather is wet. I meet a pilgrim from Poitiers, already on his return journey. Why does he walk 45 kilometres every day? Because he wants to be back in time for the baptism of his grandchild. And why does he not have a cockle shell? "Because this walk is an affair between God and me."

A pedestrian experiences a big city like Pamplona in his own way, different from the way a motorist does. For the latter it means: move slowly in low gear, stop, look for the way, get caught in one-way-traffic, swear and sigh, find a parking place at last, stretch the stiff legs, push yourself up a steep little street, "what a pity I left my jumper in the car (or not) because it is really quite chilly (or quite hot); are we not going to have a cup of coffee first? Pamplona is in Spain, isn't it? I always get mixed up with Perpignan; ah no, let's not go to the museum, the weather is far too nice; when are we going to the beach?" The pedestrian, on the other hand, does not have to slow down; he has passed through the lot in an hour's time, selecting and absorbing cultural and historical and socio-economical marvels left and right with his razor-sharp eye.

One night in the Pamplona Hotel of the Three Magi would cost something like 40 pounds sterling; that I can earn by walking another four kilometres to a refugio at Cizur Menor. There I meet a young Danish couple. "Did we do any training beforehand? No, that is nothing for us; we do it on the way; we do it the difficult way. Hahahaha." More candidates for the death penalty. On the horizon the mountains are dancing, their breasts bedecked all the way with enormous windmills.

* * *

16TH APRIL.

It is not rain that gives you the wettest feet but a walk through a dew-covered field with high grass. Slowly, in first gear, I climb up into a cloud that covers a mountain pass with a roaring sound. On the highest point, visibility is less than ten metres, even into the sheer abyss. Above me, I hear a mysterious loud swishing sound. I have reached the foot of one of the big windmills and I don't see it, not even its foot since it is more than ten metres away. A few more hours and the sun is shining again, gently drying everything, except the socks inside my boots.

The landscape through which I pass now does not know the epic extremes of northerly regions. It is more like the landscape I imagine in Saint Mark's gospel: everyday I see a sun shining there, folding itself around everything, penetrating everywhere and, at this time of the year, coaxing new life out of apparently dead recesses. I feel sure that that is how Jesus imagined the power of his message to be: an all-embracing sun. We have rather turned it into a laser-beam, good for operations and amputations to be performed in our churches.

I reach Puente la Reina at 1.30. The refugio opens at 3.30 only. All the churches are closed. The opening time of the post office is from 9.00 to 11.00 in the morning. This is awkward for I have some urgent letters to post. A good reason for James to make sure that there happens to be a nice person in the post office who opens the door and helps me in a very kindly way. When later on the church opens too, I find a very old crucifix in German style, a witness to the international character of this small town. Religion certainly left a good dose of nostalgia behind.

It is sad to see that the church of Spain is as sick as everywhere else in the West. One sees it in the villages. At 10.00, the van of the baker or the grocer arrives and hoots. Everybody who wants something from them comes. On Sunday morning, the parish priest comes with his van, hoots with the church bells, and everybody who wants something from him comes. And the latter are precious few. The Eucharistic celebrations are barren and a far cry from what they are supposed to be: a vibrating community celebrating together that Christ, alive and life-giving and brimming with good ideas, is actively present among them. Here you see a Eucharistic famine. When on a Sunday morning in these churches here the parish priest is reading out his foolscap pages to a group of nodding faithful, my thoughts often drift away to our own church at Kisumu. At that very same hour, the collection money has just been gathered: the people, and especially the children, have had a chance to exercise the legs a bit with a walk to the money-boxes. Now the mass-servers with their candles go to the middle of the church; the dancing girls are there already, wobbling impatiently. Behind them the carriers of the gifts are lining up holding the chalice, the wine, the filled ciboriums, the book with mass-intentions, the box containing the money – the biggest banknote will later on be given to the poor – the baskets with 12 loaves and 12 packets of milk for the poor. The choir falls silent. Now the big drum begins! The girls look at each other to make sure that they will all start to dance in time and the big song bursts loose with everybody rising to their feet. Slowly, the procession drifts forward, the slower the more solemn. The boys glance backwards to make sure that the girls don't step on their heels; the girls dance on the heavy rhythm; now and then they go down through their knees, raise their wriggling little hands in the air, shake their backsides a little and turn around, the way they have practised it for hours beforehand. All those that were carrying something gather around the altar together with the acolytes and the dancing girls – Saint Mary's Flower Girls they call themselves – and the Eucharistic ministers in their white robes and gold crosses around the neck. Everything and everybody disappears in clouds of incense. The great prayer starts. Nobody has a book; they have a mouth for answering, hands for raising up to heaven and a body to sing with. There they stand, there they kneel, the little saints and the little sinners, the mothers with the babies – when they lift them by the upper arm the little legs automatically open like a pair of tongs to catch the mother's waist. The hard workers trying to gain credit with God, the young girls with their bouffant hair creations; they all went on their way at an early hour to secure a good place, and afterwards, many will keep hanging around for a while. Many of them carry the AIDS infection in their bodies already. Lord, have mercy on your family.

Admittedly, this throbbing celebration is no guarantee that all is well, for they did that too in Rwanda before they went for each others' throats. But it is most certainly true that these people wait with impatience for more inspiration and illumination from above.

Everybody in the refugio courteously becomes quiet and silent at 9.00. But tonight we are all suddenly disturbed most rudely by a couple that appear to belong to the order of the compulsive cleanliness-addicts. Without recognising anybody's presence by as much as a greeting, they explode into action. Till past midnight they are splashing in the basins, bailing, scooping, and stamping through puddles in a scarcely controlled rage to get the revolting sweat out of their filthy clothes; and then they hang dozens of dripping socks, underpants, shirts, bras and trousers on the beds of the restive sleepers. When I am disturbed in my sleep by water dripping on my arms and bedding, I chuck the offending lot on the floor. So they may have some work left for tomorrow.

* * *

17TH APRIL.

In some villages on my way the streets are so steep they look like staircases. I pass a medieval bridge, broken but still passable for pedestrians. I walk on a medieval pavement. How the trimmers have made a mess of the vines in the fields, reducing them to small stumps! But the old stumps are quietly waiting for the new sun, the soft rain.

The bare wood is not dead. Nothing that still has good roots in the earth can be dead; everything is full of life germs. Many of our disillusioned Christians are like trees that have lost their leaves. Those leaves did not fall because they were mistakes but because they had played their part. We should not go round gathering the fallen leaves to stick them back on the branches; new foliage will have to come from within the old wood. There are evergreen trees but it is the fruit-bearing trees especially that lose their leaves. There are religious leaders who have time for evergreens only. Others concentrate on the new seeds, the youth. But in the new spring it is the old wood, especially, that will have to start blossoming again.

At Estella nobody knows of a refugio; this may well have to do with the fact that the people of the family-hotel San Andrés are so kind and accommodating. It strikes me that in this town; the gutters are in the middle of the streets, not along the sides.

* * *

18TH APRIL.

The land is full of surprises and not only for the walker. Just ahead of me a car comes hurtling from a side road; at the very last moment the driver brakes, so hard that the wheels scream and skid before he comes to a standstill, holding the mobile telephone in his hand. What will happen once we get mobile television? Surprises in the landscape. Before you lies an undisturbed landscape with gently rolling hills. As you approach the top of the next hill, you begin to see a small spire of a village church, some trees at the side and a few roofs. Going on a little higher still, you see blocks of flats; as you go over the top you find a big town spread out before your unbelieving eyes. The town was there all the time; you just did not see it. Things play hide and seek with people.

That kind of surprise gives the landscape a four-dimensional quality. According to the rationalists, everything is strictly three-dimensional: you can clearly see everything properly from afar. Unless you suffer from polder-blindness (would that be nature taking revenge?). Polder-blindness is a strange phenomenon that occurs in perfectly flat open spaces like Dutch polders: at crossroads, cars crash into each other as the drivers just fail to notice one another. Nature wants to play hide and seek. The same can be said of our spiritual and theological landscapes. Surely, they too are playgrounds. Will our religious leaders still allow the spiritual landscape to play hide and seek with us? Or are the guardians of orthodoxy afraid of playfulness and poetry? Everywhere their cry for clarity is heard loudly; they must be convinced that reflections on the divine are best served with precise definitions and that poetry gives scope to dangerous vagueness. This is an amazing standpoint, considering the character of ancient religious literature. Look at the Old Testament: the Psalms are timeless poetry; so are the Prophets. Even the so-called historical books are full of poetic stories. Where in the world of Jesus and his contemporaries do we find true dogmatic definitions? Perhaps you could hold that the sayings of the elders were a bit like dogmatic statements;

but no, these too were so poetic. The gospels and the epistles excel by their poetic style and teachings. The trouble started when people tried to draw logical conclusions from poetic sayings. At that moment, heresy was born. Together with her twin sister orthodoxy. I strongly suspect that doctrinaire people dislike poetry because it does not give them deadly weapons for fighting heterodoxy. Poetry is a language pulled out of joint by the Spirit. Dogma is petrified language containing fossils, which are of great scientific interest nevertheless.

Laws are reckoned to be a guarantee for certainty. Rationalists think that laws should be applied. Wisdom on the other hand, the Spirit, loves to play with laws. Lovers play with laws. This statement can be explained in a negative way and it would be an ominous sign if many people would do this. It is meant in a positive way; for playing you need playing rules. Among the church leaders there are veritable rationalists; they cannot imagine how an inspired person can make a marvellous play of liturgical rules and can reach out to the divine poetically. They prefer to call this "experimenting", which is a term taken from rationalist science, and they find that it is high time that this should end.

It is two and a half months now since I started walking and all that time I have been hog-healthy.

An odd expression: is a hog that healthy? There are more expressions like that: as sick as a dog or as stupid as an ass. In Dutch we say as hungry as a horse, as angry as a spider. Poetic.

When you pass through tiny hamlets, you may well find on many a facade snorting coats-of-arms showing that important families live here. A village nobleman became a rear-admiral or a governor of a quarter of all America. From hamlet to centre court.

It is really true that life can jump in absolutely all directions: up, down, to the possible and to the impossible, cutting people to the quick. Life means balancing at all cost, acrobatics in the roof of the circus. Ultimately, life will prove to be impossible: inescapable death is the proof thereof. One keeps alive because one manages to fend off death for few more days. Here is an illustration.

I have a friend who can prove that he can walk over the water. He proves it this way. He gets a cameraman to make a film of himself. He then takes an almighty run and as he crosses the water's edge he begins to run across the water. Because of his speed he makes quite a few steps on the water but then he sinks. If you take the film, select that small part when he was running over the water and turn that very slowly in 75 years' time, then you will clearly see that my friend is indeed walking over the water.

Progress takes place when you try the impossible; the same happens in nature. Mother Nature had a serious problem: how to find volunteers for trying out impossible schemes. For that she designed the male. The existing kind of humans – females were far too realistic to allow themselves to be used for hare-brained experiments. A male's weak side is that he can entrust himself to his logical intellect in the naïve conviction that this will keep him on the road; he does not realise that the lines of his mind are straight and the road has bends. And so he is ready to try horrifying capers, often leading to death. But thanks to that naiveté we now ride bicycles and cars, we fly up in aeroplanes and we dive down in submarines, we do bungee-jumping, we kill each other with nuclear bombs and we juggle with genes.

In Los Arcos, the streets are like deeply-eroded ravines, securing coolness by excluding the sun. This town has, like so many others, a richly decorated church. I count five altars, each of them as high as a three-storied building and completely covered with gold leaf: a cascade of baroque frills to make the gold really glitter. I heard somewhere that much of this gold came from South America. All the niches and floors of the altar walls are inhabited by statues of saints.

It is true; statues are not very well suited to pure religion, just as little as words. But we do not have much else. If you take statues in their "literal" sense, they are no longer fit to illustrate religious mysteries. But statues are able to exude a strange power; that is because statues are more than what they are. The original function of a religious statue is to be a reference, and reference has to do with the mind and with the heart. Because there is this element of referring to something else, the statue is never quite clear and unambiguous. That makes it fit to be used

102

in the service of religion to refer to mysteries that are unclear too. A problem will arise with people who insist on having a religion that is clear and distinct. The relevance of the image will be belittled, statues will be reduced to clear representations (and distortions therefore) of the divine. The result will be iconoclasm. Is it not a rationalist sin to demand that religion be clear? He who demands clarity wants to know exactly what he is dealing with; away with parables, away with poetry. He wants to know exactly who is who, who belongs to what group and who doesn't. Thus, he will be able to know who is good and who is bad, and separate them. Anathema (the sentence of condemnation pronounced over heretics) means: separated. To be able to declare who is anathema, you need borders. One makes borders by defining them (finis means border).

By insisting on clarity, one invites more problems than one solves. Mysteries, to be sure, do not have borders; they have a heart instead. He who constructs his religion along the lines of defined dogma can know from the beginning that he is wrong. He hands in his heart in exchange for barbed wire. And, as they say in Dutch, he can "feel through his wooden shoes" (it is pretty obvious to him) that there is going to be violence. To sum it up cynically, this is how it works. Somebody who understands well will need half a word only. However, half words can also be half-truths. So it is better to use whole words; then nobody has an excuse for not understanding. Those that still do not understand must be of ill will; those of ill will must be made to feel. Bring in the Inquisition.

At night, I watch bullfights on the television. It is a sport that strikes us northerners as rather unbecoming. It remains a gamble with death, which is a bit different from snooker. But at least the bull knows what is happening to him and why he dies: he is fighting an enemy. In that, he is better off than our own cattle which are, retching with fright, rammed into our cavernous chrome-decorated humane slaughtering palaces for the sake of our tender little beefsteak. (Why do the butchers never advertise: the buyer of every thousandth beefsteak will be rewarded with a free visit to the slaughter house?)

Now I have left Basqueland behind me too, one of the most ancient European nations, riven in all directions. Within itself, it is torn asunder: there are two regions in France and three in Spain. The wound in Spain is kept bleeding by the ETA terrorists and in France they do as if there were no Basque nation. The pilgrim going to Compostela will be blissfully unaware of any strife. Saint James's road looks like a way of reconciliation. From the Pyrenees, the pilgrim is carried forward along a very ancient trail, urged on by countless anonymous friends who forget their differences for his sake. Can this pilgrimage inject people with a healing unifying strength?

✳ ✳ ✳

19TH APRIL.

It is funny to see a procession of a hundred caterpillars all closely linked up. Why do caterpillars do that? Do they want to look like a snake? I have seen them do it in Africa; so they do it here too.

Africa has taught me always to watch the ground before you put your foot down. That habit helps me now so that I do not stumble on the rough path. But what I see on the ground here is not half as exciting as what I see there. No safari ants here, long columns of aggressive well-trained little bastards. In platoons, they climb up against their prey or their attacker and then all of them bite at the same time. Their jaws lock; they can't open them any more. Not long ago we had a foot journey across East Africa and one whole day long we walked over ground that was covered with the footprints of lion and leopard, and with elephant dung. Another day a big and extremely poisonous puff adder was lying on the narrow path, hidden under the overhanging grass; the man before me had stepped over it already before I saw it. I regret that I do not know more about the science of determining droppings: there are always so many different kinds of droppings to be seen.

On one field I see 40 vultures; I hear they have been introduced here.

At Logroño you will find St. James's church in the old town, a little away from the city centre. The big statue of the saint, sitting on horseback hacking Moors to bits, is so high on the facade that in the narrow street you can only see the belly of the horse – curiously it has the oversized testicles and the penis running along the belly the way a bull has. I am getting dizzy when I look up like that; would that be because I am looking at the ground all day long?

* * *

20TH APRIL.

Just outside Navarrete, I find a poignant group of statuettes fixed to the outer wall of the cemetery of the Ermita de Santa Maria de Jesus: a young woman sits resting on a cockle shell, her head turned in the direction of Compostela, and behind her the commanding figure of St. James smiles at her encouragingly. In Spanish and in Dutch the following text is added: "In memory of Alice de Craemer, died on 3 July 1986 on her pilgrimage to Compostela, and as a memento to all pilgrims of Saint James who died on the Camino de Santiago". She was a young Belgian woman making the pilgrimage with her husband and children on a bicycle; a car killed her here.

The camino to Santiago is like a long line drawn across the north of Spain from east to west. It coincides roughly with a historical frontline between Christians and Moors. The conquest of Spain by the Arabic Moors in the 8th century was a blitzkrieg. They got a foothold in Spain around the year 710 through their victory at Xerez de la Frontera; and within a couple of years, they had reached Poitiers in France, where Charles Martel stopped them around 745 AD. They consolidated themselves in Spain, founding a caliphate at Cordoba. The Christian kings managed to hold out at the northern edge of the peninsula. The whole area was turned into a cauldron of battles, raids and plundering campaigns, of which you are reminded often. The last Christian bastions of Asturia, Navarra and Aragon gave birth to the great royal families during the Reconquista. The legendary battle turning the tide in favour of the Christians was the one of Clavijo, around 800 AD. At the height of that battle, Saint James himself appeared personally on a white charger to lead the fighting lines of the Christians like a medieval bishop gone berserk, thus earning himself the honorary title of Matamoros, Moors-killer. The Reconquista was only completed in 1492 with the conquest of Granada. Many consider this Reconquista to have been a successful crusade; it coincided largely with the crusades in the Middle East, reconquistas that failed utterly. Under the Moors, the Spanish Christians developed their own so-called mozarabic liturgy. I have read somewhere that the majority of the Spaniards had joined Islam. I do not think that happened through physical force but rather by the offer of financial and social advantages, the way North Africa turned from Christianity to Islam.

Were the crusades necessary to protect people against Islam? That would be hard to prove. But one thing is sure; the crusades have given Christianity a permanently bad name with the Muslims and have hardened the mutual relations for a long time to come. Because of past violence, rapprochement has become almost completely impossible in our days. One question remains: should the Christians not have absorbed the Islam from within instead of so resolutely resorting to arms?

A hard cold wind pushes me on from behind; a bare vineyard, metal wires strung all across it, hums like a wind harp in the storm. The entrance to Nájera is ugly, as if you enter the town through its arse: all you see are rubbish heaps and factory yards.

I always eye rubbish heaps with suspicion, since I once found the dead body of a little baby on one of them in Kisumu, sticking out of a brown paper bag; it was red all over and held its little hands raised.

The Saturday evening Mass in the old cloister church of Nájera is for 40 people, none of them younger than 30 years. One hears no alarm bells ringing in the Spanish church; there is rather an atmosphere like: "Well, that is how it is; and as long as the football players still make the sign of the cross, it could be worse".

* * *

21ST APRIL.

Sunday. The way out of Nájera leads via rubbish tips too, or at least places where people throw their litter. I try to visualise how people do that: do they put their old refrigerator and two mattresses in the back of a pick-up and take them to some piece of forest to chuck them down between the trees?

When the Iberian crusaders had driven the Moorish invaders out of their last Spanish bastions, they crossed the Straits of Gibraltar to continue the campaign in North Africa. They had heard of a legendary African Christian Priest/King called John whose realm was supposed to lie south of the land of the Moors. By sailing southwards along the West African coast, the Portuguese tried to get into contact with him in order to attack the Moors in the back. And thus the voyages of colonial exploration found their origins in the Reconquista.

Santo Domingo has the church with the well-known chicken house inside it – high up on the wall next to the choir loft. It is there as an act of homage to those chickens that saved the life of a young pilgrim who had been condemned to death by jumping up – though they had been roasted – from the plate of the nonchalant but confident judge.

Miracle stories belong to the world of half-truths and half words, and those we use in order to refer to a second kind of truth. We humans are ourselves truly called "half people" and "bigger than we are": there is more to us than our physical reality would suggest. It is really part of our glory that we can speak with half words. That means with words that do not just have a literal meaning but must be understood figuratively or analogously. That is a precious gift: the literal meaning makes you to remain firmly fixed inside your own present world; but by the figurative meaning, you can reach out above your present time and space. A wise person needs but half a word. But inversely, for the half word to become fruitful, a person is required to be wise in return. Those that get disturbed by figures of speech will soon end up in a home for the disturbed. They will start checking if it is indeed better to have one bird in the hand than 10 in the bush, or if a stitch in time does indeed save nine or perhaps only seven.

Analogy is the home area of the philosophical words about God and religion. It can happen that an expression becomes too vague in the long run and that a new image is needed to make the human spirit glow when it tries to make contact with the divine. In such a case we have to ask poets to find new words that can inspire people of today. But alas, many Westerners demand crystal-clear certainties, rather than rich meaning.

Intellectually I am well looked after. In the excellent refugio I find the April/ March 1996 issue of Prana, a Dutch periodical for spiritual matters.

From one of the articles, I learn that my journey is really a classic literary phenomenon known as a Hermetic Quest.

A dream journey starting from a situation of frustration, from which one escapes through prayer and which leads via meetings and dialogues to the freedom of new insight and a cure from some human disruption, and all that through love. I furthermore hear about an interesting law, the law of Beyerinck-Baas-Becking. It says: "Everything is everywhere, but the environment selects". I think that is true.

* * *

22ND APRIL.

I have to pass over high hilltop roads through ice-cold showers of lashing rain that scourge my front because of the strong head wind. I feel no temptation whatsoever to take picturesque country paths; I have to try and get to Belorado as quickly as possible. I get there in one piece, to find the refugio still under repair. But a chain of helpful hands guide me to a somewhat dingy little pension, third floor, with a talkative old lady. The room allotted to me is filled with two almost-double beds with satin covers. The paint is peeling off, the wallpaper pulls itself into long folds and around the light switches, you find 40 years' grime from searching fingers. On the ledge behind the bed there are two small vases of gilt-edged china, three plastic border-collies, a smiling violin-playing piglet wearing a cap, a porcelain couple in Mozart-type dress and a plaster child Jesus from a Nativity crib dressed in little underpants with green dots.

At the various side altars in the village church, you are drawn into a devotional form of Trivial Pursuit. Who is the saint carrying a round tower on her hand? The correct answer is Saint Barbara. What saint lifts up the hem of his tabard so that you can see a gaping wound above his knee? The answer is Saint Rochus, patron saint against rabies. And who do you see there, a lady carrying a dish of Delf Blue and on it two amputated breasts? Correct. Saint Agatha. And the one next to her, carrying a dish with two eyes, eyelids and all? Yes, Saint Lucy. One can pass hours of gentle pleasure sitting in front of the sky-high main altar to discover ever more figures in the labyrinth of gold frills, the way you do it with the puzzle called Where Is Waldo?

* * *

23ᴿᴰ APRIL.

The Oca Mountains are gloomy, with no sign of new leaves yet, muddy, steep and bitterly cold. I see tracks of deer and swine (and wolves?). I pass a depressing monument for people that were shot there during the Civil War; sadly faded flowers show that they are still being remembered by old comrades. The path is not a path really but a fire corridor cut through the inhospitable bushes by tractors. Here and there you see a jeep abandoned in the green slimy mud. The yellow arrows give you the assurance that you are moving in the right direction through an obscure environment.

Clarity and certainty are not obligatory bedfellows. Vagueness, too, can create certainty for some people. Ignorance can be bliss. Prejudice is a good example: for a rock-solid prejudice you need very little clear knowledge; in fact the less the better. Something similar happens in the case of God: the more limited your knowledge of Him is, the more apodictic you can become in your assertions. Don't ask for an explanation of how He relates to space and time; then you can all the more easily say: "God is everywhere". Don't try to think of how God relates to Auschwitz: then you will have no problem with saying: "Everything that happens is God's Will". Don't try to know how our free will works vis-à-vis God's omnipotence; then you can wholeheartedly say: "God can do everything". As long as you don't try to really understand God's mysterious existence and keep Him as vague as possible, everything will be fine and sure. But it is those kind of certainties that cause the death of God. On the other hand, the more deeply you are allowed to penetrate into the mysteries of God, the more the magnetic needle of your mental compass begins to turn in circles.

Fundamentalism is another example of a wrong kind of certainty, a certainty fed by disinformation.

One more example occurs to me. If the statement "Jesus is God" needs defending, you had better not go into knotty questions like is there a difference between God and Jesus? For then you begin to hesitate. In my home area of Twente in the eastern part of the Netherlands, we do not hesitate. We say: "Oons lee'm Heer" meaning "our dear Lord", and that can mean both God the Father and Jesus. No problem.

The old monastery of San-Juan de Ortega, in 1971 still a ruin, it is now totally restored, and turned into a refugio. Six tall young men are lounging around in the company of two older persons. From afar, I can recognise them as being Dutch. From the fact that they avoid giving information about themselves and their journey, and are subject to strict discipline, I can conclude that they are a group of young delinquents who are busy with a form of alternative punishment. Fancy that, that is still being done. I am amazed at the huge packs they carry and the sober food they eat. They are not even staying; they continue their walk, for there is still daylight. The old priest, of whom it is said, that he is a faithful Franco-fan, entertains us with great speeches about the European unity that is being fostered by the camino; in the meantime, we feast on his garlic soup and on the shared provisions of all the walkers.

* * *

24TH APRIL.

After two hours, I fail to recognise any of the things mentioned in my route description to Burgos. I blunder across a small airfield, crawl through a culvert under a four-lane highway, come to a dead end in a factory yard, get contradictory advice and make a corrective detour of an hour.

Whoever goes to Compostela on foot is given a pilgrim's passport; this gives you access to the refugios. And of course you have it stamped everywhere so that you are entitled to your pilgrim's certificate at Santiago. As I enter Burgos, a car stops alongside me. Out gets the burgomaster of a small village I have passed today; he insists on stamping my passport there and then; he rounds off the treatment with a glass of beer.

Even when I am walking on tarmac I get pebbles in my boots; three today.

Has the graduand started his study on this topic? I want to tell him that he has to investigate if it has anything to do with the shape of the pebbles: compare pebbles that get into the boots with pebbles that don't; check also on the difference between a tarmac surface and a stony one; and whether the same happens in the northern hemisphere as in the southern hemisphere.

* * *

25TH APRIL.

A free day at Burgos. The students of the hostel where I stay rise late: between 8.00 and 9.00. One has to consider, however, that because this region lies so far to the west, the clocks are about two hours ahead of the sun. To keep contact with my friends I have organised a series of poste-restante places. Sometimes the poste-restante system is confusing. First of all, Spanish post offices are often closed, especially in smaller places. Then, the people working there are not always linguistic geniuses. When somebody has written to me as Rev. Fr. Hans Burgman, I have to ask them very kindly, will they please look under the sections R, F, H and B.

Dealing with my mail is one of my preoccupations. Another one is getting money from the bank and hiding that cleverly on my body; I like to pay everywhere with cash.

I have established quite a daily routine. My breakfast is uniform. As soon as I rise I begin to drink: before I start off I want to have drunk one litre of juice; I eat one slice of bread and two small cartons of yoghurt and some fruit. My food on the way consists of two apples, some groundnuts or some cheese or some sausage plus two cups of water in my waterbag. Usually I am off at 6.00, having risen at 5.00. I walk briskly for two hours so that I have done 10 kilometres by 8.00. Then I rest for 10 minutes and continue on a scheme of 50 minutes' walk and 10 minutes' rest. During those pauses, I eat an apple or some of the other things and take a few gulps of water. Usually, I arrive shortly after midday, ready for a couple of beers. By drinking well beforehand I am hardly ever thirsty. By buying food only after my arrival I save on the weight I carry.

I have changed over to the feeling that walking is normal, that movement has primacy. That is a revolutionary feeling. We Westerners are definitely still caught in a deceptive vision, worked out by Aristotle, that primacy belongs to standing still: everything is stationary by nature and if something moves, then there must be a reason for that. Heraclitus had been there before him, saying that everything moved and nothing was stationary, and Parmenides saying that true reality was motionless and all change was deceptive appearance. Parmenides' view supplied a better foundation for logic and the science of cognition became more acceptable and was ultimately assimilated by Plato and Aristotle. The Aristotelian theory was greatly appreciated by the Church in the Middle Ages, because the demand for a special mover led to a proof of God's existence: the First Mover. Since then, other cosmological visions have become popular, theories that hold that everything moves; and we have rationally accepted those. But many of us shelter the old theory inside some hidden corners of our mind: an emotional conviction that lying still and rest are normal. If only you rest, nothing will wear away. Look at a bicycle: keep it in the attic well oiled and greased, and after 25 years, it comes down in mint condition. Doctors kept hammering the maxim that rest cured anything. That is not so. True, there are some doctors now, that will admit that a living body is not a machine and that an organism atrophies by immobility; but their insights seep in only slowly. A body is designed to move. We have to learn again to enjoy moving. It is nice to wobble, to see-saw, to swing, to skate, to swim, to walk.

* * *

26TH APRIL.

As I pass the cathedral of Burgos on my way out of town, I see that at this hour the building is open and freely accessible to people that want to pray. In the very early sunlight the dome inside is the most beautiful one I have ever seen. Near Tardajos, I join up with two Japanese Zen monks, dressed in their traditional outfit: flapping dark robes, hats like baskets upside down and wrappers instead of socks. They had heard about this pilgrimage from a friend of theirs at the Catholic University of Japan. The Japanese Buddhists have a similar sacred walk past a hundred sanctuaries and they have done that once. Their joints hurt because of their inadequate footwear; nevertheless, they march on swiftly. Hontanas is the kind of village that suddenly comes up out of the ground in front of you: even at a hundred metres' distance, you do not see it yet. An old innkeeper entices me to enter his cave-like doss-house; there he shows me how good he is at squirting a thin jet of wine into his mouth. Well, I can do that too. But now, watch this one. He makes the wine run over his face, along the bridge of his nose to his mouth. OK, he wins. Would I not like to eat something? Meat? Sausage? Or everything perhaps? OK, everything. When I have everything in front of me on the table, he picks up my fork at intervals to help himself to the food on my plate. I ask him, can he also drink through his ear? Not yet. Farther down the road, a beautiful refugio has been opened; some enterprising ladies come in to ask what we would like them to cook for us. Splendid food and clever ladies.

* * *

27TH APRIL.

The old ruin of San-Antón's convent through which the road passes and the castle on top of the mountain of Castrojeriz, straight from the world of Don Quichote, are buildings from olden times that are preserved carefully.

They way they are treated contrasts with the way we deal with religious imagination, formulations and devotions coming to us from the past. The latter we weigh on extremely critical scales and our fingers are itching to throw them away. If they come from honest people, who worked hard to make them and keep them, we should really accept those as gifts from an inspired generation: an inheritance we should treat with respect and not judge frivolously.

In the afternoon, on the way to Frómista, I walk along the banks of a canal that is higher than the land. I thought that was a patent of the Dutch. Frómista is an ancient Roman settlement in an area that was then already rich in wheat fields. It could well be that the landscape has changed only very little over the last two 2,000 years. Saint Martin's church is renowned for being almost too beautiful, a clean Romanesque church with perfect lines and balanced proportions.

If only life were like that. Life is cluttered, tatty and full of questions. Of course a person needs clarity. True clarity comes from insight and that does not always mean a clear and sharply defined concept, an "idea clara et distincta" to speak with Descartes, the father of Rationalists. Insight belongs to the realm of wisdom and wisdom loves to dress up in the mysterious robes of poetry, analogy and imagery; the rationalists list these categories under vaguenesses. Yet it is through them that a person will have clarity and certainty. Certainty is the fruit of trust and faith. And those again reside in the realm of love and good personal relations. A person can be certain even if his statements are vague.

The parish church of Frómista has a statue of Saint Telmo, the patron of navigators. The little flames that play on the ships' masts now and then are named after him: Saint Elmo's Fire. On his arm, he holds a man-of-war; its little cannons dangle from its sides like drones of a bagpipe.

* * *

28TH APRIL.

To help the pilgrims they have made a gravel path along the main road. To prevent tractors from using this path they have put concrete pillars on it every hundred yards; the result looks like a tank barrier. Not very pretty.

Jacobean purists are disgusted with it. They would have preferred a mud track next to the normal road, so that they can plod on in the medieval fashion as they imagine it to have been. It seems to me a case of erroneous nostalgia. Pilgrims of all ages have preferred a well-paved road over a mud path; and if possible they would make use of a horse or a cart. The modern equivalent of the horse is the bicycle. Well, let them push on; using a bicycle also means going by your own strength, even more than when you ride on horseback. But there are limits. Travelling by car and by train and by aeroplane gives the journey a completely different character: it has little to do any more with feet, muscles, circulation, heart, skin, the whole moving living body.

Baroque statues are always in motion; they freeze the action at a certain point. Somewhere high up in a niche of the church at Carrión de los Condes two life-size figures sit, the one behind the other, with their hands raised aloft. They look like two bus passengers bracing themselves for a frontal collision. The Eucharistic celebration is matter-of-fact; there is no need felt for anything inspiring; the people in attendance seem to be content with the guaranteed supernatural effects of the liturgical function.

Like in other parts of southern Europe and France; it is especially the women that attend church services. The church seems to be for old women; many sharp-thinking citizens feel that that very fact disqualifies the church from being taken seriously. In my opinion, such a conclusion shows a profound contempt for women.

It is remarkable indeed that so few women's names have gained a place in the ranks of the philosophers. I would not be surprised if that was because the men never gave them a chance to talk seriously: women should be silent in a gathering.

If women are given a chance to talk, they will quite possibly start a whole new trend of thinking.

A woman's constitution offers a wonderful starting point for philosophical thought. Philosophy has to do with affirming or denying concepts in regard to day-to-day reality; it is the world of identity and being different. Pregnancy is a fascinating starting point for this. Women tell me that they experience pregnancy as something identical to themselves and at the same time as something that distanciates itself from them. Even with animals, you can see how the mother identifies her young with herself. A pregnant mother experiences right inside herself unity becoming multiplicity, identity becoming otherness. That must be an extremely fruitful point from which to start a metaphysical reflection, a point to which no male has any access at all.

Does male gender set any good ideas going? A man's penis spreads vitality and thus becomes a symbol of power, a power that tends to deteriorate into aggression, finding its ultimate form in the gun, spreading death. In our masculine kind of world, human philosophising seems to begin at the moment where a baby discovers his own hands and starts talking to them as if they were strangers; which means that we start with badly perceived multiplicity that makes a problem of unity. It is high time we invited the women to lead us along new paths.

* * *

29TH APRIL.

Yesterday, some unwise Frenchmen behind me allowed a small dog to walk along with them and now it does not want to go back. Early in the morning, the crafty little fellow has taken up position on the bridge at the edge of the town; now it wants to join me. I chase it away with exaggerated hullabaloo.

I walk for hours over the straight path across the flat meseta; in a few months' time, the heat will be murderous here. Two American girls on bicycles overtake me heaving big sighs. "How are your backsides?" I ask with sympathy. They shout back: "Everything that touches the bicycle hurts". At Sahagun I find a place with the Madres Benedictinas; with them all the religious images from the past appear to be fully alive still.

All the same, I think that the dogmas and the religious formulas that have been bequeathed to us should be no more that a back-drop and wings for the stage of our own act. Dogmas do not catch the great enigmas of life. For that, you need parables. And parables we make ourselves, with the adventures of our own lives. And we need new images of God; these do not sprout from the old formulations.

* * *

30ᵀᴴ APRIL.

Free day. Nowadays they drink a lot of beer in Spain, albeit from tiny bottles. In a bar, I see two people drinking beer from wine glasses.

To get new images of the divine you have to beg poetic spirits for help. A poet who has intrigued me for many years in this respect is the German Rainer Maria Rilke. I carry his *Stundenbuch* – Book of the Hours – in my rucksack, read to shreds and festooned with attempted translations. Sometimes his God is a blacksmith hammering on his anvil every Sunday morning. Sometimes He is a high church tower around which I circle and circle for ages as if I were a falcon, or a storm, or a great song. Sometimes He is a silent farmer who saves. Here is the first poem from that collection that I could not shake off any more.

> Dear neighbour God, I know I often spoil
> your nights by banging loudly on the wall;
> the problem is, I hardly hear you breathe;
> I know there's no one with you in that ward.
> And when you want a thing, no one is there
> to put your tumbler in your searching hand.
> I always listen. Give a little hint.
> I am quite near.

(*Das Stundenbuch*: 'Du Nachbar Gott, wenn ich dich manchesmal')

THE FOURTH MONTH

MAY

1ST MAY.

The camino crosses a high and almost empty plain called the Meseta. They have planted long rows of trees along the path; it will take years before they produce shade. The isolated tiny villages have grandiose names such as Bercianos del Real Camino and Calzadilla de los Hermanillos. Here, too, development is getting ready to strike: new roads are being laid out, an embryonic little airfield appears, marked with old car tyres.

In the year 1971, these boundless plains with sand tracks made a deep impression on us. But the only things I remember are silly trivialities. On the path we saw lots of small grasshoppers jumping up when you put your foot down; some of them had pink wings, others had blue ones; somebody said that showed they were girls and boys. Hour after hour, we heard the high-pitched and at the same time rasping sound of an insect, a sound that seemed to have no dimensions; we called the insect the Coarse-Haired Drivelling Beetle. The obese girl called Catherine got such sore chafing spots on the inside of her thighs that she had to walk with her feet wide apart. The merciless sun gave the boy John second degree burns in his neck. A support car, a tiny Fiat, got stuck in reverse gear somewhere at the back of beyond. I had to drive it back to the main road in reverse, 25 kilometres. Aunty Nanny, one of the two old ladies, left her cheap plastic raincoat on the door of our sleeping place and got damages paid by the insurance later on.

At El Burgo Ranero the motherly owner of the pension joins me for the evening meal – with her own plate. I visit the brand new refugio and there I find a simple Belgian boy with frightening wounds on his feet, caused by new boots that he did not properly break in and a rucksack that is far too heavy. I bandage his fee and advise him strongly not to continue walking.

* * *

2ND MAY.

When I have walked for about an hour I realise that senora Mercedes Lozano has made a mistake when settling the bill, and returned 1,000 pesetas, about four pounds, too much. I will give them back to her on my return journey.

What is all this about the untrammelled careless stroll through charming fields? It occurs in my dreams only. On the road there is always something to urge me on; let me speed up a bit, for there is a shower of rain coming; let me hurry on a bit, for it is still nice and cool; no, this is not a good place to rest, it looks awful.

The romantic carefree pilgrim sauntering through the glades is not me. Restlessness itches in my bones continually: when I walk I want to arrive; when I arrive I want to find a place to stay; I want to know tomorrow's route; I want to depart early; I eagerly reach out to the things lying ahead of me; I cannot rest until I have completed this journey. At the same time, there is much peace and quiet inside my soul. I have confidence; I know I can do what I set out to do. I know that I am well-equipped and that I am not burdened with superfluous things. Deep down inside my fibres I enjoy the myriad little things happening to me and above all the fact that there is only one thing to worry about and that is: to complete this journey. Still, the whole venture is framed in a cadre of restlessness.

Restlessness is quite clearly an important factor in my existence. Why that should be so, is not so evident. Am I looking for something? It would be hard to say for what. There must be something that I miss; some say that we are looking for the other half of our being.

The theme of a person being only half a being occurs in many versions. It is significant that husbands and wives call each other their better halves. The Spanish philosopher Ortega y Gasset sees two halves in each one of us: the way we are born is one half and what people and the environment make of us is another half. I myself and the others. Again, you could see those as two halves; it would mean that everyone who withdraws within himself becomes half a person; thus Western individualism would lead to the establishment of a continent of half people. The past and the future, they could be taken to be two halves, like two legs on which we walk. If you dig yourself in in the past without embracing the future, you become semi-human, and likewise if you sell yourself to the future without carrying your past, you become semi-human. Old people and young people need each other like two halves. Recently, I read about a Benedictine monk who went to India "to look for the other half of his soul". The Hindu are very much opposed to our ego-centricity; according to them the isolated self is the root of all evil. Self has no meaning except in relation to others, including God.

But there is no getting away from the fact that all varieties of life are shaped in the form of an "I" and in the form of "here" and in the form of "now". For those who lose sight of that the Delphic oracle has important advice: "Know Thyself". But the pilgrim continues to yearn, for elsewhere, for others, restlessly, restlessly.

I have to reach the post office of Mansilla de las Mulas before closing time; just as I nip in at 12 noon, they lock the door behind me. Along the road I find a big traffic victim: a full-size wild boar. At Villarente, in the lounge of my small hotel, I see once again how the Spaniards shamelessly chuck any amount of rubbish down in front of the bar.

* * *

3RD MAY.

Like a silver magnet, León lies there in the early morning light. Many a walker halts for a moment to absorb that sight. Although León proudly displays rampant lions, the name has nothing to do with these animals; the name is derived from the Latin word for legion; for here was the place where the "Legio VII Gemina" was stationed. For hours I sit in the cathedral in the shower of colours cascading from the windows; mostly they are the pure Vermeer-type hues of yellow, blue and red. On one of the altars I spot a medieval statue of Saint Luke; he is wearing spectacles.

Near the banks of the river I see a local variety of skittles: 12 pins are put up in a square of three by four pins, and they try to upset them with a half ball thrown high through the air.

* * *

4TH MAY.

Rest day. The most luxurious hotel of the town, San Marco, the one with the famous façade of cockleshells, is originally a doss-house for pilgrims, founded by the Reyes Catolicos "ad recipiendum pauperes Christi", to welcome the poor of Christ. Long ago I have sworn the solemn oath that once in my life I was going to spend the night there; and now the day has come. Being an old age pensioner, I even get a 35 percent discount. I think I have never slept so beautifully.

For a moment I am back in a different world, a world of television and supermarkets. A French channel has a circus show from Paris; one group of acrobats comes from Kenya. I happen to remember that the Republic of China invited young people some years ago to train them in something as exotic as acrobatics; this is probably them. But the commentator informs us that since olden times every Kenyan village had a group of acrobats, that there used to be village contests and the most popular feat of those acrobats was forming a human pyramid. The things you can learn from television!

Supermarkets flourish through the widespread infection of Buying-Aids: customers cannot resist the offer of a bargain. A German magazine suggested recently that the public suffers from Information-Aids: they cannot resist the offer of any information. In this way you can probably identify still more types of Aids.

* * *

5TH MAY.

Sunday. Two friends have joined me for two weeks. This gives the journey a very different character. It is cosier, you chat a lot. But I have to adapt myself too. They like to have a big breakfast on the balcony in the sun; so no early departure before sunrise, more heat on the way. I have to adjust to different needs of resting, a different marching tempo, a different appreciation of nature, different rituals for dressing. I never change clothes on the way. In the morning I put on the clothes of the day. For my upper part, that means just a shirt made of fleece. Initially that may be a bit chilly but after a few minutes the body thermostat has hit on the correct temperature and from then on you feel exactly right. Only a heavy shower of rain can make me put on more. Most other people decide to put on (or off) different clothes for every varying shade of temperature. That means interrupting your marching rhythm, taking things off your back, opening your rucksack, putting off your boots maybe, then putting on the new assortment and getting going again. Today's walk is tough, along the main road. I am lucky I have good company now, two cheerful but determined ladies.

I have no problem with unpleasant sections in the route. The pilgrimage is an image of life and so it should contain unpleasant and awkward parts. He who demands a pilgrim's route of nothing but beautiful parts is like somebody who eats the raisins out of the bread.

The company in the refugios is becoming more and more international: Belgians, Germans, Dutch, English, Spaniards, Italians and yes, Brazilians. The latter are so numerous because of the best-selling book of the Brazilian Paulo Coelho (O Diario De Um Mago). Today for the first time I do not find a blanket, in the refugio of Villadangos. I make use of my astronaut's sheet of aluminium foil. The thing crackles like a bush fire but otherwise it is all right.

* * *

6TH MAY.

One of our two ladies can be so unhandy that you cannot stop laughing any more. Today we want to buy some bread from a baker's van. She is our treasurer. The rucksack comes off and is put down on the pavement. The zip is opened and the hand goes inside to locate the moneybag. The zip of the moneybag is opened and the zip for the department of the coins; then the fingers take out coins one by one to count. When it is seen not to be enough, the zip of the banknote department is opened. A note of 5,000 pesetas is taken out to pay 130. The baker has no change so the search starts for a smaller note and so on.

When you are walking in company, it is much more difficult to philosophise and to meditate. The two Japanese monks kept a distance of 20 yards from each other; perhaps that was the reason why.

The Puente de Orbigo is a remarkable bridge. It is long, some 20 arches, and not quite straight, and why would it have to be? There are heavy stone balustrades on both sides, making the bridge into a veritable bottleneck. In 1434 AD, Don Suero de Quinones felt the irresistible urge to do something memorable; so he blocked the bridge with nine other knights and defied all blue-blooded knights of Christendom to fight their way across. After 30 days they had defeated all candidates. The names of the 10 stand chiselled in the pillar in the middle of the bridge. In the restaurant of the campsite the waiter gives each of the ladies a red carnation.

* * *

7TH MAY.

Along age-old tracks, our path leads to Astorga, a town more than 2,000 years old, from before the time of the Romans. The refugio is small but good and friendly, and is looked after by Dutch brothers. Brother Frans from Denekamp in Twente has an encouraging word for each pilgrim personally. I meet again with the two Dutch girls from Roncevaux; the one with the cuddling bear is tortured by a painful nerve from the back to the knee. She considers giving up.

* * *

8TH MAY.

After Astorga, the pilgrim's path crosses the Montanas de León. In 1971, that was still a very rough area with steep gravel paths. One of our girls slipped and fell into a shrub so that a branch penetrated her leg between the shinbone and the skin; three people held her down whilst I quickly dug out the piece of wood. Now the track is covered with tarmac. While we are sitting by the side of the road, a beautiful hare with black-tipped yellow ears passes by, jumping high above the heather. He is followed closely by a fox jumping in the same way. Can a fox catch a hare that way? We are curious to know the end of the story but it remains hidden to us.

When we arrived at Rabanal del Camino in 1971 with 35 pilgrims that was such an unusual event for the out-of-the-way hamlet that the burgomaster organised a procession with local musicians to lead us into the village. Now you will find a small hotel there, an excellent refugio (taken care of by England), several other sleeping places and a restaurant. The leading musician of 1971, called Maximilian, is still there; he remembers us and he comes to give us a small concert, playing the flute with one hand and beating the drum with the other.

* * *

9TH MAY.

On one of the high mountaintops you find an iron cross; every passing pilgrim casts a stone that he has brought from afar at its foot. There we meet a French lady called Odile. She is an invalid and she travels, or rather lives, in an adapted small car. All she does is drive up and down along the Compostela route from Puy; she meditates and encourages the pilgrims with coffee and talk. She regrets that all the ancient wells along the route have become taps. The great thing about a well is that you have to bend down before it. Formerly she worked in West Africa as a midwife. Her father had been a journalist; he had been shot after the war because he was "in favour of European unity".

You feel truth shifting about uneasily inside the ill-fitting words. According to my categories, her father was a traitor but he does not fit into this category because he was a good man. On the other hand, nobody is shot just because he is in favour of European unity. What do you do with clumsy words? Our very word "lying" is clumsy and ill-fitting. We give truth the character of barbed wire and then everything that lies beyond this barbed wire is supposed to be lying. But surely, that is not so. Genuinely living truth is not the fruit of a perfect human copying machine but comes from a faltering human mouth. Truth becomes real truth only when you save it from suppression; he who cannot lie cannot speak the truth either. Truth is there because untruth can be there, just as life is there because death could be there, and vice versa. It is really nonsense to say that a stone is "dead": if it is dead, it has died. Death belongs to those that can live. Life belongs to those that can die. Life needs support. Truth needs support.

A little farther on, I visit a group of hermits who offer pilgrims an alternative type of refugio: mattresses on the floor and in the loft. An invalid old gentleman potters around and also some young people, a couple of babies, four dogs and a man with a cap who by himself constitutes the society of the Guardantes del Camino Santiago. This confraternity has to develop into a corps of protective vigilantes who before long will patrol along the route of Compostela on light motorbikes. On the wall you find evidence of their first campaign: a photograph with a warning text helps us to identify a "ladron de peregrinos" (a robber of pilgrims) who hides behind a number of disguises. Sometimes he pretends to be a doctor, at other times a seminary professor.

This is the land of the extinct villages. Some of them, however, show faint signs of life again, be it through the pilgrims, be it through communes that have established themselves.

Communes have an old-fashioned ring: they are a remnant of the 1960s. In those days, communes made people think of "free love"; they had overtones of licentiousness. When people abandoned themselves to lust you could not take them seriously, everybody said. As a movement, they were looking for new forms of relationships of course.

The lower slopes are covered with a profusion of white broom and shrubs full of creamy white flowers, five red dots around a yellow heart and smelling of balm. You are put under narcosis by the overwhelming and sultry beauty.

What really happens here is this. Mother Nature wanted the vegetation to secure its future by procreation. To make sure that procreation would really be effective, she hit on an engaging formula: put next to femininity a separate male pole creating tension. The tension occurs because the two poles are separate but want to be united. That is very clever. The urge to overcome spatial separation is inherent in both poles. Now Mother Nature plays the role of the matchmaker who leaves no trick untried to seduce male and female to join together. Thus, this sultry spring valley is the vegetative equivalent of a red light district.

As things developed, several other possibilities presented themselves to make the sexes join, especially the possibility of force: the one overpowers the other. In nature, force has another line of descent than seduction, the way gravity is distinct from magnetism. (Or are they the same very deep down?) But if procreation rests on mutual magnetism, then brute force enters the equation as a foreign element. Among objects, magnetism goes against gravity; so also love runs counter to force.

In the world of living beings, love of acting is mysteriously rooted in the individual, whereas force finds its origin in the application of universal cosmic powers like gravity or centrifugal force. Sex is alive and copulation ought to come from the individual wellspring of love; copulation though force reduces the victim to a dead thing. Copulation through force can very well be a sign of utter contempt, oppression and even hatred. The penis looks like a sword or a spear: that has been clear to people from the beginning; its very appearance seems to justify the subjugation of women.

The fortress of the Templars at Ponferrada is a monument of domination but it lies in ruins. The nearby basilica of the Virgin of the Oak has withstood the ravages of the ages much better. Before the entrance lies a cosy little square with budding plane trees and wooden benches where I sit for a couple of hours to watch children playing with balls, shopping people being picked up by shining limousines and girls going to a music school. Would there be many people who still recognise the sacred place of this church as a spot where you can play with spiritual thoughts? Where you can renew the store of your spiritual provisions and where you can learn how to make your life sing?

It is much easier to keep church buildings in good shape than to keep a church community alive. Strict rules favour rigor mortis more than living resilience. Take the question of obligatory celibacy for priests. The Eucharist is a command from the Lord, in the words of Scripture. Celibacy is, in the words of the pope, a gift. It is clear that the Holy Spirit does not give this gift often in our present time. To say now that we will not observe the command of the Lord unless He gives us the gift of celibacy more often would be an indication that we do not have our priorities right; one could even say that we are blackmailing God. But our leading shepherds are quite clearly not impressed by this argument.

At Ponferrada I get to know a new recipe: fillet of chicken in a sauce made of Roquefort cheese. It tastes delicious but is very, very heavy. In the refugio, the beds have been put too near to each other. Next to me lies a cyclist with a bad cold; the whole night he sneezes and coughs all over me.

* * *

10TH MAY.

I belong to the generation for whom this day will remain a day of calamity till their dying hour: the day on which our world collapsed in 1940 when the German armies attacked the Netherlands.

As we leave Ponferrada we are treated to a chain collision right next to us. A police car stops in an exemplary manner to give right of way to pedestrians who try to use a zebra crossing but the police officers do stop quite suddenly and the five cars following them crash into the police car and each other. What a way to start your day. To be honest, the policemen were driving dangerously. But on the other hand, it would not have occurred to any of the others to stop for a zebra crossing. So who is at fault?

All around us, nature is sweet and tender. How on earth did Mother Nature hit on the idea of male and female beings who play the game of seducing each other. Our clothes are a continuation of the theme of seduction. It is the same game of hide and seek that is being played all the time, the old philosophical game of no and yes: it is not here, it is here; I have no sex organs, I have sex organs. The most important function of clothes is to hide sexuality and thereby stress it. Even that seems to have been discovered by Mother Nature: I think that the first example of human clothing is female pubic hair.

The name Villafranca shows what happened when Spain was being reconquered in the Middle Ages; many people came from France to repopulate it. The devotion to Christ in the grave is very popular here too. At the back of many churches, you will find a life-size statue of the dead Christ lying in a glass coffin.

* * *

11TH MAY.

The apotheosis of today's trip is the long and steep climb to O Cebreiro on the mountain pass of Piedrafita, the border of Galicia. The land bounces upwards along steep slopes or slides downwards in unfathomable valleys. Here and there, I have noticed for some time – actually already since Conques, I realise – messages from four Belgian girls. They call themselves the Oikoten girls; they designate their journey as "the Winter-walk from Oikoten". Through inscriptions on posts, walls and in pilgrims' books, they let other pilgrims know that they are from Louvain in Belgium and that they "are the best". I wonder if they are perhaps Louvain students and if the name Oikoten is perhaps student patois for Louvain.

Across this countryside one of the famous retreats took place of which the English armies have shown to be such masters. In 1808, Sir John Moore had to withdraw before the troops of Napoleon; he fought all the way from Sahagún to La Coruna. There is a story that deep down in one of these ravines lies a great treasure which the English could not prevent from sliding down the snowy slope and which was never recovered.

The higher we go up, the lower the temperature goes down. Right at the top we are assaulted by a furious wind and after that an ice-cold mist envelops us.

Making such a formidable climb gives me great satisfaction: I can do it.

I have not been able to do it for many years. When I was 55 years of age, it looked as if my walking days were over because of severe arthrosis in my right hip. After different kinds of treatment, they gave me an artificial hip when I was 63; and now at 67 I stride up this majestic slope without any pain. It is wonderful to experience the healing powers that are hiding in the human body. An interesting additional detail is that an X-ray done at the time of the operation showed that the original arthrosis could be traced back to my right ankle which I must have broken as a 12-year-old boy and the broken bones of which had grown together in such a bad way that they were still a little apart.

The great promoter of the Jacobean pilgrims' way was Elias Valina Sampedro; he was the parish priest of O Cebreiro. He was the one who checked out the route in detail and marked it with yellow arrows. He has given a very important impetus to the revival of the old Jacobean pilgrimage.

O Cebreiro is renowned for a number of reasons. It is a unique prehistoric village with houses built in ancient Celtic style. It is even more renowned because it is the place of the "Galician Grail". According to legend, it happened a thousand years ago that a simple farmer made his way through the deep snow to attend Mass. During the Mass, the priest thought the farmer to be a bit of an idiot to tramp through the slippery snow for a tiny piece of bread. At that moment the host began to bleed and the chalice began to overflow with blood. In the same old church the same old chalice and blood-soaked cloth and pieces of the host are exhibited in a reliquary. On these same cold grey slabs of stone people have knelt down for centuries in the throes of great emotion: great people, small people, big names – El Cid, Jan van Eyck, Saint Dominic, Charles V – and forgotten names, but all of them pilgrims.

There are many places in Europe where the same kind of miracle is claimed to have happened. This is a clear sign of the great veneration the faithful felt for the Holy Eucharist. This veneration directed itself to the miraculous presence of Jesus under the appearances of bread and wine. All Christians believe that Jesus is present there in a very mysterious but real way.

A few centuries ago, the explanation of this presence became a razor-sharp edge of conflict. An issue over which fierce combat is raging is seldom inspiring. The sorry thing is that Eucharistic renewal is still being judged according to its relevance to these old battle issues; hence, renewal evaporates. Nobody dares to offer a refreshing new vision because one fears to be accused of denying the doctrine of Transubstantiation, a medieval term that up till today nobody can explain convincingly. And so the Eucharist as source of inspiration is drying up. The results of this situation can be seen in all parish churches. The Eucharistic celebrations along the route are depressingly dry and barren, correct and boring, without a noticeable desire for renewal, without participation of the faithful. Formerly you had Mass-servers at least; now everything is arranged in such a way that the priest at the altar does not need any help any more. All ingredients are put on the altar beforehand: food, drink, plates, cups, washing basin and towel. Since time immemorial, the altar represented Jesus Christ. They got rid of that symbolism; now the altar is just a dining table, kitchen table and washing table. "Communion under both kinds" is really considered superfluous. In other words, the pre-Vatican II theology about the chalice being superfluous has re-established itself. The prohibition for lay people to drink from the chalice rested on the argument that under the species of bread as well as under the species of wine the whole Jesus was present, both times with His body and His blood. So, those that received the chalice after having taken the host did something superfluous.

It has never been clear to me why then the priest should have to drink the chalice.

That warped theology has worn away much beautiful symbolism. What is left of the image of an agreement signed with blood as if it were living ink? What is left of the agreement at all? Of the chalice as a healing drink? Or as a drink to celebrate? Celebrate what? What is left of the sign of blood-relationship? Of the divine dimension of our daily food? One gets the impression that all those images are being discouraged because all one wants to hear is about the "Transubstantial" presence of Christ. It is not rare to see the champions of this kind of orthodoxy unwittingly slip into heresy when they proclaim with impunity that Jesus is "physically" present in the holy Eucharist (that means: subject to the physical laws of gravity and chemistry). They intend to say that He is "really" present but that is not the same as physically unless you are a total materialist. They are not content until they have reduced the mystery to a platitude.

You hear everybody say the sacrifice of Mass is the same as Christ's death on the cross. Who is able to illustrate this a bit? This is how I venture to explain it to our people. By virtue of the consecration of the bread, the body of Christ as such becomes present; by virtue of the consecration of the wine His blood. For the moment I refrain from further logical implications. By virtue of sacramental symbolism you now find on the altar the body and the blood of Christ separated; and that is exactly what happened on the cross. With this sacramental separation of the body and the blood, which we offer to God on the altar, we remind God – and ourselves – of the terrible things that happened on Calvary. After that, both are united again at the moment of holy Communion under both species: the symbol of the resurrection, taking place inside the person receiving holy Communion.

My old parish priest shook with suspicion when he heard my theology and did not want to hear of it at all. I was disappointed, for I was so proud of this explanation, more so since the people understood it, even the devout riffraff in the prison.

* * *

12TH MAY.

When we left O Cebreiro in 1971, Don Elias played Wagner's Pilgrims Choir from the church tower; it moved us to tears. I am getting troubled more and more by the cold that was passed on to me by the cyclist of Ponferrada. This is really the first physical discomfort that I feel during this walk. I have done more than 2,000 kilometres and my body feels fit and resilient. Every day I see people around me who are a lot less fortunate.

But one has to admit that many people do stupid things with their bodies. Many do not seem to understand their bodies any more. Take the case of the skin. Incessantly the advertisements tell us that sweat is something revolting and that calluses are reprehensible blemishes: two functions of the skin have thus been discredited. According to nature's plans, the skin has a thermostat that works with water cooling. Many people who feel they have a wet shirt on their back now feel like somebody who has wetted his pants: they have to wash and clean themselves to rid themselves of this embarrassment. Many walkers confuse their thermostat by constantly changing their clothes. It is easy to spoil your thermostat. Many people have lost it and laugh at me for having it. I even shy away from soap on this journey so as not to spoil the oils on the skin; I use plenty of fresh water all the time. Then, where there is friction on the skin, nature reinforces the skin with extra thick layers. The digger gets calluses on his hands; the walker gets calluses under his feet. And what do I see walkers around me do? They smear ointment on their skin that counteracts the formation of calluses! Because the girl at the chemist shop said it was so good. And thus, whereas intensive walking should join the big callous areas nicely and gradually with the areas that have no calluses, these walkers see ugly and painful blisters appear on those very spots. Away with that ointment! Use clean socks every day, put a little talcum powder in them, wear boots that are rather too big than too small: rather fill up too much space with a second pair of socks. Your feet, believe it or not, are actually fond of walking and can cope with it very well.

At Triacastela, the refugio lies far away from the town centre so we settle for a small hotel. My fellow pilgrim gets the awful message over the telephone that her mother has had a heart attack and is now dying. The people of the hotel help as much as they can to arrange for sudden transport home. There is so much goodness in people.

* * *

13TH MAY.

Once again I am by myself, alone with the crystalline sunlight, the hill climbs that are just a bit too steep and the hamlets in deep valleys. I spot pilgrims in the landscape the way a dog spots other little dogs a mile away.

Pilgrims around me get hurt or discouraged, too, by the excessive weight that they have burdened themselves with. That has to do with lack of discipline. You weigh something in your hand and you think it really weighs hardly anything and is so handy to have it with you. But one tends to forget that all loads are composed of many light things. Another point to realise is that you can get almost anything you need along the route: medicines, food, drink, paper. Never ever change wet clothing on the way: the wet clothes are very heavy in your rucksack; rather make sure you keep warm and then the body warmth will dry the clothes quickly. My trousers dry in half an hour after the rain has stopped, provided I keep moving.

On a walk like this, you are really preoccupied with your body. You feel how everything functions and what it is your body wants. You begin to ponder over its construction. Our human body has been derived from a quadruped, a quadruped that started walking on its hind legs. That was a risky experiment on the side of nature. Think of all the bad backs, the worn out knees and the ruined feet; but clearly the advantages were worth it. What a strange, mysterious and wordless mechanism this is: nature that tries and experiments and deducts and adjusts. Even the very word "mechanism" is wrong.

It is also clear that everything had its preceding phase. Take the mammals. One wonders how Mother Nature got the far-out idea of breast-feeding. I think the breast is an adaptation of the placenta. The placenta filters the mother's blood and feeds it into the baby through the umbilical cord. The breast filters the mother's blood too; but since the baby is now detached from the mother, the umbilical cord has to be replaced with a loose joint: the nipple and the mouth. (The same system is used to make a passage with the penis and the vagina.) Thus breast feeding is a continuation of the feeding system already installed inside the mother's womb. The child continues to float in the safe warm arms of the mother; far away, he still hears the familiar sound of the mother's heartbeat; he feels the sweet nourishment entering effortlessly; he tastes a little more now with his nose as well; sounds that he used to hear from afar and indistinctly now have come nearer and clearer. The touch of space has changed gently: not any longer the hollow forms, this time forms are convex – the round breast; and above that the round friendly head of the mother. What kind of madness has inspired modern Western humans to deny all this to the child and replace it with a dumb bottle with a rubber tit in order that the adults may reserve the female breast as a nice little toy for themselves.

Galicia is the land of seafood, calamares and pulpa; yes, you learn to like cuttlefish and octopus. Fish soup smells like low tide, the land smells of toiling pilgrims and old-fashioned religion.

The pilgrimage to Compostela has seen a remarkable resurgence recently. Nobody in Holland talked about it in the 'sixties; when I went in 1969 I was an oddball. Soon after my journey my fellow tribesman Hans Annink went, calling himself a late pilgrim on the Milky Way. Now there are thousands of us. Is it romantic nostalgia for the Middle Ages? I personally don't feel it that way. To me it looks more like a bodily and liberating challenge to the ordinary man who finds himself locked up in a technical merry-go-round. It has something to do, too, with finding your roots. For the previous generations, the Middle Ages had had their day, they were a station we had passed on our way to progress. That was an erroneous idea: you never pass any stage of your development; you drag it along and you might as well have a look at it.

The Middle Ages certainly were an experimental garden of knowledge and culture. (Formerly they had experimental gardens, now we have laboratories!) Our world owes a debt of honour to the dedication of the people of those days.

The Middle Ages definitely had their dark sides. Pious men made philosophy a humble handmaid subservient to theology: ancilla theologiae. The Church made use of Platonic concepts so as to describe her doctrine more strikingly and around 1200 AD Aristotle became popular. The great Scholastics in the era of Thomas Aquinas (1270 AD) constructed a breathtaking synthesis of Plato and Aristotle and set up a body of knowledge in the shape of a huge scientific skyscraper with the twin wings of philosophy and theology. A growing number of scholars like Roger Bacon (1290), Duns Scotus

(1300) and William Ockham (1340) pointed at weak spots in the construction but their criticism was rejected vehemently: whosoever tampered with philosophy, was unscrewing theology. The point these men tried to make was that concrete investigations were more fruitful than processes of reasoning, for the latter overrated the reality value of concepts. Rather than describing concepts as eternal essences they would see them as handy titles for collections of similar thoughts. They said there was no "Iron" as such, only pieces of iron; there was no "Horse", only horses. Iron and Horse were no more than handy names. That was the reason why the followers of Ockham were called "Nominalists", names people. They were the forerunners of the future scientists. And they undermined the world of Scholastic thought.

At Sarria, I quite accidentally come across the erstwhile prison where we slept in 1971. I remember. In one of the cellars we found a bull's ear and a human skeleton; we had boiled fish for supper, something quite a few people did not like; the toilet flowed over into the sleeping space. Aunty Nanny suffered from diarrhoea; when she tried to sleep she had a coughing fit, with disastrous results. "Good God, what do I do now," she hissed. "Just wait," I whispered and quickly fetched her plastic bag with clothes.

Scholasticism was a very imposing system. Everything was fitted into a huge logical scheme of reality and defined sharply, especially human things; and the whole scheme was put into the perspective of good behaviour, which was also defined sharply. The ideal human was an honest person: righteousness became the central pillar of reality, the ethical parallel to logic.

For many people this ideal is still valid today. Being upright means that their outward appearance is a true reflection of their interior; and then this interior is supposed to be a nicely cleaned inner habitat without dark corners. But here lies a hitch. For 40 years, I spent time in confessional and consultation rooms and ever so many people have poured out their hearts' troubles. And so I know what every doctor and every psychologist knows: that there are very many people who keep carefully chained monsters of bad memories in their inner living rooms or bedrooms. To use another image: many people's interior looks like a chaotic kitchen and the surprising thing is that they manage to prepare tasty dishes there. Many people with damaged interiors look for help from somebody who they suspect has experience of interior damage himself and knows how to cope with it in a fair way.

We should allow people to have their dark corners: these are part of human life. There are moments when the chained monsters are shaken awake. On a walk like this, they are shaken loose slowly but surely.

* * *

14TH MAY.

The day of the bombardment of Rotterdam in 1940, always. The path is so rough that I make slow progress. Often the narrow track is blocked by slowly strolling herds of incontinent cows. The old town of Portomarín has disappeared under the water of an artificial lake. The old church was salvaged and rebuilt, stone by stone in the new town: that is the only thing of the past that was saved. The rest lies on the bottom of the lake with all the dark secrets that will never surface again.

Let me talk about a dark secret in my own life. To speak about it I have to make a detour, via a Scholastic explanation of the validity of sacraments. A sacrament is "an external symbol instituted by Christ that gives the grace it signifies". Very long ago, an interesting notion entered the world of the sacraments, the notion of "validity". Certain conditions had to be fulfilled, otherwise the sacrament would be null and void. These conditions had to do either with the words that were being used (let us say: the formula, the "form") or the material that was being used (the "matter"). If you would say at the moment of baptising: "Be life-giving like water", then the baptism would be invalid or null and void because the form is faulty. If on the other hand you would pour salt over the candidate, the baptism would be invalid or null and void because the matter is faulty. By attaching such a decisive value to a correctly pronounced formula, one moved very closely to the field of magic. Scrupulous people could have great problems with pronouncing sacramental formulas: a small but vital omission due to inadvertence could render the whole ceremony invalid.

A curious incident occurred at my ordination to the priesthood. The English cardinal who was to perform the ordination of the 28 candidates was suffering badly from senile decay. There were rumours that recently he had made such a mess of a priestly ordination that they had secretly re-ordained the whole class afterwards just to make sure. The cleverest theologian in our ranks toyed with the idea of refusing ordination by this cardinal but he did not press on and so the big day arrived.

Now you have to know that the forma for the priestly ordination is: "Infunde in eis, Domine, presbyterii dignitatem" (pour forth in them, O Lord, the dignity of the priesthood). It so happened that ordinations to the diaconate and subdiaconate coincided often with the ordinations to the priesthood. The form for the ordination of a deacon had "diaconatus dignitatem"; of a subdeacon, "subdiaconatus dignitatem". All these formulas were printed in the pontificale, the book of rites used by the bishop. To avoid too many duplications in the book, they had printed the formulas thus: "Infunde in eis, Domine, subdiaconatus/diaconatus/presbyterii dignitatem"; and it was left to the ordaining bishop to select the right formula. When in our case the cardinal arrived at the essential formulas he lost the way. I remember him saying something like: "Infunde in eis, Domine, subdia... eh, eh... diaco... eh, eh... pre, pri... ignitaaaaatem". I thought to myself "well, well" and the others probably did too. But what could you do? You entrusted yourself to God. But I think it would not be a difficult job for even a minor theologian to prove that I am an invalidly ordained priest. That would mean that all the Masses I ever said in the past 43 years have been invalid, that all those thousands of people have been given unconsecrated hosts for communion. All the people whose marriages I blessed live in concubinage; all their children are bastards, etc. When one link is missing, the whole chain falls, like in the apostolic succession. We have never talked about it afterwards but recently I heard that one of my classmates is now getting scruples about not having been ordained validly. Fortunately it does not bother me at all. How do I get around it? I just don't believe that those theories work like that with God. Finished.

Matter, too, can cause trouble. Thus it is absolutely essential that for the Eucharist you should use wine made from grapes and bread made from wheat flour. In the Latin rite, the custom is to use unleavened bread. They make a soft mixture of water and wheat flour and from that, they bake wafers called hosts: small thin white officially approved wafers.

Well now, let me in my turn corner some orthodox theologians. The bread used for the Eucharist has to have the "species panis" to be real bread. But species panis really means: if you look at it (spicere), then you are made to say: that is bread. This is ad validitatem, required for validity. However, the purely white hosts do not at all have the species panis. If you show them to people and ask "what is this?" they will in all honesty say "plastic" or "cardboard". And if you say "this is bread", nobody will believe it. It just is not bread to the ordinary people. That really means that all the Masses ever celebrated with this kind of hosts have been invalid, right from the 13th century or so, in the whole Latin Church. If you call this absurd, then call those theories that lead to it absurd as well.

We nail ourselves down with theories because we do not dare to play with the gospel. Whenever it happened in the past that the church nailed her doctrine down with theories, things went awry. Neo-platonism turned the church into a theocracy; in rational Scholasticism God died of logical schemes. I learn a lesson from all this: the church should not sell herself to any theories but should continue to play with the divine child outside and inside us, and sing children's songs like "Glory to God in the Highest and Peace on Earth to People of Good Will".

* * *

15TH MAY.

Yesterday's steep paths have given me a pain in the groin and my cold is growing into real bronchitis. At Ventas de Naron, a graffito tells me that the Oikoten girls are called Linsay, Elke, Herma and Christel. The route I am following now should be familiar to me: I have walked this section four times already, albeit 20 years ago. So much has changed: you cannot walk through the same landscape five times. I spot a farm where we have slept several times; it is a ruin. Stopping near the dilapidated house to greet some old people I mention the names of the dogs of those days – Satan and Trotsky. That makes them really laugh and now they can remember us. A little farther there should be another farm where I was once welcomed most cordially by an old farmer with two daughters, one of whom was lame and skipped though the house like a squirrel. Isn't that the house there? I slow down. Behind the house, a lame woman is hobbling around. It is her! Hesitantly she stumbles back along the crooked paths of her memory and then she begins to smile. She invites me in again. The father died three years ago; the brother does not work in London any more; her sister Trinita has married; her mother has gone blind and she herself is an old woman now. At last she also has a name for me: Lucia Garcia Castro.

In one or other way, I feel closely related to these people. I know the statues on their walls, the medals and crucifixes around their necks. I know their words. These are things with which my generation grew up. The old people had their psalms, the young people had their parables. And these things meant something to them. During the War, my generation prayed: "My shield and my support, that's you my God and Lord; on you I do rely, don't leave me ever more", words from our national anthem; and that was real. My friend, military policeman and parson, was condemned to death together with ten other policemen for having refused to arrest Jews. As they came out of the court room they were counted by a German officer. Eleven; correct therefore. "No," said my friend, "twelve." The officer counted once more: eleven. "Twelve," my friend repeated. "God is the twelfth one."

What kind of words do the young generation have now? I really do not know. I hear them quote catchy phrases like "We're here for the beer". Do they still learn things that inspire a person? Fifteen years ago, I was talking to a friend who thoroughly disliked things religious. I asked him: "Would you not feel worried that we might get a generation of children who have no idea any more what the Prodigal Son might be or the Good Samaritan?" No, that was quite fine with him. Has that generation come now? They and their words are strangers to me. Sometimes I get the feeling that I know my young nephews and nieces less well than the medieval peasants who built their little chapels here. Or is this the normal generation gap? Perhaps it has always been like that. One day I may discover that I have very much in common with the present youngsters, except that we use different words and ideas. Perhaps it has to be like that, for we are educated with static ideas and the world is moving. On this pilgrims' route there are as many young pilgrims as there are old ones. It is as if our heads grow apart but our feet and our hands remain together. All the same, you can discern different forces at work in education now. Formerly the educators were the parents and members of the clan; now we also have the school, the peer group, the media; and many youngsters come home like strangers.

Palas de Rey is a second-rate little village. Apart from the name, there is nothing that indicates that this was a royal residence once upon a time: a Visigoth king lived there.

The Goths were a Germanic people; they played a very important part in the dismantling of the Roman Empire. The Eastern Goths or Ostrogoths invaded Italy and replaced the Roman authorities there. The Western Goths or Visigoths did the same in Spain. Other Germanic people had gone there ahead of them: the Vandals or the Walkers. They pressed on to North Africa, leaving in Spain only the name of (V) Andalusia behind. From what is now Tunis, they even attacked Rome and ransacked it. The Visigoths stayed in Spain and became the ruling class, like the Franks in France. It was the Visigoth kings that were defeated so roundly by the Moors a few centuries later.

Palas de Rey has a comfortable refugio. The interior is lovely; a big sitting room with polished wooden furniture and a very useful kitchen. And you are assisted by courteous ladies. There are pilgrims who find this quite wrong: they remember the good olden days when you had to be content with a small corner in a farmer's shed. I like the present comfort. And it is not as far removed from the facts of history as some people would have us think. Formerly, you had religious houses all along the route ready to receive you. And what really matters, making the rugged walk through weather fair and foul, has remained the same as ever. No one else can do that for you.

The food in the Casa Curru is splendid, for all the family eats the same and guests get a special treat: the best pieces of meat and a big helping of ice-cream.

* * *

16TH MAY.

At 12 noon, I reach Mellid and pass a pizzeria. In a fit of recklessness I order a big one. It appears to be big enough for a family with three growing kids; I eat it all nevertheless. When I arrive at the end of today's stretch, at the village of Ribaldiso, I find it has only one building and that is the refugio. I am the only visitor, it is pouring with rain and there is no food to be had anywhere. Now I bless the mega-pizza in my stomach.

The name Galicia teaches us something about the history of this region. When the Angles and the Saxons conquered Britain around the year 500 AD, quite a number of the original Celtic inhabitants fled. A number of them emigrated to France, to a region that became known as Brittany. Others crossed over to the western tip of Spain and called their new homeland the land of the Galls or Gaelics or Celts. Many of the farmers have distinctly Irish heads.

* * *

17TH MAY.

The last day before Compostela. Twice I pass a memorial for a pilgrim who just did not make it and died on this last day. "Guillermo Watt, peregrino, abrazo a Dios a los 69 anos a una jornada de Santiago, el 25 de agosto de 1993, ano Santo. Vivat in Christo." His shoes are there, cast in bronze. "Mariano Sanchez-Covisa Carro, peregrino a pie, fallecio aqui 24.IX.1993. D.E.P." So he died exactly in this spot. Some way back I saw another monument for a deceased cyclist; it looked as if it was made from the parts of his bicycle.

Arca has a refugio with a washing machine, a drier, a refrigerator, heating that is on and delightful ladies once again. In the route descriptions, the refugio is not indicated as being in Arca but in O Pino.

* * *

18TH MAY.

This is the day of the entry into Compostela. As I set off the rain comes down in torrents. The path passes through dripping forests over slippery muddy ground. On this day, every pilgrim is filled with joy. The last hill is called Monte do Gozo, the mountain of joy, because it is from there that you get your first view of Santiago. I have read somewhere that the pilgrims used to race each other to the top; the winner was proclaimed king and he was given privileges during his stay in the city. It is said that names like King or Le Roy can be traced back to this custom. This time I am a king without rivals but Santiago is invisible on account of the squalls. Besides, on this same mountain a monstrously big complex of campsites, bungalows, monuments and congress facilities has been erected on the occasion of the visit of the pope. When I have passed just beyond this depressing eyesore the rain clears and I march into the city in fine weather, feeling quite normal: the anticipated solemn emotions are not there, yet.

There is the fat German! On the way he popped up here and there like a long-haired skinhead but after some weeks of civilising pilgrims' existence he has become much more normal. He has retained his style of speech: he delights in the hackneyed phrases of television advertisements. He is now going to the coast "to de-stress himself".

Near the cathedral, I do get overwhelmed by the monumental proportions of the whole entourage and also by the emotions that go with the completion of a big task. Suddenly, I find myself surrounded by Dutch people, friendly as if they knew me. I ascend the steps to the Portico: in the middle there is a pillar with the genealogical tree of Christ; at the bottom the sculptor has left five holes. Everybody puts his five fingers in them but nobody knows why. At the back of the same pillar there is a stone head named "the head-butt-Saint", Santo dos Croques. They say that it is the head of the architect and by butting your head against it; you can get some of his wisdom. Then you float forward through sacred space, Romanesque in form, Gothic in height, Baroque in decoration, straight towards the main altar where the immense figure of James stands, staring like an idol, covered with gold, silver and precious stones. Everybody climbs the small stairs behind the statue and taking the good saint around his shoulders from behind, gives him a hug. And whilst you do that you should think of all the people on the road that sent you on with the classical greeting "Give James a good hug for me". In the crypt under the altar the tomb of James is venerated, a tomb that was discovered around the year 825 AD.

From the earliest times there has been a tradition that the Apostle James worked in Spain for some years and that after he had been beheaded by King Herod, his body was buried in Spain. What happened in 825 was that mysterious light and angelic music appeared in the shrubs that covered an ancient Roman burial site. Thus the tomb was revealed which was identified as Saint James's by the local bishop. You are invited to believe it all and if you do, then everything becomes much more interesting, That event coincided with the beginning of the re-conquest of Spain from the Moors. James became the great patron of this Reconquista. Charlemain had a dream in which he saw that the Milky Way was a reflection in the sky of the holy way going westward through the north of Spain, to the end of the earth. That is why the French like to call this pilgrims' way the Milky Way. The innumerable pilgrims have made Santiago big. They came in such numbers that they were allowed to sleep on the balconies of the cathedral. To freshen the air, incense was used. There lies the origin of the swinging of the Botafumeiro, the man-size thurible. By means of a long cable it is suspended from the top of the dome; eight men get hold of the other end and tug at it in such a way that it swings higher and higher, until it comes swooping out of the high vaults like a sparks-belching dive-bomber. A spectacular and popular show.

The cathedral of Santiago de Compostela is a place of crossroads where the paths of many unusual and special persons are intertwined briefly, people full of strange stories, people who still have the rough weather in their tousled hair, people that wake up momentarily from a deep dream. Because the path itself is one long drawn-out church, these people are veritable church-goers. They have been living in a church for weeks on end; that has imprinted on them a strange and authentic seal. A Protestant Dutch pilgrim, who had started from Taizé in France, said to me in the cathedral: "What a shame that we Protestants have no saints any more".

One thing is very clear to me: the way of Saint James is a way for the child in us. In Mark 10:15 we hear Jesus say: "Let me tell you one thing: if somebody does not accept the Kingdom of God the way a child does it, he will never get inside". Have we really assimilated that word fully? Sometimes I think not. Not at all. How often do we not look down patronisingly on the more childlike expressions of faith. I have heard people say: child-like religion is all very touching but it solves nothing. We should stop once and for all seeing everything in terms of problems and solutions. We can turn a new leaf by seeing things, events, mysteries and even persons as newly offered opportunities. If we insist on solving everything, then before long we will have dissolved Christianity itself.

I register myself with Don Jaime Garcia Rodriguez, canonico delegado de peregrinacion. He calls for the photographer and for the reporter of El Correo Galego who distils an article from her interview in which I emerge as a second Francis of Assisi. And then, finally, I get my compostela, the official certificate of the completed pilgrimage. It is my fifth.

Somewhere the Oikoten girls have written down that they arrived on 12th April. They had started from Tildonk in Belgium on 14th December. Tough girls. I also learn that Oikoten has nothing to do with Louvain. It is a Belgian organisation that makes it possible for young delinquents to have their prison sentence commuted into a walk to Compostela. The conditions are laid down in a contract that describes in great detail all the particulars, such as the daily distances and the weight to be carried.

After a long journey, the migrating stork is drawn by a mysterious force to the place of his nest. So I also am drawn by an irresistible force to the Hostal de los Reyes Catolicos. The previous times I only went there for a free meal in the servants' quarters and the servants' company. Now I want the full treatment: staying in a luxury apartment with a bath of gel and body-milk, dining from a table with silver and crystal, and lackeys in turquoise and gold in the company of fragile dowagers and puffing millionaires.

* * *

10ᵀᴴ–28ᵀᴴ MAY.

Vacation. How do you celebrate the completion of a 2,437-kilometre walk? You stroll around a little. You feel the short-lived intoxication of the champion, dwelling on the highest top for a moment, and after that the only way forward is downward. I am so happy that I still have an extensive walking programme to tackle: I am not even halfway. The heavy work still lies ahead of me: the tropical summer heat of southern Europe, the crossing of the Alps. After the extravagant night in the ancient pilgrims' hostel, I find hospitality in the Casa Sacerdotal on the Preguntorio, the same house I stayed in in 1969. In 1971, we all stayed in the soaking wet campsite, of which there is no trace left now.

On that campsite I came across two girls, one from California and the other from New Zealand, and they were playing virtuoso violin duets of Haendel in the laundry place with its perfect acoustics thanks to the ceramic wall tiles. They had gone on holidays with their violin under their arm and they met here. Next to my tent, a young American couple had settled down; they were travelling with their two small children on a donkey. They reminded me of Joseph and Mary on the flight to Egypt. They had no tent, just a plastic sheet tied to the fence. Quite adequate, they said. But when it started raining in the night I heard Joseph howl: "Mary, the children are getting coooold!"

I disappear for a couple of days for a rendezvous in a secret place.

Santiago de Compostela, some 50 kilometres from the Atlantic Ocean and Cape Finisterre (the end of the world), is the turning point of my pilgrimage: from here, I start the way back. It makes me think of turning points that have marked history. They are not abrupt, they build up slowly and long in advance. Just the way a super tanker that wants to turn into Rotterdam harbour begins to adjust its speed and its course as far away as somewhere near Dunkirk in France. The Western world has

taken a gigantic turn towards a de-Christianised society; that
did not happen in a few days. It is possible to indicate some
periods of time at which the direction changed.

One such moment occurred around the year 1400. It is then that
people became aware of "history" as applicable to mankind.
Up till then they had been thinking in a more cyclical fashion:
the same events tended to return, the way the seasons returned.
And if in the course of the years new trends had become
visible, they had been denounced as some kind of decay. But
at the time mentioned there arose a trend of thought saying
that new things stood for development of something better,
progress. The term "modern" became fashionable, derived
from the Latin "modo", meaning "now", with the overtones
of "better than before". The new philosophers round William
Ockham called themselves promoters of the "via moderna",
in contrast with the Scholastic "via antiqua". The philosopher
Durandus boasted of the title Doctor Modernus. In the world
of the church there was widespread fermentation caused by
the incredible Western Schism, the thirst of power among the
highest authorities and the scandalous life-style of many of
the clergy. The first "reformers" appeared, Wycliff and Hus,
and not long after that there arose in the Netherlands the great
renewal movement known as the "Modern Devotion". "Ars
Nova" was the name given to the new type of polyphonic
music developed by Flemish musicians. In later years they
would call all this the beginning of the "Renaissance" or
rebirth, a cyclical term, funnily enough.

Once you let go of the cyclical way of reading history,
confusion is likely to set in, for the future is not predictable
any longer but open. At the time of the early Renaissance,
many thinkers in Europe began to sow the seeds of new ideas,
ideas that were to develop into modern points of view. Eckhart
came out with ideas about the enigmatic and dark character of
God. The art of printing made it possible for ideas to circulate
freely. The vernacular languages became respectable, which
stimulated popular thinking, which stimulated nationalism,
which stimulated national wars. Copernicus disseminated the
idea of heliocentrism (the earth turns around the sun). Vasalis
shattered a big taboo by dissecting the human body. Paracelsus
disseminated homeopathy, Montaigne modern scepticism,
Macchiavelli political amorality. Soon after the year 1400, the
Western world was awash with wild ideas about the World-
Soul, Monads (creatures are contractions of the Godhead) and
Utopias. The church leaders could not cope with it. They felt
threatened, they felt much more at home in a cyclical world,
they dug themselves in in their "perennial" ideas and began

to fight bitter rearguard actions. Loudly acclaimed church philosophy slowly collapsed.

It is significant that Geert Grote, the founder of the Modern Devotion and the real author of the book known as the Imitation of Christ, found himself at the end of his life barred from preaching by his own Archbishop of Utrecht. Church leaders did not know any longer, who were their real supporters and began to shoot at their own soldiers. When the urges for renewal became too strong, the body of the church fell into a state of cramp and was torn asunder. Reform began to lead its own life, under protest. The church has not yet recovered from that trauma.

* * *

29TH MAY.

The journey continues. It is high time for me to go back to normal after those nine days of rest and put in six to eight hours of walking every day. At my last visit to the grave of James, I put the royal gift of 40 pounds in the alms box and as I leave the city, I am made uncomfortable by the strange feeling that I am walking in the wrong direction. At times, people let me feel even that a returning pilgrim is an anomaly.

That is nonsense of course, for long ago all pilgrims had to walk back.

The walk to Santiago is clearly a symbol of life. One wanders over meandering ways and paths that do not differ from any other paths, it would seem; yet every day brings the pilgrim nearer to his cathedral behind the horizon. Arriving at Santiago is the equivalent of reaching the heavenly Jerusalem. This moment is surely a magnificent apotheosis. Nowadays, however, it is followed immediately by sobering disenchantment: the game is over, the magic spell is broken, train connections and flight tickets back to the fatherland have to be secured immediately. It would be so much better if the way back would not be so disruptive and if there were a gradual return to normal life. If the process goes too quickly, there is a danger that the unique experience of the pilgrimage will be encapsulated like a foreign body. I am very grateful that I can walk back gently and that one day my faithful feet will quietly carry me through my own front door. It seems to me that more people will choose to do this in the future.

The way back seems shorter. I meet many pilgrims. On one day I note: a Frenchman, a man called Dick van der Velde from Vlaardingen, two Danes, a Spanish couple with their young son, two Spaniards on horseback, 50 Irish who cover large stretches by bus, a Brazilian boy, two Frenchmen again, two Frenchmen with mules, two unknown pilgrims. We often stop to exchange a short word of greeting; this makes me think of ants which sniff each other quickly as they meet, to establish their mutual identity.

A pilgrim is in a way an extraterrestrial being. As he walks, he gets shaken loose from the mould of "today" and of "here". He does not belong any more; he is the odd man out. His feeling for time vanishes: what happened to him 50 years ago may suddenly become actual again and urgent. His historical platform begins to sway and to shift: he suddenly fits into old churches again; he belongs to old roads again; he can change into a medieval person if he so wishes. When he resumes normal life and accepts again the imprisonment of the "now", he may well feel that the practical and everyday activities of that "now" are a form of sleepwalking.

On the one hand, the pilgrim gets rattled loose from his space, his surroundings, relations; and yet he remains attached to them. That creates duplicity in him. He does pray but with his eyes open. He withdraws but remains present. He goes to where he has always been; he walks away from something that he takes along; he enters more and more deeply into himself. A pilgrimage is a poetic combination of going and not going, it is a dance.

* * *

30TH MAY.

I have to be fully concentrated to find the way. The markings have all been put down for people going towards Compostela: thus the arrows are always found after the crossroads. On top of that, on the way back the landscape can look quite different. Fortunately, I had put some annotations on my map. But the clearest indications are the footprints of the other pilgrims.

Looking for the right direction can be a difficult task, especially when nobody has been there before. That is a problem you get when you do not think any longer in a cyclical way. That is the problem that begins to affect the Western world around the year 1600. Soon after the stormy start of the Renaissance, many people lose their bearings; they find no firm ground under their feet any more. Descartes (1640) desperately looks for an indubitable and unshakeable foothold. He is overjoyed when he finds one: "Cogito, ergo sum"; I think, therefore I am. It is indeed a new and very fruitful standpoint, albeit a one-sided one.

The one-sidedness of this exclusive attention for the "ego" will lead to disastrous consequences. It is, for instance, completely alien to the Hindu convictions: there the independent self, the individual I-by-myself, put on an exalted pedestal is the root cause of all misery in the world. And so, at the very moment when the West establishes close links with the Eastern world through the efforts of adventurous sailors, those very links are spoiled by its new philosophy. From now on, the intellectual treasures of India are being rejected expressly: the Indians themselves are relegated to being heretical and semi-barbaric strangers by the arrogant European vanguard. What a missed opportunity.

* * *

31ST MAY.

The sun reaches its full strength. I am now walking from west to east; that means to say, against the morning sun. That has its own charm: it often makes the colours of the flowers brilliant. The yellow flowers of the broom become so bright that they seem incandescent.

People tell me that a new form of condition-training has been launched, called "walking", and that means marching over a fairly long distance. That is indeed correct, it is excellent for your condition. Scientists have made it modern by attaching technical frills. The biggest refinement is this: you can make this walk under carefully-controlled conditions on a moving belt, so that you do not waste any time in nature, and you are able to watch your favourite TV programme in the meantime.

I meet mechanised pilgrims, an English group. Their journey has been organised completely by a travel agency. A bus carries all their burdens and an official leader arranges for their stay in comfortable lodgings and solves all their other problems. The tourists themselves walk for a couple of hours a day, are picked up and taken to their hotel. No, that would spoil all my fun. It does not seem to be a jolly group: they are wrangling and bickering and talking in harsh tones like football supporters. Surely, the pilgrimage to Compostela has to be an affair of the feet and an adventure where you yourself have to solve your problems and make your decisions.

My preparations for this walk have taken me two years. I am somebody who cannot just walk into the wide beyond; I want to know where I am going. For a very long time, I have been busy looking for the most fitting route. Once I was happy with the route, I started buying the maps. I always walk with one eye on the map and one eye on the road. I hate losing the way and that happens very rarely. It does happen. What should you do when you realise that you have lost the way? First of all you would do well to find where you are: search hard, ask people. You may be on the wrong way but it is very useful to know which wrong way. Then you can begin with the next question: how to get back to the right track? You can retrace your steps to the point where you went wrong and that can mean a long walk. Most people will try to cut off a corner but that can lead you into a labyrinth.

A really strange experience is arriving without knowing that you are there. If you continue after that you are always wrong. Admittedly, this does not happen very often on a pilgrimage; but all the more often during a spiritual or an intellectual journey. Both the church and the intelligentsia try to demarcate the land they are walking on. Church people sometimes reassure themselves that they have the compass of God's Word to rely upon; but in a labyrinth a compass is of little use, more so if you do not know in what direction you are supposed to go. Often you do not even know what you are looking for until you find it. Only then can you say: that is it. On the other hand, it is also quite possible to continue searching with fierce determination whilst you have the answer already, except that you do not realise it. People can walk past God, can pay no attention to the voice of the angel, fail to recognise the angel, and plod on relentlessly.

Rilke has a marvellous poem about this: how we trace God, but strictly on our own terms. Even a flash of genuine insight will not make us give up our efforts.

I know you are a riddle hidden
behind Time's shimmering mirage.
But I created you unbidden:
with arrogance my hand was driven
as I composed your apt collage.

I draughted curves with cautious grace,
and lines as delicate as lace,-
but something ruined my design:
like brambles lines got intertwined
with ovals, triangles and planes,
till somewhere deep in my domains
where I was groping in a daze,
emerged a shape truly divine.

It's hard to see what work I've done:
It's now complete, I know. Instead
I firmly turn away my head:
I cannot stop and doodle on.
(Rainer Maria Rilke, *Das Stundenbuch*:' Ich weiss, Du bist der Raedselhafte')

THE FIFTH MONTH

JUNE

During the month of June, I walk along the Camino in the opposite direction as far as Estella, spending the night in the same places as on the way to. That reinforces the feeling of being on the return journey. Now I have a little more time to look around a bit. The daily distances should have seemed shorter now but that is not so, on account of the much greater heat. It is high season and all the refugios are open. The most remarkable one is the one at Villafranca del Bierzo. It is an elaborate construction of sheets of yellow plastic; these are being cooled continuously with a running hosepipe. It can accommodate 50 people in its cluttered interior; there is also a bar with cool beer and complete meals and lots of unusual customers. During this pilgrimage, I meet some 12 fellow countrymen who have come all the way from Holland on foot. A very special occasion was meeting my friend Jaap van Rooijen, also from Hengelo. He had started at roughly the same time as myself but followed a more westerly route. Once he had reached Lourdes, he was struck with such a heavy dose of homesickness that he gave up and took the train home. Within days he was struck with an even heavier dose of remorse that made him rush back, like greased lightning as they say, and continue his walk as if nothing had happened. At El Burgo Ranero, we fell into each other's arms. In the same village I surprised senora Mercedes by returning the thousand pesetas she had given me by mistake on the way to. She remembers and is enchanted.

I should not forget to mention that my path crosses that of two other Dutchmen who, like myself, go both to and fro. There is a man from Simpelveld who makes enormously long daily marches. The other one is Jan Kengen from Venray. The latter is an imposing character: a patriarch with a long beard and radiating piety. Everybody along the route talks about him and all the ladies want to cuddle him. By worldly standards, he should be a marginal figure: he is old and redundant therefore; he is pious and abnormal therefore; he has very old-fashioned ideas and is a retarded fogey therefore. But in the refugio, crowded with a multicoloured collection of adventurers, he plays a hero's role just by being what he is and doing what he does. Among the pilgrims, one tastes democracy of true and high quality.

There is more than one kind of democracy, and has been ever since democracy began. The term makes us think first of all of ancient Athens. The Athenians developed a democracy of government by pursuing order and fairness, and by their determination to make a maximum number of citizens participate in governing the city. On closer inspection, it turned out to be an elitist kind of democracy, restricted to free Greek citizens. The inheritors of this movement were the rationalists of the Enlightenment, the French Revolution and the Marxists.

In that very same antiquity, there is another kind of democracy to be found, namely a religious one: the one found in the mystic cults. Everybody was welcome to attend those mysteries, including women and slaves. This movement has found its way into the heart of Christianity; it is ironic that church leaders sometimes do not know what to do with it.

Early in the morning old Jan is pottering around the refugio of Nájera, muttering sotto voce; he wants to preen his long beard nicely but he cannot find his small brush anywhere. He sets out in the pitch-dark and returns after five minutes, afraid of being unable to find his way in the dark. A moment later I depart in the opposite direction. As I leave the town, I see Jan Kengen's small brush on the track: I can recognise it from the grey curly hairs. One of the things that I regret about my walk is that I did not pick up the small brush to return it to him afterwards in Holland.

Truly speaking the Gospel contains a democratic constitution: the coming of age, the power and the responsibility of God's People on the Way. Power has to be granted to the powerless. This is something you do see in the church regularly. From the most improbable quarters, persons emerge to take on important positions. Many church people offer all their possessions and their whole being to support those that have no voice. Mary keeps appearing to simple rural children. All the more surprising then is the fact that church leadership often had and still has problems with democracy.

In the past, leaders of church communities had no problems with autocratic monarchism, especially where they themselves were in power. They did this notwithstanding the word of Jesus that this was not to happen in the church. I am sincerely convinced that many of today's rulers of the church are thoroughly unhappy with their monarchical status. The message they emit is: we are stuck with it, there is no alternative, for the only alternative is democracy; and democracy is incompatible with a religion as ours, because God's Will is not determined by a majority vote.

This argument, I fear, gets you into even deeper water. Democracy is not about counting noses but about the shared responsibility of the people. In that sense the church has the duty to make herself democratic. All of God's children ought to speak up: did not all of them receive the Holy Spirit and most of all the little ones? The sensus fidelium – the "instinct" of all the faithful you could say – is open to a minimalist explanation: it is only valid when it agrees with the decisions of the authorities. To me, that sounds hollow. Bishops encourage us not to consider the church as "a democracy" but rather as "a mystery". But democracy and mystery do not exclude one another. Would this dislike of democracy not rather be a pagan residue of the adoration of power, unconverted paganism therefore? For this dislike is the opposite of what the gospel says: "For you are all brothers and sisters, children of one Father".

The gospel formula is the family; relationships of authority should resemble those you see in a functional family. (Although, even those can be corrupted into the direction of a Big Brother figure.) There are conservative faithful who like to use the image of a club. You are members of this club and if you do not like the rules of this club, you had better look for another club. This image, too, differs sharply from the family-model of the Gospel: children are not told to get out and look for another family when they disagree with a parent or with a big brother. Yes, I am sold on the family model. There definitely is a kind of democracy in a functional family. And there is mystery, too. The mysteriousness of love: the folly of the old father who welcomes back his lost son, the unreasonable behaviour of the master who wants to reward the workers of the eleventh hour, the irresponsible action of the good shepherd who risks life and limbs and the wrath of the 99 good sheep to find the lost one.

In the refugios, the people are tolerant. Once I am woken up rudely at 3.00 in the morning – it is at Mansila de las Mulas – by the Dutchman from Waalwijk next to me who shouts: "Now the goddam idiot is pissing on me! The German here above me, he is pissing right through the f- mattress! What will happen next? What the f- hell am I going to do now!" The tiny light is switched on. Everybody is awake and holds his breath. In the feeble light, I see how the portly German sits up on the bunkbed and quizzically explores his crotch. Well, how do you solve that one? Some people walk to and fro, drag mattresses about and curse, and after half an hour everybody is asleep again. People are sorry for the Dutchman; it is said that his life is already stressful enough on account of an impending divorce, without any German pissing on him.

There are people that see the pilgrims' practical comradeship and mutual respect as humanistic leftovers of what used to be a religious event. I do not see it that way at all. To me, religion gets the hallmark of authenticity only when it mixes in with the ordinary things of daily life, like salt in the food. One could start a discussion about whether religion as such has to be tasted: the whole idea of religion is to give true human relish to ordinary life. And a pilgrimage like this proves the point; for this journey religion is like the salt in the food.

The church towers, the small chapels, the crucifixes along the road, the sacred images on the facades, they still salt the landscape, whilst most people have said farewell to traditional religion. The landscape has remained religious the longest.

God has seen tough times. When Descartes chose his own ego, in the 17th century, to be the unshakeable foundation for a new philosophical edifice, he really sat down on the chair of God. His choice was bound to lead to theoretical atheism. God does not tolerate others next to himself, certainly not on his own chair: "Ego sum Dominus et non est alius". Just as God has a problem with others, we (who are like Him) have a problem with Him. And with everything other than ourselves. Reconciliation is needed and possible. A beautiful example of reconciliation between myself and the other is my body: my body is at the same time myself and another. Reconciliation takes place but how can you translate that into thought?

The Western way of philosophising is to turn everything into an object to think about; objectivation as it is called. Objectivation means: to make into another, to "alienate" it as being distinct from yourself. You do that also when you think about yourself and about God. Once you are in that position, most of your profound searching about the principles of reality will be a desperate effort to save either yourself or God.

Plato gives the primacy to the divine, to God and all that has been His from the beginning. Now he has a big job on hand:

that of saving his individual ego. He does that by making his individual ego a part of the divine super-ego. The divine in us recognises the divine outside us. Five hundred years before Plato, Homer had said it already: The gods can disguise themselves but not for one another. ("Ou gar t'agnootes theoi alleeloisi pelontai")

Despite his exalted religious tone, Plato does not manage to salvage the individual human person. In his Republic, he idealises a centrally planned economy that shows an uncanny likeness with the old-fashioned Eastern European communist state.

When you identify the human personal reality too closely with the divine, you have to brace yourself for another dilemma: the problem of evil. Inside me evil is quite tangibly present and incompatible with divine reality. Should we then not grant evil also a comparably high pedigree? Should we accept that there is an independent, superior, dark and evil power at work? The rival world of matter perhaps?

Aristotle tries to start with human reality. He puts the creative, formative power (entelecheia) in the soul of the individual person. Many medieval theologians did not like him, considering him to be a crypto-atheist, compared to Plato. Scholastics tried to Christianise his philosophy by postulating that each particular human soul is created by God. That is not an elegant construction, such a constant interference from God's side; and besides, it does not solve anything. The heart of the problem is merely shifted a bit. Is the human person autonomous or not? Does he have a free will and can he decide for himself?

With those questions you tumble smack into the middle of the Reformation.

At that point, the philosophical discourse stops: as if people feel that quite possibly, no rescue actions can be taken to save God. God refuses to put on the lifejacket of a human argument. Where God is concerned, one will have to be content with parables and children's words and riddles and chance-happenings.

But we do have another task: to liberate matter, bodiliness, from the prison of darkness. Aristotle can be of help there. He makes room for matter amongst the good things of creation: matter is the mine of potential forms. Inspired by him, the Scholastics refuse to call matter bad. On the contrary, it becomes a space-time equivalent of the divine. Those who ıw Thomas Aquinas also hold that "being" should be ьıdered to be an analogous term: all beings show the same essential dimensions of being one, being true and being good, but in varying degrees. In that sense, they are all the same and different at the same time.

Let that be enough. Even if we cannot construct a fortress for God where we can defend Him until death, we can play with Him; and really, that is all He wants, it seems.

Corpus Christi at Astorga. I join the great procession in the town; the bishop and the canons make me dress up in a gold cope The centre of the procession is a float, a decorated old-fashioned cart on which the Blessed Sacrament, exposed in a precious monstrance, is mounted. The foot of the monstrance is secured with a strong pin and from above the monstrance is covered with a baldachino from which little bells are dangling. The pavements are decorated with tapestries made of flower petals; we shuffle over them nonchalantly. Two acolytes steer the front of the cart by means of a shaft; the propulsion is supplied by a number of sturdy pushers hidden inside the chassis. Interested onlookers line the route; the eyes of the children, held on their parents' arms, are sparkling. Teenage girls come out of a bar to have a look; one of them has a plunging neckline; an old woman taps the girl's breastbone with her fingers and the girl hides quickly behind her friends. The clergy in the procession and the old people along the route sing, slow and loud, popular favourites of questionable quality with texts as: "We honour the Blessed Sacrament of the Altar and the Blessed Virgin conceived without sin". People enjoy it the way they have done it for centuries; what do you want all this renewal for? Afterwards I inspect the cart: the fellows get in through a loose panel and on the inside there are six hooks on which they can hang their clothes.

The solemnity revives many dormant memories: of other processions through the streets in liturgical vestments that were completely out of place there; of little bridesmaids carrying cushions with symbolic objects such as an anchor signifying hope; soldiers saluting the sacred. I remember a church in the Tyrol where we passed the local shooting company and the commander shouted: "Present Arms... Blesseeeed Sacrament!!!!" Formerly processions were popular; nowadays people prefer not to walk in procession, except children and at carnival time.

The memory is something very wonderful and extraordinary: it means moving backwards in time! The memory is something very precious. It gives everything a fifth dimension, next to length, width, height and time. Our human problems are such that we can solve them properly only when our memory works properly. Thus, our future can be said to depend on our memory. The companion of remembering is forgetting. Because we find "remembering" so very important, we are inclined to call "forgetting" a bad thing. And we have worked out many methods to do away with forgetting.

But forgetting can also be good. Forgetting has a healing function. There is, however, still another thing. Truth is dynamic, sometimes even more so than we ourselves. Sometimes nature has to correct us on her own initiative in a harsh and illogical way: bitter experiences make us wise. People who cannot forget their former convictions may well become immune to improvement. In that case, not forgetting is harmful. Also, if somebody would describe wisdom as remembering everything you ever learnt, then he is not describing a sage but a know-all.

Writing plays an important part in all this. Writing has several functions. We use it to communicate with each other but also to save something from oblivion. Scripta manent: what has been written down, remains. This may spoil the therapeutic function of time and it may even create the possibility of blackmail. Once my evil deeds are committed to paper, I cannot undo them any more with good deeds. Paper can thus be very threatening. In the medieval Lauda Sion-hymn about the Last Judgement, we used to sing "Liber scriptus proferetur, in quo totum continetur, unde mundus judicetur" (Then the written book will be produced, in which everything is contained, and by which the world will be judged).

Illiterate cultures do not know this menace; but on the other hand, in the absence of writing, truth can be more easily manipulated. What about debts? In our Kenyan cultures, even if debts are not supposed to be forgotten, at least they have to be forgiven as debts; after that they are transformed into a vague kind of friendship. I feel this is relevant to the question of the international debts of Third World countries: it just is inhuman to remember debts after such a long time. My Kenyan friends have integrated the mechanics of forgetting into the process of problem-solving. We Westerners get irritated with them when we see that in dealing with problems, they like to put things off all the time. I am convinced that this is not some kind of lethargy but something like: let us give forgetting a chance. It could well be that in the matter of the written word we Westerners should curb our compulsion for registering everything and put more stress on the communicating power of writing. Incidentally, this underlines the value of literature: literature is not aiming at registration but appeals to recognition, to understanding, all the time offering the joy of entertaining imagery.

More things happen to me at Astorga. In the cool of the afternoon, I visit that strange Episcopal palace of Gaudí; and after that I sit on the old city walls to enjoy the prehistoric view. At 6.30, I saunter back to the gate to find it locked. Passers-by gesture that there must be another exit at the other side. Alas, that one is not there any more; there is a metal circular staircase but I would have to make a jump of six feet to reach it. So, back to the main entrance. You feel a real fool, shouting at passers-by through the iron railings; what can they do? The fence is a few metres high with big pikes on the top; since I got my prosthesis, my clambering technique has been reduced to zero. After a long time somebody brings a ladder. They shift it over the top of the fence, so that I can use it from the inside, putting it slanted against a pillar. I climb up till I can sit on top of the pillar, pull up the heavy ladder and put it on the outside; of course I hurt my shins in the process. Nobody recognises in me the dignified prelate who, adorned in gold damask that very morning, strode majestically in the procession. Standing on the other side of the fence is a great relief and I walk off with a true feeling of liberation.

At the campsite of Puente de Orbigo I meet some Dutch girls and soon we discuss in depth what it is that animates the pilgrim and what happens to him. I share some ideas with them that I distilled in my heart long ago.

People undertake the journey to Compostela for a variety of reasons. Some see it as a kind of sport. Others are motivated by devotion; again others want to have a rather cheap kind of holiday; others again go because they know that this journey is permeated with culture and history; then there are those who are looking for an entirely new experience. I have met them all and I have seen how they departed as a motley collection of divergent characters. As they went along it was the road that turned them into pilgrims. They realised that they needed each other. They also noticed that the journey became much more pleasant when you surrendered to the religious folklore that formed part of it. It also happened that a farmer came rushing after us on his old motorbike; he had seen that we were on our way to Saint James, and would we please light some candles in the cathedral for his brother who had been lost for four years. Another time an old woman came out of her hovel, greatly upset; she pressed some pesetas in our hands to be offered in the cathedral and would we then please pray for her very sick cow. We smiled self-consciously but we knew that we had become the carriers of the gifts and the prayers of simple unimportant people; and I do not doubt at all that when the moment was there, we all prayed for the lost brother and

the sick cow. In whatever condition we had left home, we all
arrived as pilgrims.

*A feast in Sahagún; how could that be without bulls? In the afternoon, the
festivities start with the "encierro": fighting bulls are made to storm through
the town along wooden fences, the poles of which are fixed in small pits that
are permanently dug out in the pavement. After 6.00, the fights in the arena
begin.*

*The solemn preparations are those of the liturgy. Sacristans lay out the
glittering vestments and the shiny instruments: the decorated pikes and
the various swords that are being honed all the time with an emery stone;
and when the time is there the celebrants enter dressed in brocade. One
of them is a woman, to be sure: Christina Sanchez. The women cry at her:
"Torero! Torero!" It is remarkable how many children there are among the
public, mothers with toddlers, granddads and grandmothers with their young
grandchildren. Like a thunderbolt the bull appears in the ring, snorting with
fury. Suddenly mortal danger hangs in the air; not just danger but death.
What I find most frightening about the bull is not his horns – these are just the
bumpers – but the tautly strung huge buttocks that propel the fighting machine
of 500 kilos of rage towards an enemy. Or towards the horse, blindfolded and
its sides covered with mattresses, that slowly drifts into the arena like a float
in a procession, with a Don Quichote on its back. The bull concentrates on
whatever moves, such as the cloth of the torero. Sometimes the torero stands
right in front of the bull and moves the cloth behind his spread legs: the bull
looks at it right and left past the legs as if they were trees. Whilst the bull
gets exhausted, wounded by the lance of the horseman and the stings of the
pikemen who, elusive like hornets, plant long arrows into its back, and dazed
by the taunting red capes, the torero takes ever more outrageous risks. At long
last he sinks the sword into the back of the bull by reaching over the horns
and piercing the heart. He does not always manage: Christina does not thrust
quite straight and the sword comes out through the flank; she has to make a
second thrust and the high nobs on the VIP stand do not like it.*

*Is it sad for the bull to have to die like that? It seems to me that "sad" is a
rather inappropriate word for a raging bull. It does happen that the bull has
had enough and wants to run off; it is then the task of the acolytes to stir up
his fury so that he wants to go on. Do they suffer pain? Not by the looks of it.
They are probably numbed by a copious amount of adrenaline in their blood.
Nor is there any sign of the agony you see in the eyes of an African buffalo,
which is ripped open alive by some lion. Is it destructive of man's dignity? If it
is, I find it less so than a hen battery or a pig farm or artificial insemination.
The public does not come to enjoy the sight of spilt blood but to see men in
satin and glitter play with excessively provoked death; as such it is similar to
acrobatics in the roof of the circus or Grand Prix races for motorbikes.*

Pain is not only something that you feel inside – you can also see it. Images of pain are etched into our memories and come back to our conscious state like uninvited guests. Thus, I harbour an indestructible old image going back to the year 1945. We were travelling by train, a group of boys whose ages varied between 12 and 15; the train had no passenger carriages, for they had all been shot to pieces during the war; we were travelling in freight wagons. The doors were open and the passengers liked to stand near the door for fresh air; the front row was sitting in the door opening with their legs outside. There was no harm in that, except that there were Bailey bridges here and there, constructed by the military. These bridges were very narrow and the space between the train and the bridge was only just enough for legs. At the railway station of Udenhout it was announced that there was such a dangerous bridge just at the beginning of the next town, Tilburg, and everybody had to stand up. But very soon people forgot and sat down again. In front of me a fellow student was sitting, a boy from Delden called Dick Falke. Suddenly, the bridge appeared in the door opening; I shouted a warning. The boys threw their legs up in the air but Dick was late. The bridge caught him by the feet and pulled him out; he rolled over a few times and then before our horrified eyes he slowly fell between the train and the bridge. Flesh and iron, an impossible encounter.

Another image that breaks into my mind regularly is that of Ben, the six-year-old son of our African family in the centre where I lived. One day a pan of boiling water fell over him. For a week on end, he lay dying in the hospital with a sadly scalded body. He could not lie still with pain, and when at times he lifted himself up a bit, his little body would go up but his skin stayed behind on the bed. It still makes me cry. The only consolation is that it is over; except in the memory of my heart, an image that refuses to go.

Whenever the Spaniards built a gothic church in days gone by, they discovered after a couple of years' work what everybody could have told them from the beginning: that the church was far too big. They solved the problem by putting a smaller building in the middle of the nave. Apart from that, the churches they built were magnificent. And the very buildings contained a lesson: if religion can transform pieces of stone into something like the cathedral of León, you are left wondering what it can do with human hearts! The cathedral of Burgos has been proclaimed a monument of humanity. The first and at the same time the lasting impression one gets in this church is: this is complete; you can not add anything, you cannot take away anything, this is the Mozart of gothic architecture. In nature there are no vacuums, everything is full. If you have a good look at a square kilometre of land you find that it is teeming; if you have a good look at a square millimetre you also find that it is teeming. The same you can say of the cathedral of Burgos: it teems on all levels.

For the rowdy youngsters it is good to know that Santaclause has a cool church in Burgos, with a high altar that gives you a pain in the neck from looking upwards. Mary is sitting there in a flowerbed of little angels.

An irresistible theme in the world of gothic sculpture is the Last Judgement, with the inevitable weighing scales, devils hanging on them like monkeys trying to rock them; and the panoramas of hell with plenty of bare backsides ominously exposed to frightening treatment. The sight of it amuses us but formerly it had a sinister message for people.

In Africa, I have seen that the gospel can be a potent antidote against fear. It would seem correct to say that many people in that continent find fear to be an element they have to face all the time. At the same time, I have seen there that the Christian message is for many a powerful support not to allow themselves to be intimidated by tyranny, aggression and display of power. One finds many new and courageous persons there. Religion, on the other hand, is not without dangers either, for it is quite possible to make people afraid through religion, to make capital out of human fears. That goes against the essence of Christianity. Time and again we hear Jesus say: "Do not be afraid". A frightened person is a person in fetters. Fear does not give a good motivation, not even to do something good. Prudence is quite a different thing, of course.

In matters religious, it is not possible to gain control over the supernatural; for that reason religious fear can easily degenerate into the terror of scrupulosity. Sometimes I think that in former years they were not averse to making children fearful so as to make them faithful. In the area of religious education, images were used that were terrifying for children, especially in the explanation of "mortal sin" and the "eternal damnation" attached to it. Hell, for instance, was the pain of being burnt alive that would go on for ever and ever, never stopping.

My sister came home from catechism class with a striking illustration of the eternal duration of hell. Imagine that the whole earth is made of iron. Every century a bird comes and touches the earth with its wing. When the earth has been touched so often that it has worn away completely, eternity has not even begun. As a child, I could not stand such an image: it triggered panic. I am quite sure that many children, by the time they had grown up, swore an oath that never ever would such a thing be done to their own little children. I did too. And that is one very important reason why the traditional view on sin is being rejected by many Christians.

The assortment of pilgrims becomes more and more colourful: two Finns; a Swede; a German couple who spend all their free time washing whatever they carry with them because they do not want to smell of sweat. A Belgian of Hungarian extraction who wants to walk to Mongolia; two French ladies, one of whom is afraid of the devil all the time; an Amsterdam lady who shows signs of serious dehydration but who says it cannot be due to drinking too little for every morning she drinks a glass of water. At Portomarin, I meet an Englishman named Ralph. Formerly he was a sailor; then he became a fashion photographer. He contracted multiple sclerosis and decided to go to Compostela on horseback and do interviews for the BBC on the way. In the same refugio, I meet two Swiss Evangelical ladies, one of whom had been bitten by a shepherd's dog when she tried to kiss the shepherd; a Belgian from Kortrijk who covers daily distances of 40 kilometres; a Frenchman with a withered arm; a group of Belgian children with Down's syndrome; a German boy who had started from Clervaux with 20 kilos on his back and who is suffering now from very painful joints; and a really very heavy German lady from Essen who pushes herself up a hill puffing and almost exploding with redness, eyes popping out menacingly – she is surrounded by worried friends who had not had the courage to tell her in time that she really was not fit for this.

The assortment of churches is as varied as that of the pilgrims. Next to gothic architecture, one sees in Spain a lot of baroque as well. The transition from gothic to baroque is a mystery to me: the difference is so big. It is as if baroque fell upon the land like a sudden storm. The audacity of Spanish baroque! The pillars are twisted like corkscrews, festooned with bunches of grapes. The cathedral of Santiago has a sanctuary like a forest of gold bushes through which giants push their way. Sometimes things go awry, like at Sahagun. There they wanted to represent the Assumption of Our Lady into Heaven three-dimensionally with lightning-filled thunderclouds; but alas, the clouds became black pudding-coloured intestines and the thunderbolts toothpicks. Recent renovations have made the contrasts even more stark: the walls have been made plain, making the high and polished altars still more exuberant.

The churches are too small for the accumulated treasures; these even choke the museums so that you get tired and blasé looking at them. Seeing all that ostentatious gold and those precious stones, I am reminded of a poem by Rilke, running more or less like this:

When you were guest to gold, God, you refused to stay.
To please an epoch that liked adorations
with precious clear-cut marble formulations,
you showed yourself like king of constellations,
your forehead flickering with blinding rays.
That epoch melted; you just went away.

(Rainer Maria Rilke, *Das Stundenbuch*: 'So viele Engel suchen dich im Lichte')

God is not dead; He has just gone home!

A well-to-do family is having dinner in an expensive restaurant at Burgos and a small girl of ten is allowed to eat a whole dish of bonbons all by herself. The man who marries her later on will get a wife for whom one single bonbon is grinding poverty. A few more people like that and a daily dish of pralines becomes one of the human rights; and everybody who does not get them falls below the poverty line. And thus misery grows.

Baroque was a reaction to the widespread scepticism of the 16th century, a reaction that took on the character of a feast. But since it was art, it did not offer much to systematic theology.

After the year 1600, there are not many philosophers any more that will take up God's case. Spinoza makes a brave try, around 1650, to inject new life into the God of Philosophers with a lot of platonic infusions. In that same period Pascal tries to save God by disconnecting the concerned and cordial God of Abraham, Isaac and Jacob from the unmoved theoretical God of the philosophers. Around the year 1700, Leibniz makes God play the role of creator in a most remarkable way. God created all beings as "monads"; that means, they all are contractions of the actual universe and they have no contact with each other ("Monads have no windows"). But they are perfectly synchronised so that all developments take place in all of them. That synchronisation is called Harmonia Praestabilita, a fantastic concept. Thus, with each human person the universe is born again but with the light on in a different place. The monads only appear to influence each other but they don't. When I hear my alarm clock go off, this is really what happens: the alarm clock has reached a point of internal development whereby it begins to ring. I also have reached the same point of internal development whereby I hear the ringing of an alarm clock. The alarm does not cause the hearing of the sound in me, my internal development does. God, then, is the great synchroniser. An impossible job, seemingly, but God can do it because He is almighty.

These last three thinkers who tried to deal with God were eyed with extreme suspicion by the church authorities, who considered them dangerous marginal acrobats. Eventually they became the precursors of 18th century Enlightenment, whilst the church leaders slowly but surely lost philosophical significance and became the "Dunkelmaenner", the Obscurantists, of Western civilisation.

Storks' nests are to be seen on all Spanish churches, sometimes two or three of them. The young ones stand there all day long, bored stiff, in the merciless sunlight: flapping their wings now and then, wobbling on the edge at times, clattering with their bills once or twice, and for the rest waiting till they are grown up. I always considered them such dignified birds until I saw 30 of them together on a rubbish tip. The fact that they dare to put their nests just like that on public buildings is a sign of great courage; and they are, strangely enough, even welcome. Would they themselves have spread the story that they take care of delivering new babies?

After the ebb tide of winter, nature has now gone back to work at full tilt. Everything has unfolded out of something very tiny. It is amazing to see that every plant knows how to subdivide the available space in such a way that all its flowers, leaves and twigs are positioned at a fair average distance from one another. The plant world as well as the animal world has geared itself completely to the expected raids of thieves and parasites. Plants have different ways of reacting to marauders. Some defend themselves with spikes, poison, stickiness or hard surfaces. Others make use of the raiders to gain some advantage. Bees may think that they are stealing honey but they are in fact servants of the plant looking after its fertilisation; humans and birds imagine that they are snatching fruits but they are being used secretly to spread the seeds. And whatever happens in nature, the method is invariably through overwhelming numbers, according to the axiom: "Much and often must be effective". We weep with aesthetic joy when we see a tree laden with blossom; what we see in fact is the lowest form of efficiency at work. By the way, talking about efficiency, are we still allowed to say that something is being done in nature? Is something afoot in nature? Are plans being executed? And if so, what plans? Our scientists refuse to face these questions and the churches' information bureaus are closed on account of renovation. But if you want to maintain that nothing is being organised in living nature, you have to keep yourself strictly aloof from reality and hole yourself up deeply inside the cave of your own mind.

Very rarely a meeting with fellow pilgrims turns out to be unpleasant; but it does happen. In the early morning sun, two French walkers stop me for a short chat, a couple brewing a cup of coffee on a burner. Where do I come from? Oh, from Holland. And why do they make such a mess of the church there? I answer that the church in Holland has to wrestle with the same problems as the church in France: an immense number of sheep are leaving the flock and that is something to worry about. Oh no, I am completely wrong; there is no question of lost sheep, they never were sheep in the first place: the flock is simply being cleansed. The only sheep that are going to be part of the true flock are those who are willing to subject themselves to the laws and the authorities. I continue my walk grumbling, continuing the argument within myself, which is not a good thing, for when you talk by yourself you will be right far too easily.

Originally, Christianity was synonymous with freedom, with liberation from slavery of different types, down to the slavery of the law. Often that is still the case. Go to Africa and you will see that church membership entails an impressive form of liberation for women. I am thoroughly convinced of this: if we mix the gospel with the local cultural values in the right proportions, we will get an inexhaustible supply of nuclear energy of freedom. It is all the more surprising that the concept of freedom seems to be a difficult companion for the Christian faith. After the Renaissance, all thinkers agreed that the human person had to be sovereign, free in his thinking and in his acting, free from all authoritarian dogmatism. This led to clashes with the church authorities all the time. They were irritated by the fact that the new views on human existence left no more room for God within their systems, systems of autonomy or even atheism. And then all that freedom! All this clashed with the hierarchical character of the church where people saw themselves invested with divine prestige and burdened with the task of protecting humanity against error, if necessary with force. The only thing the church could do was reject the new philosophies. Would that also be the reason why philosophy emigrated northwards to the more Protestant parts of Europe? The modern philosophers had the feeling that they had escaped from ecclesiastical darkness and that they could now bask in the brilliant light of free reason. They called themselves "enlightened" and their era was henceforward named the Enlightenment.

It was both ironic and tragic that when the French Revolution promulgated the ancient Christian ideals of freedom, equality and brotherhood (albeit with force), our church did not recognise them any more and threw in its lot with the opposing side.

In the small towns, I see a system calculated to make cars drive at no more than 50 kilometres per hour. The traffic lights are permanently red; if you approach them with a speed of 50 kilometres or less, the light will change to green just before you pass it; if you go at more than 50, you pass through the red light and can be booked.

Any number of clever tricks have been thought out to get people to stick to measures that protect the lives of all. On the other hand, it never ceases to amaze me that nature has surrounded that all-important phenomenon of procreation with so few rules and regulations. Plants, animals, they all have to sort it out themselves as best as they can. People too? And why has sexuality such a difficult relationship with our religion? The answer that many would give is: presumably sexuality is something inferior or even sinful in the eyes of the Christian religion. That is probably not altogether wrong. But that would have to be written on the account of ancient Manichean dualism: spirit is good, body is bad. This idea had penetrated into Neo-platonism at the beginning of our era and via Augustine (400 AD) and Bernard of Clairvaux (1150 AD) it saturated Christian devotional life. We should realise, however, that this dualism clashes with the ancient Jewish and Christian doctrine that the material world, too, is a valuable part of God's creation. True, the Jewish scribes promoted some kind of dualism regarding purity and impurity; but Jesus left us in no doubt that this impurity should not be coupled to the material world but to the corruption of the heart.

I think there was still another factor favouring the denigration of sexuality. Nature has organised sexuality in such a way that it works through a mysterious magnetism. The individual has only partial control over this magnetism and experiences it therefore as powerful seduction that causes the person to "fall". Surely, it is unthinkable that a powerful character like a pope or a bishop or a parish priest or a reverend mother would experience the powerlessness of "falling" to sexual attraction. Sex and power do not go together. The person who boasts that "All power in heaven and on earth has been given unto me" cannot surrender to the overwhelming power of sexual seduction. So, whoever shares in the church's power should stay away from the regions of sexuality. And that is, I bet, the hidden ground under the legislation of obligatory celibacy. Women are by their very appearance agents of seduction, so they should be kept at a safe distance.

Add to that the fact that sex is very demanding in respect of energy, attention and time. Church authorities will consider that a dangerous waste of time and energy that could otherwise be used for almighty God and His glorious church.

In one refugio I share a room with a man who happens to be a missionary priest: he has worked in Chile and now he is a parish priest in Brittany. In his church, four people attend his Mass, three of whom are members of a religious order. If ever a young person attends his celebrations it is either a tourist or somebody who has walked over from a nearby psychiatric institute.

When I walked here in 1969, fascist policemen were in evidence everywhere and an atmosphere of oppression could be felt. The victors of the Civil War presented themselves as faithful Christians and the losers as subversives tainted with atheism. One would have expected this to lead to an explosion of pent-up anger later on. Still, that did not happen. It was as if religion was not a hot topic any more.

I have noticed how many people in Holland cannot get rid of their religious rancour; they dwell on their scars. Some keep saying: "How they have bamboozled us formerly!" Others cannot talk about religion without bitterness. Periodicals will print any nonsense about the church and it will go uncorrected. Recently I read in a magazine that in the Catholic Church there used to be a spirit of sombreness formerly, no joie-de-vivre, for everything was forbidden. Also, according to Catholic doctrine, you had to earn heaven by much suffering on earth. Surely, that is a caricature. Rancour leads to caricature (which means that there is an element of truth in it).

The truth lies in exactly the opposite direction. The Catholic religious attitude often gave rise to an exuberant lifestyle with feasting and music. Distrust of the body and disapproval of pleasure did not have their origin in the gospel but in the spirit of the times, like Neo-platonism. The church absorbs the spirit of the times rather quickly; that is why we have now to cope with an inherited spirit of rationalism and bureaucracy in our church. It is a pity that the church loath to admit that by taking up some rigid standpoints in the past she has been responsible for quite a lot of misery and that she was wrong to do so.

When a sheep is troubled with a sore leg it throws its head around; would that take some of weight off the leg? I am often puzzled by the way animals move their heads. Why, for instance, does a pigeon move its head forwards and backwards when walking? Chickens do the same. With chickens I can understand it a bit: chickens have very sharp vision and it may be necessary to hold your head momentarily still for maximum vision.

For hours on end, a tune floats along with me, inside my head. I picked it up at Astorga from a girl on a bench behind me in the park who was playing with a child. This is how it went:

Un! Dos! Tres!

Un pasito patrante Maria!

Un! Dos! Tres!

Un pasito patras!

I am told it is an Argentinean dance.

If you want to admit to having made blunders and mistakes, you need to have friends around you. A true church community ought to be like a family; and a family is only worth its while when you can afford to make blunders there. Where people feel affection for each other, they will help one another to learn from their mistakes. In many of our church communities, that is indeed the case. It is all the more remarkable that the church finds it hard to cope with her own mistakes. That is a real pity. If only the church would not find admitting mistakes such a hurdle: her own in particular. Surely making mistakes is the normal way for humans to learn?

I have been intrigued for many years to know what kind of mistakes Jesus made in his learning process. A remark like this can make pious people quite angry. You cannot even say it in all languages: in our Kenyan Luo-language the word for making a mistake and for sinning is the same: ketho. Frightened people argue thus: Jesus was God; God cannot make a mistake. Ergo Jesus could not make a mistake. But with that same argument you can also prove that Jesus did not die. So you prove too much; qui nimis probat nihil probat. The following sequence of thoughts brings you nearer to the heart of the matter. Let Jesus be both God and man. We do not really know what it means to be God; but we know very well what it means to be human. And according to the old scriptural expression, Jesus was human in exactly the same way as ourselves, except for sin. To make a mistake is not a sin; so Jesus made mistakes. Popular devotion will go to great lengths to make divinity shine out of His pores. We used to sing the old Dutch song: "He ate porridge from a dish and He did not make it dirty; He fell on the ground and He did not get a lump". That is engaging and touching children's heresy. In reality, we have to hold that Jesus made all the small mistakes of all small children. Did He make mistakes later on, when He did the work of the Messiah? I am sure He did. I can think of several. Before He started His public life, He withdrew into the desert to think about it. He decided not to try and do spectacular miracles, like turning stones into bread thereby giving his listeners gratis food. Yet, a little later He made the mistake of giving free bread and fish to more than 5,000 people; He evidently could not stand seeing people suffering from hunger. But the results, which He had so clearly foreseen in the desert, followed immediately: the crowd tried to get hold of Him to make Him their king, no doubt crying "Jesus of Nazareth, King of the Jews!" He had to flee into the hills, probably kicking Himself. The following morning He was still rattled and greeted His audience saying: "Ah, here we are again, ready for the next batch of free bread". That the testy exchange resulted in the famous address of "I am the bread of life" does not alter the fact that the whole episode flowed from an initial mistake. I find it a beautiful lesson of how the Holy Spirit can turn honest mistakes into divine mysteries.

At Granon I visit the old church. They have put so many lilies there that I have to sneeze. I count them: 400 of them. There is also a small box on the wall; when you put a coin in it, the illuminations switch on for one minute.

I think that the Good News is something that you have to try. It is not a-priori clear how it will fit into your life; but now and then a light goes on suddenly. Whilst I recite the gospel of Saint Mark I am often struck by new insights.

Take those temptations of Jesus in the desert. At His baptism in the river Jordan, it had been made clear to Him that the task of being the Messiah was put on His shoulders. But He wondered how to go about it. So He spent time in the desert to think about it. His thoughts went to Moses, another deliverer of the people. Should He follow in his footsteps? Moses had given the people in the desert bread from heaven. It occurred to Jesus that He Himself might be able to feed hungry people by changing stones into bread. He realised that this would give Him plenty of followers but for the wrong reason: free bread. So He rejected this idea as a suggestion from the wrong corner.

A second possibility was to make a spectacular leap from the top of the temple, forcing God to save Him with a miracle: a type of blackmail and not acceptable therefore. That it was a real temptation for Jesus may be clear from the advice He would give later to His disciples: pray in such a way that you take it absolutely for granted that your prayer will be heard. Sometimes we as a church community fall for the second temptation, I think. When the number of seminarians began to lessen dramatically, quite a few people would react to that with the decision to build a big new seminary as a sign of faith. The present official policy regarding obligatory celibacy for priests has a whiff of that too: just continue in the old way in the unshakeable belief that God will make the tide to turn when He sees a devastating eucharistic famine strike His faithful.

The third temptation, of securing his dominion over all kingdoms by adoring Satan, is difficult to place. Would Jesus really have contemplated the possibility of cooperation with the devil? More probably, He might have thought of possibilities of co-operating with worldly principalities. In those days, different from now (?), the rulers were not nice people; certainly, in the eyes of the Jews, the pagan potentates were accomplices of the devil. Was Jesus thinking of agreements and concordats with ruthless rulers and powerful criminals,

people who determine the world's course of events without
any reference to justice?

*My rucksack is disintegrating. I try to repair it with very soft technology –
needle and thread, matchsticks and staples. Often this leads to some respite
but not now.*

*At Logroňo, I amble around in some low-class neighbourhoods. There is a
small bar intriguingly decorated with exploding gaudy lights, and I hop in.
In the exciting semi-darkness, an aromatic lady soon begins to rub herself
against me with sweet words and extraordinary proposals. An ordinary chat
from person to person is not really possible and a small bottle of coke costs 400
pesetas, almost two pounds. So I get out into the fresh air, where there are lots
of other entertaining things to see. Logroňo, like Burgos, has grand manners.
Kings donated boulevards and squares with statues to such cities. It strikes
me that I know comparatively little about Spain. I can think of some important
religious personalities but I do not know many historically significant names,
like El Cid. But they all had grandeur. At Burgos I visited his grave; on the
coffin was written:*

Even if this casket made of wood
Contains a heap of simple dust,
It's dust in which I had entombed
The gold of my integrity.

*These are words of grandeur. Don Quichote. Whatever he lost, not his grand
manner. Theresa of Avila, John of the Cross. I have been told that they were
mystics of grand style. I should read some of their writings. Decades after
the Spanish empire had disappeared, the Spaniards flattered themselves with
the thought that their kingdom was one of the great powers on earth. I rather
like that, that unruffled self-assurance: the cock crowing every morning on
the dunghill because he is sure that otherwise the sun will not rise. National
self-assurance modulated to personal self-assurance that grew everywhere in
the 17th century.*

From the days of Descartes the "ego" begins to play its part
as subject. And straight away you find yourself settled with
a huge problem: once you take yourself as the starting point
of your thinking, how are you ever to reach others? Granted
that you are unshakeably sure of your own thoughts, how can
you ever be sure that these thoughts refer to something outside
your own thoughts? For nobody can, by thinking, step outside

his thoughts. This is the famous Problem of the Bridge, the Quaestio de Ponte: the bridge between my subjective thoughts and the objective world of things.

Descartes found this way out: if I think in all honesty that the other beings exist, then surely the good God, who made me this way, will not deceive me! But others soon said: "Well, then let us limit ourselves to our thoughts and ideas." They became known as Idealists, the opposite numbers of the Realists. But if you really limit yourself to your own thoughts, then you will inexorably arrive at Solipsism: I am the only one existing and all other beings are the products of my imagination.

Others again would say: "Let us limit ourselves to our simple observations and not allow ourselves to get caught up in abstruse questions." These are the Empiricists with their acquired knowledge or "a-posteriori cognition".

Leibniz had put in a plea for in-born knowledge that unfolds itself inside your mind and is therefore "a-priori cognition". You can make a case both for a-priori and for a-posteriori knowledge: the fact that all people come to the same kind of ideas points at an a-priori structure; the rule that all knowledge must come through the senses points at an a-posteriori set-up. Kant (around 1775) constructed an imposing philosophical theory explaining that we are born full of a-priori categories; that our reflection makes us detect those categories; and that we dress up our experiences in those categories, thus leading to a-posteriori knowledge. You could compare those pre-existing categories in our mind (such as quantity, quality, relations of cause and effect) as an extensive wardrobe; and then you invite your perceived impressions to chose from this wardrobe the outfit that fits them best. Then you can ask: if that is so, what kind of grip do you have on the objective world the way it really is? According to Kant, that grip goes via ethics, or Practical Reason as he calls it: the rules for practical behaviour. Your ethical grip on reality lies in your sense of duty, which he calls your Categorical Imperative. The most elementary rule of Ethics is: your behaviour must be such that if everybody did things that same way, the world would be a good place for every person to live in.

I attend a Sunday morning service in the church of San Lesmes, patron saint of Burgos, a born Londoner. Two priests are involved: one offers up the Mass for some hundred people; the other sits in the penitential box at the back with his little light on and receives a couple of sinners, no hardcore criminals so to see.

On that morning there are nine such thinly-attended services. I sense a lack of inventiveness. And what is really wrong with that statue of San Lesmes? He lies on his back, with his mitre on, and reads a book; that is a bit odd. Ah, I see: the folds of his garments hang the wrong way; originally the statue stood straight up.

The ornaments of our churches constitute an immeasurably rich inheritance of culture and history. They can teach us much. The world of symbols is a very ancient world, connected to primitive expressions of human emotions. The oldest symbols have probably to do with sex, danger, water, fire, death. It is no surprise, then, to see so many phallic symbols in and around the church. Take the candles, especially when they are burning; think of that venerable ceremony in the Easter Night Vigil when the big burning paschal candle is dipped in the basin of baptismal water, the symbol of the female womb, three times up and down. Take also the church tower. And what to think of a bishop wearing his mitre? I find it marvellous and even moving. They are remnants of ancient fertility cults that have died long, long ago and have been stored away in the memories of the devout as scandalous idolatrous rites. But on Easter day, when everything that had died in failure, everything that had been written off as hopeless, comes back to life in an unexpected way together with Jesus, the first-born of the dead, these rites are allowed in again, to play an honourable role in our liturgy, in deep disguise, alongside the holy water and the holy fire. All we still have to wait for are the holy women.

There are still Maecenases. Inside Burgos cathedral, Rhône-Poulenc (the chemico-pharmaceutical industry) advertises itself as the benefactor who is repairing the Golden Stairs, after having restored the imperial Vietnamese city of Hue in 1995, Roman remnants in 1994, the Venetian Basilica of Saint Mark in 1993, the Arc de Triomphe in 1988 and the horses of Morly in Paris in 1984.

Gothic cathedrals are numerous in the north of Spain, no doubt evidence of French influence. But they must have been popular, too, for the simple reason that it was great fun to build them, so high and so fragile. If you compare them with the older and much more heavily-built churches you begin to wonder if for every church building the same amount of building material was available but successive generations made the walls thinner and thinner. In the final days of high gothic, they even left out most of the walls and replaced them with glass.

Would God also adapt Himself to the kind of building He is given to stay in? Would He become a God of light and high majesty in the gothic cathedrals? I remember Durham cathedral: a heavy and somewhat clumsy Romanesque building, dark and grey; when I went there it was half covered with snow. Entering there to wander in the chilly twilight between gigantic pillars I felt like a gnome who had crawled inside a mountain. The God who lived there was a God of deeply mysterious presence, a God of basalt and earthquakes and indestructible roots reaching into the living core of the earth.

My health is first class but often I feel small pains here and there. Of late it is my big toe that hurts a bit but it looks entirely normal. And I have some nerve pain in the hip. Furthermore, a corn is appearing on one toe (isn't it funny that in Dutch we call that a magpie's eye). That spoils my gait and that again causes more pain in the hip. I manage to remove the magpie's eye, my gait improves and the pain in my hip disappears.

The end of the month of July has come. At Los Arcos, not far from Estella, I stay in the pleasant hotel Ezequiel; the proprietor is a painter and he gives me a T-shirt of Saint James. I meet there also Mr. Admiraal from Egmond who has started from Heilo together with his daughter Mrs. Kuiper; we drink a lot of cool beer together, discuss all the important issues of church and world in one wide sweep, and after having found satisfactory solutions for all of them we conclude our harmonious togetherness with an excellent meal. Yes, one meets lots of interesting characters on this walk, persons who are ready for a solid talk with serious contents rather than just bubbly chit-chat. I also meet many people who have a positive attitude towards the Christian faith. That could mean that the people who decide to walk to Compostela are often people with a more positive attitude. It could also mean that, since I am a believer myself, believers seek contact with me. Maybe if I were a convinced atheist, many happy atheists would come my way.

The well-known Dutch publicist Herman Vuijsje thinks that the pilgrimage in reverse, from Compostela to Holland, is more suitable for a "pilgrim without God". He has written a most delightful book about that and uses every opportunity to tell his readers that he is an atheist and how remarkable it is that he makes this pilgrimage, albeit in reverse order, as homage to his view on life.

It strikes me that some atheists like to give themselves a jaunty profile. At Kisumu, we had some young Dutch visitors who assured the people that they did not believe in God but that they believed in themselves. The people almost died with laughter.

Running away from God, meeting with God or not, denying God's existence, it is all based on a clearly-defined idea of God, a concrete figure who is somewhere or who is not somewhere. That figure is really the aboriginal idol. The great classical religions do not want an image of God. They call Him Light, Life, Love, Grace and, if you really want an image, Daddy. The mystics refer to Him as a hidden light somewhere behind your back which you notice on account of your own shadow and which you can approach by walking backwards only; the trouble is that we have not been made for walking backwards.

THE SIXTH MONTH

JULY

During the month of July, I walk linea recta to the Mediterranean. Just north of Estella, I will turn sharply to the east to enter an unknown world. Exciting! First, I will walk a few hundred kilometres along the foot of the Pyrenees. In Andorra I will cross the Pyrenees and continue my way eastwards, along the northern edge of the Pyrenees, to the Mediterranean. During the first week, as far as Jaca, I will walk along a classic Jacobean pilgrims' route, the so-called Somport way. After that, I will become a solitary eccentric. There will be no more refugios; I shall have to find hospitality in small hotels. Andorra has been a kind of dreamland for me ever since I collected stamps as a young boy. Beyond that there are the beckoning names of Montaillou and Carcassonne and after that Narbonne and Narbonne Plage. I will have to face the fierce heat of summer. With my African background, this should not worry me, and besides, the Pyrenees ought to be relatively cool.

I have been walking for half a year. Walking does not make me tired any more. It even seems the normal way to pass the hours of the day. I can notice that the human body has been designed for walking. Of course, I knew that all along, otherwise I would never have dared to start this journey despite the prosthesis in my hip. By way of precaution, I had been careful not to consult my doctor: you should not settle a person like that with such a responsibility. Another doctor volunteered some unsettling prophecies beforehand. In a quietly scientific manner he sketched the misery the future had in store for me. The lower part of the prosthesis, the pin so to say, has been hammered into the marrow of the thigh bone. Well now, bone grows on the outside, whereas on the inside cells disappear; thus the hole of the marrow becomes bigger and bigger. For that reason, the pin will rattle loose after a while. I nevertheless stubbornly cling to my idea that by walking quietly and rhythmically for a long period the whole muscular suspension system of the leg will become beautifully buoyant and strong, so that the prosthesis will be saved from damaging shocks. It looks as if I am going to be proved right.

The refugio of Puente la Reina is more than full; they are opening up spare buildings and another municipal refugio. They will not easily leave you out in the cold. There must be more than a hundred pilgrims sauntering through the small town. Once I have left the town there are no more walkers: the Somport route is much less frequently used. The yellow arrows, too, are not much in evidence any more. The ones that are there lead me over small tracks, far away from the big roads. The tracks are not without risk because of the loose gravel on steep sections. All the time I am very much aware that I have to be careful. I do not mind taking risks from time to time but I weigh them up carefully. The cautiousness is probably part of my age. Young people take different risks.

Without risks, you will not get anywhere. Life itself is risky. Marriage is risky. Religion is risky. I must admit, however, that for many traditionally-minded people religion is a kind of insurance against undue risks, through a divine cover. In that case, religion will make you avoid risks and then you are certainly wrong.

Even Jesus, in spite of His divinity, liked to play 'Winner Takes All'. Paul says that Jesus turned off the switch of His divinity so as not to have a head start on us. The risks that Jesus took are legion. He invited Matthew the collaborator to become his disciple and also violent types like James and John, the Sons of Thunder; plus Simon the Fanatic; plus even Judas the guerrilla-man (is Iscariot "dagger-man"?) Then, that holy man allowed Himself to be cuddled by a prostitute. He denounced high religious authorities and sabotaged their temple trade. He encouraged pagan and Samaritan women to lecture to Him. He promoted children to being teachers. He spoke in riddles to give the malevolent a chance to misunderstand Him.

What about the entry into Jerusalem? Did that not backfire? He allowed Himself to be convinced to make a quasi-royal entry into Jerusalem and if possible to proclaim the new kingdom there. He felt He was carried along with an irresistible flood. A few friendly Pharisees tried to dissuade Him at the last moment, saying "Don't do it" but He replied that the very cobblestones cried that He had to do it: "Hail to the King of the Jews". There was no way back. And true enough, within a week He hung dying on the cross with the triumphal cry of Palm Sunday over His head.

The greatest risk He took was handing Himself over to the Spirit, that wind that blows wherever It wants, unpredictable and uncontrollable. It is not often that His followers can match His courage in this respect. Church leaders much prefer clearly marked areas of faith, behaviour and policies. They appear to be afraid that if you let the reins go a little, chaos will set in. Is that not lack of faith? They firmly believe that the Holy Spirit works in themselves; but they hesitate to believe that the same Holy Spirit works in the faithful, in His stubborn and erratic way.

After a while, I see to my left very far away the high-rise buildings of Pamplona in a blue haze. A big commercial aeroplane slowly descends in that direction: there it feels at home. Straight ahead of me, the mighty Pyrenees come nearer. At Monreal, I find the refugio closed; fortunately, there is a small hotel. There I meet the first pilgrim from Jaca, Liedeke, a girl from Antwerp. To lower the cost we decide to take a double room, a refugio with two beds as it were.

Is it normal for a priest to share a hotel room with a strange lady? One has to understand that it is entirely normal for a resting pilgrim to find a strange lady in the bed next to his. The rugged lifestyle leads to a fading away of the more frivolous aspects of the relations between the sexes. Men and women, they all walk side by side. They all wear more or less the same practical clothes. They all are equally dirty. They all sweat to their hearts' content. Along the route, they rest leaning on each other. They rub one another's sore limbs. The women don't have to be coquettish any more, the men don't have to be stalwart any more. They eat in the same place in a mixed crowd and in the refugios they sleep in the same place in a mixed crowd. There are no gender-sensitive toilets; on the road, the men pee in front of the bushes, the women behind the bushes: some difference there has to be.

Liedeke's pilgrimage is therapeutic: she wants to start a new life. When she was 12, her parents divorced. Her mother developed an alcohol problem; her new father became frisky when drunk. She has tried to commit suicide five times and she had twice been committed to an institution. She is 20 now. She has started in Lourdes, all by herself, determined to regain the lost time of her life. She is very curious to know what you feel when you enter Compostela at last. In the morning, our lives continue in opposite directions. I strongly advise her to expect small miracles only.

When I started in the month of February, nature was dormant; now she wants to make up for lost time. Procreate, that is the motto. Gain space! Nature resorts to orgies of colours and smells. But no sounds! Is it not strange that plants do not make use of sounds! Or do they whilst we have not discovered their wavelengths yet?

Mother Nature has offered me the first wild strawberries and blackberries. Excellent food for a walker, just like figs. For hours afterwards you are trying to get the little pips from between your teeth; and that is the idea of course.

If nature managed strawberries and figs so cleverly, you may expect that she has done wonderful things with us humans. And not only in as far as we are strawberries and figs but especially in as far as we are thinking figs.

Emmanuel Kant dedicated his whole life to the effort of trying to figure out how the mechanics of our reason work. It is significant for Kant that he spent his whole life in far away Koenigsberg in east Prussia. His world was his study room plus the landscape visible from his windows.

When Kant had completed his very insightful philosophical explorations about what goes on inside a person's mind, his fellow humans began to feel the strong desire to leave the study room where the thinkers had locked themselves up and go outside to visit Mother Nature. Their first visit concerned the part of living nature that we ourselves are. It had occurred to people that when you say "I", you say "You" at the same time: both are the two halves of "We". Fichte (1800) picks up that thread. He stresses that to be is not just a quality of a substance but an "I" in action. Every being says "I", because the whole of the universe is one huge "I", that is saying "I" through each single individual "I"; and all individuals say "I" and "You" to each other in order to build up a human society, a huge "We". Lo and behold, we are back with Plato. Schelling (1825) joins Fichte; he strongly reminds us that action is intrinsically tied up with impulse or urge. This means that "Willing" is a primeval reality. Hegel (1825) develops these ideas into an imposing construction, which makes us understand better why things happen the way they happen. The mechanism inside change, according to Hegel, is "dialectics", the threefold jump from Thesis via Antithesis to Synthesis. Thesis means that something is stated or asserted. Antithesis is the denial of this statement and the assertion of the opposite. Synthesis is a new statement, containing the reconciliation of the thesis and the antithesis in which both are somehow vindicated. These dialectics can be seen at work in many different instances. Consider, for instance, the following trios: I – You – We; Spirit – Body – Person; Humanity – Divinity – Christ. Reconciliation is a fundamental value for Hegel.

At Sangüesa, a message reaches me that I should contact Kenya immediately. When I manage at long last, there are only a few seconds left on my telephone card – just enough to hear from my colleagues there that they are in great financial difficulties. This news gives me a number of sleepless nights. What could have happened? When I left, everything seemed secure and well taken care of. Is it true that things collapse when I am absent? Should I stop my walk and go back to Kisumu? If things go really badly, I want to be there.

Considering all in all, we should feel that making mistakes is part of human existence. Still, when they occur they give us a shock. It remains true that mistakes are even functional and therefore good. We learn from making mistakes: improvement means the correction of shortcomings. Infallibility does not fit into the process of learning. Humanly speaking, infallibility looks like a defect. In the story about Paradise we understood as children that Adam and Eve never had any pain, could not hurt themselves. Only much later did we begin to see that such a condition would be a situation of pathology, of sickness, rather than of beatitude. Could infallibility turn out to be a similar condition? Why do popes and bishops rate infallibility so highly? Quite honestly, that is a mystery to me. Another thing that I fail to understand is why they are so loath to admit their own mistakes. Never have I heard a pope say: "Sorry, my brothers and sisters, I made a serious blunder". It is as if they owe it to themselves to gloss over all their own imperfections. Thus, they distance themselves from all of us who stumble and stand up again; they leave us alone with our weakness and sinfulness. This contrasts sharply with Jesus who publicly joined the ranks of the sinners in the river Jordan and who told

John the Baptist to wash Him clean from sins: the Lamb God that takes upon Himself the sins of the world, calling them His own.

At the end of June, the farmers started the harvest; now the new straw lies on the land in the shape of huge toilet rolls.

When you walk quietly through the countryside, hour after hour, quite a number of problems get solved spontaneously by thoughts that come floating to the top, shaken loose by your footsteps. Take this question: why are women beautiful? The answer seems somewhat obvious: because they must not give babies a fright but attract them instead. The Luganda language has a funny saying about an ugly person: he is so ugly that he makes his food cry. Ugliness spoils the food; and ugly mothers are bad food. The next question follows immediately: why then do grown-up men find women beautiful? Again, the answer is surprisingly simple: because the psyche of a grown-up man is that of an over-grown baby. That explains also the besottedness with which men fixate themselves on the female breast.

The way along the artificial lake called the Pantano de Yesa takes many long hours; first you cross the high dam and then you follow a lonely track. I do not feel safe. Going by the prints in the sand, you would say that somebody passes here once in two or three days; so if I were to dislocate a foot, I would be in serious trouble. An artificial reservoir is rarely nice; where the water touches the shore you find a dead, rotting zone.

Water reservoirs, once monuments of progress, provoke a lot of resistance in our time. Some people reckon they are now monuments to ecological barbarism. What is progress for the one can easily be a nightmare for the other. Similar cases of contradictory evaluation are not uncommon in the world of art and certainly in the world of philosophy. One of the few booklets in my rucksack is a small volume of philosophical texts. It contains remarkable thoughts. I see there a touching contribution by Kant, just before he becomes senile. Not without conceit, he disqualifies the new insights of Fichte as sterile squabbling. On the next page, young Hegel flings Kant into the rubbish bin by stating that the Kantian philosophy was but a type of pseudo-knowledge that supplied the intellectual nakedness of the Enlightenment with the fig leaf of a good conscience.

Modesty is not often the philosophers' strongest suit. Hegel could really be preposterous. They say he sometimes concluded his lectures with the remark that the evolution of the human spirit had reached that moment in time. And when somebody tried to make clear to him that the facts did not agree with his theories, he is supposed to have retorted: "So much the worse for the facts".

The whole village of Ruesta is a rotting zone all by itself. All the inhabitants fled when the new reservoir filled up in the 'sixties and destroyed their arable land; they were victims of "developmental barbarism". The houses – the ground floor for the cattle, the first floor for the family – the town hall, the church, they are all in a state of collapse; weeds fill the open spaces. The government has made restoration plans to resurrect the village over a period of 50 years. So far they have laid out a campsite, transformed a big building into a refugio with restaurant and bar, and repaired a few houses and a bridge. They aim at something they call "turismo social". It is all depressing, hot and full of flies.

The publican of the bar is an engaging anarchist. When I come in he says to me: "You are a priest". A man with a sharp nose. I am truly curious to hear more about his anarchistic ideas but we get stuck in the beer.

In every refugio you are likely to find a pilgrims' book; visitors are encouraged to write something. It contains a potpourri of remarks, from elated contemplation down to rude graffiti. In the Ruesta book, somebody complains that this is not a genuine pilgrims' hostel because the pilgrims' spirit is missing. Had he been quarrelling with the anarchist? The contributor is patently wrong. A pilgrim has no house of his own; he is always a guest, can never make demands, always needs help and always should be grateful for any assistance he receives. But as a quid pro quo he also brings something: he is a person on the way to an inspiring place and with his radiation he encourages those that are stuck in a rut.

When you are using two walking sticks, you will miss two hands. I noticed that immediately with my leaking nose; by the way, it has stopped completely, strangely enough. Now I notice it with the flies. All you can do to defend

yourself is stopping from time to time and whipping a handkerchief around.
Now I appreciate why horses and cows have tails and flapping ears.

I belong to the dying species that has seen workhorses walking in the streets. Do today's children still know that horses have soft velvet noses? That you have to be wary of their rear end? That you can scratch them on their forehead (which gives you fatty fingers), that you can smack them on the neck and that you have to open your hand flat out if you want to give them a small thing to eat? And that a horse has a repertoire of means to chase away flies: shaking the head, banging the feet, rippling the skin and swishing the tail, to mention but a few? Would horses ever hit a fly with those eco-friendly tail-whisks? In those days, we humans had our own clever tricks to catch flies. A glass bell comes to mind with an opening at the bottom where the edge of the glass curled inwards; the space between the inner rim and the outer wall was filled with sugary water, made almost solid with the black bodies of the drowned victims. Most popular were the sticky ribbons which you pulled out from a small paper cylinder or cartridge and stuck to the ceiling. They capitalised on the flies' strange preference for sitting on things that stick out. But was it quite ethical to expose very young children to the sight of dozens of whirring flies desperately trying to get their wings unstuck, for hours on end? Thank God we now have aerosol squirts and poison gas.

Nowadays I take good care not to step on insects; in this I have begun to resemble the members of the ancient Eastern Jain religion. I also have developed a close relationship with Mother Nature.

Mother Nature, I would call her crafty. Just see how she got things done. In her youth she could not think. And so she thought: let me develop a human being, so that in and through the human person I can think about myself. That is indeed what happens: in the human person nature reflects on herself. The human person is 100 percent natural and whatever he does is natural. With this at the back of your mind it is difficult to see what the real meaning of "artificial" is supposed to be. Is it a non-word? And is the distinction between natural and artificial a fictitious one? The only thing a human being should really do is use his brains well.

Clothes that have become superfluous I put along the road on a stone, for the lucky finder. Berdun is a sympathetic little town. It lies on top of an oblong hill with a flattened top and is approached via a climb that gives cars more trouble than pedestrians. It looks like one of those pre-Roman fortified towns. The main road bypasses it at a few kilometres' distance; the same was the case, I noticed, with old towns along one of south England's pre-historic roads, the Hog's Back. Thus the rabble on the road would not have to go through the towns: they could be observed from afar and even be controlled from the stronghold. At Berdun, I find a sympathetic hotel, called Rincon de Emilio. It is really full but nevertheless they find a nice room for me. Sitting at my table near the open window, I have a view of the sympathetic little church square where small children kick a ball. When I tell the owners that I want to depart really early next morning they insist that I should be given a sympathetically-prepared breakfast in the evening, a breakfast that I can eat in my room the next morning. In my mind, I combine all those pleasant experiences and thus I compose a happy memory of a wonderfully charming little town.

In the same way, you can also join a number of less pleasant details and construct a memory of an inferior hole of a place. It depends very much on the spirit with which you are animated, whether a place is good or bad, including the people living there. Somebody with a positive attitude will always come across many fascinating persons and lovely places. We have to be on our guard against people that always meet unpleasant characters and find disgusting places.

One text of Saint Mark that has begun to vibrate within me has something to do with the foregoing. Jesus warns us that there is only one unforgivable sin and that is: to attribute bad things to the Good Spirit (3:29). Let us say: starting from your own negative attitudes, you interpret a problematic situation or personality in a damning way; and then you do not relate that rejection to your own wicked self but you ascribe it to the Holy Spirit. It occurs to me that this constitutes a problem within our church. What we like best is to paint over our church's human blunders with the whitewash that it was all the work of the Holy Spirit. But that is wrong. The church has made many a faux pas. Those should be accepted as our own and not be put on the account of the Holy Spirit; otherwise they cannot be forgiven and will continue to fester.

Jaca has many attractive things. In the first place, there is a beautifully dry hotel where I can recover from splashing through heavy rain for hours on end. There is, furthermore, a fine Italian restaurant where I can make a beast of myself (due to the way I eat spaghetti). And then there are many wonderful old buildings, especially the cathedral.

It is noteworthy with how much care they preserve everywhere the cultural inheritance of medieval art. And there is still so much of it. The paintings on the wall often touch a soft spot in us.

Between brackets, mural paintings present a special challenge to the artist: they are painted at arm's length but they have to look right at a distance of more than ten metres. Poor artists end up with an almighty mess; the good ones step back every so often in order to check, a difficult thing when the paintings are on a high wall; the real masters are able to calculate that element of distance straight into their work. In the cathedral of Jaca I find several examples of the latter; they have been painted in almost monochrome burnt ochres and at close quarters they seem a confused muddle but at a distance they have exactly the right depth.

I buy two new walking sticks at Jaca. The old ones are worn away beyond repair. I need another pair with shock absorbers; without them they bounce too much on the pavement. It breaks my heart that I have to buy another rucksack as well and discard the old one, faithful servant of over 30 years. All the metal parts have corroded, all the zips are gone, the canvas tears, the leather parts disintegrate.

It was such an excellent rucksack, the ladder-type, which had just appeared in the shops. You carried it nice and high on your back and it had many compartments. It was easy to attach other things to it and it was not too big. It had been my familiar companion on all my walks: to Compostela five times; to Canterbury twice; a Christmas walk from London to Walsingham; a walk from the Polish border to Cestochowa and Cracow; a winter's walk from Salisbury to Glastonbury; a walk in the snow from Hengelo to Munster; from Heilo to Brielle in Holland; across Turkey to Tarsus; once from Nakuru to Kisumu; and twice across East Africa from Mombasa to Kampala.

What is the correct way of saying goodbye to a friend like that? I am allowed to leave it behind in the shop; the smart-looking young men keep on assuring me that I will not get any discount for it. My old sticks I just leave behind in the rubbish bin of my room. These dramatic changes tie in with the character my route will have from now on. So far I have followed the Somport route but that one turns north at Jaca, crosses the Pyrenees and continues to Toulouse. I continue straight eastwards. Now that I do not follow a classic pilgrims' route any more, I somehow lose the classic character of a pilgrim. Indeed, no more refugios, no more yellow arrows, no more descriptions of the route, no more fellow pilgrims. I spend a whole Sunday afternoon searching for the best way. It is going to be the 'Transpyrenaica', the N260 from Jaca to Andorra. It proves to be a lovely route. Off I go, all on my own. But there is plenty to keep me busy.

Every morning, after I have hit the road, I spend the first three hours in prayer. My prayer scheme is the Rosary, all the 15 "mysteries". Since I walk with two sticks, I cannot hold rosary beads in my hand. So I use my ten fingers as rosary beads. Because I am walking, I can not take on a prayerful pose: I must keep my eyes open and pay attention to the road, the traffic and to other people. Praying with your eyes open is an art by itself. On the one hand, you are distracted often and for long periods; but on the other hand, you can relate your prayer to the ordinary things of life: the things and the people around you. Then again, the regular footsteps and the rhythmic breathing constitute a more favourable setting than frustrating struggles with sore joints when on your knees or with your nodding head when sitting on a chair. And often I burst into song. For the crucifixion I have a beautiful old Dutch folksong where Mary laments: "Oh beautiful above all beautiful, how can it be/ that you hang here, nailed, for all to see!"; for the resurrection I have the Plain Chant "Resurrexi et adhuc tecum sum"; for the Ascension "Viri Galilei"; for Pentecost my favourite "Veni Sancte Spiritus"; for the Assumption a song for Our Lady, "Salve Regina" or "Regina Coeli" or "Virgo Dei Genitrix". Words stored away decades ago come back when I try to recall them often enough. And singing aloud along the path is good fun; nobody else does it and you feel odd but the birds and the trees understand.

It is striking to see how nature wallows in plurality and variety. I wander through green fields, through rugged forests, across impregnable mountains, through cool moist ravines. All of them different biotopes with their own norms, their own flora and fauna. All of them different improvisations on the same theme. And even if I walk here with my well-tamed and well-trained mind, I am and I remain a guest, and neither the flowers nor the butterflies are in any way impressed by my intellectual eminence.

Hegel identifies the spirit of the world too much with reason and so he creates a world of ideas and reasoning. But that is not quite in alignment with nature: there is much more afoot. Look at all those tiny ants running around, all those birds flying, all those mice and cockroaches scurrying about: a world of ideas? Hard-headed rationalists will stick to their guns: all those small animals are just robots. Nobody will buy that, of course.

One and a half centuries ago, a new term was created to give a better grip on nature: the word 'instinct'. That term is so vague; however, that it does not explain anything. The original meaning was: impulse or stimulus. A little later it got the meaning of: an automatic and built-in and more or less infallible urge. Schopenhauer (1850) picks up the thread of Fichte and Schelling about the primordial urge or will that lies at the foundation of the world. Reality, he says, is insatiable will; the body is a solidified urge; the stomach is hunger become incarnate; sexual organs are the procreative urge turned into flesh. Thus I am intimately related to the animal and the plant world. If you want to lead a reasonably good kind of life, you will have to bring the urges under control by ascetical discipline.

Along the roads you find texts: mostly traffic directions and advertisements. Now and then there is something special, like a prayer. Or that poem about the beauty of Andorra, chiselled into a big stone at El Tarter. However, one word, and a rather big one at that, was wrong and the correction had been hacked right across it. Oops. The funniest in the field of corrections I saw was in a convent of the sisters at Nkokonjeru in Uganda. Somebody had embroidered a solemn text on a big cloth; afterwards she discovered that she had forgotten a word; she embroidered that one in addition above the spot in question and added a small 'v' under the word to indicate where exactly you had to insert it.

I find an interesting stone at Biesca, where Franco Suarez tells us he wants to pay his thanks to the Almighty because exactly in that spot He had protected him and his family from death in an awful car accident. Dated: 14th August 1911.

I experience on my walk that the traffic regulations are reasonable and that they work pretty well. For most complications they have found a ruling; but not everybody is aware. Thus, there is the prescription that a pedestrian should walk against the traffic and here that means on the left hand side. This fills some drivers with irritation. One of them came at me, slowing down on the extreme left hand side of the road and stopping the car touching my legs, to force me to go to the other side.

Insoluble cases are very rare. I think I came across one in Africa, on the border of Uganda and Congo. There was a long road and the border was the middle of the road over a distance of a couple of kilometres. Now, in Uganda the traffic keeps to the left and in Congo it keeps to the right. When cars meet on that road, how do they have to pass each other? Is it possible to drive correctly on that road? When you keep left, you are in Congo and on the wrong side; but when you move over to the right, you are in Uganda and again on the wrong side. The only possibility is this one: you are allowed to use the road in one direction only, with Uganda on your left and Congo on your right, and nobody is allowed to overtake.

Dangerous situations occur in a multitude of unexpected ways. On the day from Biesca to Broto I set off very early to avoid traffic. At the cool break of day I climb 700 metres. Then I reach a very narrow tunnel, utterly dark and one kilometre long. Thank God there is no traffic. What, no traffic? When I am halfway along the mouse-burrow, I hear the sound of a car engine. Looking round I see two cars entering the tunnel. And at the same time another car enters the tunnel ahead of me. Exactly at the spot where I am they all have to pass each other. I flatten myself against the wall like a piece of onion-skin paper and escape by a hair's breadth; the cars probably never saw me, for they were blinding each other with their headlights.

The Rosary is a meditative prayer dating back to the Middle Ages. The string of beads is subdivided into five times ten beads or 'decades'. For every bead you say one Hail Mary, the prayer that is directed towards the Virgin Mary. For every decade there is a mystery or a religious 'secret' on which you can meditate. Five mysteries make a rosary. Strictly speaking the five-mystery rosary is only one third of the complete one: the complete rosary has 15 mysteries. The 15 mysteries are subdivided into three groups of five: the joyful mysteries, the sorrowful mysteries and the glorious mysteries. The joyful mysteries refer to the coming of Jesus: the visit of the angel Gabriel to Mary in Nazareth (Annunciation), Mary visiting her cousin Elisabeth (Visitation), the Birth of Jesus in Bethlehem, the Presentation of Jesus in the temple and the finding of the

12-year-old Jesus who was lost in the temple. The sorrowful mysteries concern the passion of Jesus: His agony in the Garden of Olives, His scourging, the Crowning with thorns, the Crucifixion and His death. The glorious mysteries have to do with the wonderful happenings after the death of Jesus: His Resurrection from the dead, His Ascension into heaven, the coming down of the Holy Spirit, the Assumption of Mary into heaven and her Crowning in heaven. Formerly all Catholics knew these mysteries. When you pray the rosary, the endlessly-repeated Hail Mary's serve as a kind of mantra, a soothing repetition of mysterious words, whilst the mind thinks of the gospel mysteries. Not so very long ago the rosary was prayed in very many Catholic homes, all the members of the family kneeling down in front of chairs. It is now almost impossible to imagine that every evening hundreds of thousands of Dutch people would kneel down in their homes to meditate on religious mysteries. That is altogether out of the question now. In this day and age, they meditate before the TV set on 'Bay Watch' and 'The Bold And The Beautiful'. This is bound to have a tremendous effect on our common religious thinking.

Good luck, too, can surprise you at any moment. The distance from Broto appears to be much shorter than expected: I have already completed it at 9.30. "I suppose you are not open yet," I say to the hostess of La Ara. "Why not?" is her answer, "come in." I say, another free day thrown into my lap! From 10.00 to 12.00 I am submerged in a comatose sleep, complete with nightmares. Great!

Once you are in good condition, climbing and descending on foot is really quite easy; a thousand metres up to the top of the hill, no problem; and a thousand metres down again, like the noble Duke of York. Deep down below you, you see a village, you pass it after an hour, an hour later and you see it behind you on a mountaintop. Setting off very early, in the dark, is very important to me, because of the cool temperature and the ever surprising rising of the sun, that gigantic orange globe, new every day. Sometimes the air force had manoeuvres at that early hour and the circling planes with their fluorescent comet's tails resembled cosmic spermatozoa looking for the cosmic sun-egg.

As I make my way to Ainsa, I pass a large area totally devoid of any sign of life. They have planned a big water reservoir and in preparation, they have created a valley of death. Hour after hour, I vainly look for any sign of human presence; it is as if a neutron bomb has exploded here.

I have come to realise that not all the mysteries of the rosary are fitting for a prolonged meditation. Sometimes the sorrowful mysteries were too crude for that. I could not think about scourging for a quarter of an hour or about pressing a crown of thorns on somebody's head. Soon I started designing my own sorrowful mysteries. Here they are.

The first mystery: Jesus is abandoned by his disciples in the garden of Gethsemane;

Second mystery: Jesus is rejected by his religious leaders at Caiphas's place;

Third mystery: Jesus is rejected by His own people before Pilate;

Fourth mystery: Jesus feels abandoned by God;

Fifth mystery: Jesus dies, supported by women, pagans and criminals.

When thinking of the crucifixion, a question comes up all the time: why was Jesus nailed to the wood? Was it not the custom simply to tie the tortured condemned naked to the cross beams, break their bones and leave them to die slowly? I suspect that the nails were a contribution from a nasty zealot saying: "Just nail him to the wood properly and then we will see what tricks he has up his sleeve to get himself free, as he promised he would do". Hence the hilarity of the religious leaders who came to have a look; this is exactly what they shouted at Him.

The glorious mysteries I change a little as well. The last two, Mary's Assumption and Mary's Crowning, are almost identical. For the fourth mystery I take: the pagans are admitted to the New Kingdom. For the fifth: Mary becomes the new Eve, mother and queen of all the nations.

A few years later the Pope added another cluster of five mysteries, Mysteries of the Light; referring to important events that happened during the ministry of Jesus.

Near Castejon de Sos they are having championship hang-gliding. The whole sky is dotted with gaudy flying inflatable mattresses. Sometimes it happens that the village indicated on the map does not exist at all. And that there is nothing 10 kilometres before that spot or 15 kilometres past that spot. All you can do is walk on steadily, until senora Carmen welcomes you in her boarding house called Ventura at Adrall after 45 kilometres – and without any payment, for you are a pilgrim. Well then!

In a periodical I read that "Circulo de Lectores" has held an investigation in Spain, together with UNESCO, to find out how highly public institutions are esteemed. The Catholic Church did not manage to get beyond a poor 30th place. In the evaluation of various professions, priests and religious orders came in 18th place. Of the Catholics interrogated, 6.3 percent described themselves as "zealous", 27.6 percent as "lukewarm" and 38.5 percent as "baptised but not practising". What about the other 27.6 percent?

I go through areas where there had been heavy fighting during the Civil War. Here and there I see bombed churches or a bridge blown up long ago. People do not talk about it; why would they? Too many horrors have happened. In the crypt of the cathedral of Seu d'Urgell you can find the "Grave of the Martyrs", 16 priests "murdered during the war of 1936-1939" as a mural text shows. The word "murdered" has been scratched out and crudely replaced with "killed because they were against the Republic". Inside the major seminary there is a marble slab showing the names of 111 priests, fully one-third of the diocesan clergy, slaughtered through anti-religious hatred during the Spanish Civil War.

That was a war about social ideas, which had climbed up to the level of religion. We know by now that if you have a conflict and you blend the right amount of religion with it you will get a most explosive mixture that can be used in a good way as well as in an evil way. The Spanish Civil War was about revolutionary ideas concerning human society, ideas that were inherited from 19th century philosophers.

Where Hegel and Fichte indicated the broad outlines of changes in the world, their pupils began to formulate more exactly what happened. Once you know how the mechanism works, you can control it; in the case of human society, you can control its future. Human society had become mouldable.

Feuerbach (1860) brings Idealism back to earth. He teaches that what is evolving is not some nebulous spirit but tangible and material and dynamic concrete reality. The spiritual is but a projection of the human mind. God is the projected dream image that man has of himself: "Homo Homini Deus". True dialectics do not find place above our heads or behind our backs but are really a dialogue between persons. Marx (1860) pushes that theme a little further. He makes an analysis of history to show the misery humans have brought upon one another as they preyed on each other like wolves: "Homo Homini Lupus". For Hegel, reality was spirit and matter was a sediment of that spirit; for Marx reality was matter, and spirit was vapours wafting from that turbulent matter. Matter develops according to the dialectical leaps sketched by Hegel; hence the official name of Marxism: Dialectic Materialism. The leaps are revolutions. Progress is like a mill grinding on relentlessly and dragging everything along. The poor human person has only one way to survive: reconcile himself to the unavoidable. Marx has not only lost God, he has lost the human personality as well. Blood will have to flow. It is high time for a new prophet to appear.

Ask the people of Andorra why their tiny state is independent and they will tell you it is so because around the year 800 AD they helped the armies of Emperor Charlemain to cross the towering mountain passes of the Pyrenees. As a token of his appreciation, Charles granted them full autonomy. And he entrusted this autonomy to the nearest potentate, the Count of Foix to the north, who was to look after their material wealth; and to the nearest bishop, the one of Seu d'Urgell in the south, who had to look after their spiritual health. And so it came to pass that Andorra has two co-princes up to the present day: the French president as the legal successor of the Count of Foix and the bishop of Seu d'Urgell in Spain. Until recently, Andorra was no more than a Lilliputian mountain enclave made up of tobacco growers, shepherds, postage stamps and smuggling. Now it dreams of becoming the Switzerland of the Pyrenees. It is well on the way with its 275 hotels (and a population of 60,000), tax-free shops and fleets of Jaguars and Harley Davidsons. From the one end till the other, Andorra is a paradise of consumption. At the one border post, you break your neck over the supermarkets, at the other you are swamped by people trying to smuggle electronics. Gluttony and avarice is beaming from everyone's face, the irresistible compulsion to consume superfluous things, to buy harmful articles.

One can wonder how long such a mania can go on. By the rules of nature, superfluous things are harmful: too much food and too many superfluous articles bring physical harm in their wake. For how long can you ill-treat your body with impunity? It is not just a question of how much poisoning or mutilation your body can take. There is another aspect: we are betraying the trust Mother Nature has in us.

Mother Nature has a profound respect for our intelligence. She observes our behaviour attentively and tries to tune in to it. As soon as people stop using certain bodily functions, thereby declaring them to be superfluous, Mother Nature lets that function wither away. When you start wearing shoes, the heavy calluses under your feet disappear. Once you start wearing an overdose of clothes, the thermostat of your skin withers away. Mother Nature is deeply impressed with human planning and tries to play her part in it.

Take our economy. Modern Western man has decided that maximum prosperity will come his way if he destroys as many of his products as he possibly can so that he can make them all over again, for prosperity comes out of producing; his most cherished form of destruction is consuming the products. Here Mother Nature picked up a hint. And what does she do? She enlarges the human body to such an extent that everybody will consume and use much more material than before. For the rest there is no point at all in having a bigger body. In our naiveté, we think that bigger implies healthier and better; but in that we resemble the mother bird who proudly feeds her huge cuckoo-child.

Indeed, if our bodies would go back overnight to the size of our medieval forebears, then our economy would collapse forthwith because we would use only half the amount of textile and food and furniture.

There must be limits though. For example, how much food can the human alimentary canal cope with? That is a frightening question. If you stand in the middle of a supermarket and you see those immeasurable amounts of food, then you realise with a shock that all that stuff has to go through bowels! Can the poor intestines manage all that? Is it fair to ill-treat them to such an extent for the sake of the economy? True enough, if it makes the alimentary canal sick, that is good again for the pharmaceutical industry. Although we have to admit that the pharmaceutical industry does not really need diseases for its welfare: never in human history have we been so healthy and never in human history have we consumed so many medicines as we do now. All that is needed is fear of diseases. So there are advantages attached to almost all situations; even early death is a boon for insurance companies.

But the nagging question remains: where is the limit? Deep inside ourselves, we still hear weak impulses and alarm signals calling for true health and alignment with nature and the use of sober un-manipulated reasoning. We should use our brains again. Where supermarkets are concerned, my brain offers a clear solution. Near the exits of the supermarkets they have to put a number of very big toilets into which the shoppers can throw all the food they have just bought and flush it away without having to go through the trouble of eating it first. The customers will remain healthy; the joy of buying things is retained; and the economy can continue to grow by leaps and bounds. And we are not any longer making a fool of Mother Nature, for sooner or later she will find out. And what then? Was it not the wise old man who said: "God forgives always, a human being forgives now and then, but nature forgives never"?

Not long ago Andorra became a UN country. The ambassador gave his maiden speech in Catalan Spanish, the first time that this language was used in the United Nations Assembly. Andorra has taken part in Olympic Games (sailing), it boasts of a colourful flag (blue-yellow-red) and a national anthem glorifying Charlemain.

Avarice is extremely ancient, a primordial item in nature. Charity and respect of others have much younger papers. When did these start? With a mother who stands up for her offspring? Each one of us started his life's journey as an avaricious parasite. A foetus is a parasite carefully nursed. In the very first stage of our lives, our parasitical behaviour coincides with limitless affection on the part of our mother (unless she is contemplating an abortion). Altruism, that letting go of deeply ingrained selfishness, does that occur for the first time in a mother's pregnancy? And does that mean that mothers are the only ones who can really teach us charity? Our own initial experience of life is that it is a lazy "dolce far niente": as a baby we are spoiled rotten. That is the reason why babies, once they are born, scream blue murder if they are not served immediately with what they want. Some people never progress beyond that point. But you can't blame the babies, you can only pity them: they are the victims of the system. They have never been taught the difference between what is useful and what is just pleasant. It is all the same to them. Small wonder that dancing comes before walking.

Andorra can give you a very attractive souvenir: a cigar in the form of a corkscrew. If you have three of them they will fit snugly into each other. The problem is: what to do with them? Put them on the window sill or the mantle piece with all the other rubbish?

In a restaurant, I happen to meet an Andorrese nationalist. He makes himself very angry about denigrating remarks concerning Andorra, uttered by an elderly Spaniard who lived here in the 1930s. After the end of the skirmish he comes over to me and puts his card on my table with the words: "The people of Andorra welcome you". My friend is called Artur Homs Fernandez, living at the Av. Carlemany. Where else? And a free cup of coffee to boot.

The prophet so badly needed on account of the Hegelian and Marxist ideologists had come and gone before anyone noticed Kierkegaard. The Danish thinker clearly saw that the idealistic thought systems, but also scientific rationalism, were leading to a kind of massification that would utterly stifle the poor individual. He commenced battle to defend the concrete existence of the threatened individual. He compared human life to a long journey upwards via various stages. By doing so, Kierkegaard picked up a very old theme: the road of purification, something we find already with age-old Orphism, the mystery religion of 1,000 years before Christ. Plato knew about it too. With him, it is the Eroos, the yearning for the ideal, that propels a person upwards. Plotinus (250AD), the Neo-platonist, sees three stages in this "erotic" journey: human virtues, then science, then religious ecstasy. Scotus (875) fills in the three stages in a different way: redemption from sensuality, contemplation of ideas and finally mystic union with God. Roger Bacon (1275), too, discerns stages that lead from the turning away from this world to religious beatitude. The scheme of the three stages fits perfectly into Hegel's thinking. The dialectics of cognition run like this: first there is logic, then philosophy of nature, and finally philosophy of the spirit. Comte (1800) believes in nothing but sober and positive knowledge; he, too, cannot resist the attraction of the three stages but he makes them run from high to low. First, there is the stadium of faith in supernatural beings; then there is the stage of trust in abstract and theoretical philosophy; finally, there is the liberation of positive science. Kierkegaard describes the stages in his own way. First, we are attached to the aesthetic level of material enjoyment; then we reach the ethical level of doing our duty; and finally we arrive at the religious level of personal commitment. A person tries to climb higher and higher by an ever more personal dedication. But the passage from the one level to the other is made by an "existential leap": jumping desperately into the darkness as the only way out of the painful alienation that your surroundings induce inside you; it is a leap without logic. This is the only way to lead an authentic life; the only way to avoid being lived by impersonal forces.

During his lifetime, Kierkegaard was a voice calling in the wilderness. A century later, he was recognised as the pioneer of those that call themselves Existentialists.

It was a Saturday when I walked into Andorraland; on the Sunday I rest; and on the Monday I leave the country near the pass called Port d'Envalira, 2,407 metres high. Patches of snow lie here and there. The border crossing is a town made up of shops with luxury articles and fashionable items; the people surging past them have eyes that glisten with craving for the latest fashion.

Mother Nature must become utterly bewildered now and then when she finds us running after modish trends of which she understands nothing. Take the present day ideal figure of a woman. Since time immemorial, women have enjoyed gorgeously grand hips and backsides. That is sensible: when those body zones that have to do with sexuality give pleasure, then Mother Nature will happily comply and give them really generous proportions. But in the Western world a most remarkable notion has formed itself: that female backsides had better be as small as possible. And now a large number of women find a great fundament embarrassing. Trade has tuned in on this in a crafty way and supplied the market with underpants that are so elastic that they shrivel up to next to nothing. The ladies then appear to argue as follows: this is such a diminutive pair of panties, if I fit in there, I must have a diminutive backside. There is a roaring trade now. I am ready to accept that an element of sexiness comes into it as well. But why would a woman want to sport sexy underwear in secret, invisible to anybody who is interested in it. I can think of one explanation only. The wearer says to herself: "I know for myself that I am quite a saucy girl and not the boring frump that people suspect me to be".

Once across the Pyrenees I pass through a van Gogh-like landscape: fields with yellow wheat and sunflowers and cypresses in between, fir trees, swarms of black crows and above it all a blaring sun. The long alleys of plane trees swarm with cicada insects, stuttering circular saws making a tunnel of noise. These cicadas do with sound what Vincent does with colour: cut it all up in minute bits.

The Quaestio de Ponte – how can we make a logical bridge between what we know to be inside our mind and the objective reality outside – became more and more irritating as science continued its tempestuous progress. How on earth can you earnestly maintain that we know nothing about the objective world outside us? At long last they began to see that Descartes' saying "I think therefore I am" was misleading. If you want to be exact and complete, you should not just say "I think" but "I think of something", or better still "I am aware of something". Surely, our experience is not that I am thinking about thoughts but that in my thoughts I am thinking about things. It is part of the character of all beings that say "I" that they are geared to something else. Husserl (1900) tells us that we should call this character trait "intentionality". He also points out that all such beings try to make themselves known to others, to show themselves to others. "Showing yourself" is called "phainomai" in Greek; and so this type of philosophy is named Phenomenology. It is an insightful position to adopt. We have to make our acquaintance with all beings. You make your acquaintance by listening to others and find out what they have to say. We have to "shake hands with the trees". It is not up to us to tell them a priori what they should be looking like. Tell me who and what you are and I will name you accordingly. A true dialogue cannot start without affection. You can get to know others only when you love them, otherwise they will not reveal themselves to you. Only those that love you can give you your true name.

In that case, would it be true that all general ideas are prejudices? Is it true that essences are no more than boxes into which we try to squeeze beings willy-nilly? That will be the position of the Existentialists: they want us to forget about essences but concentrate on concrete existence instead.

Everywhere in the Languedoc you find references to the Cathars. Everybody knows them as heretics burnt at the stake by the church. Their name is milked commercially in ever so many ways: The Land of the Cathars; The Scenic Routes of the Cathars; Cathar Music; Cathar Delicacies; I even spot a Cathar Burial Company. (For a moment I thought it was a cremation service, but no.)

The beginning of their story is to be found somewhere in Egypt in one of the first centuries of the Christian era. Groups of Christians, by the name of Gnostics, tried to catch the mysteries of the Gospel in cultural concepts that were popular there. These concepts belonged to a world vision that believed in two masters, a good one and a bad one, each with their own creation. The good master had his spiritual world (good), the bad master had his material world (satanic). The gospel of John fitted nicely into these categories. A grim fight broke out about the question whether all that was really true; nobody took into account that all our words about God fall short of the mark. The theological war between the Gnostics and the Orthodox was won by the latter; the victors destroyed the Gnosis utterly, including its popular gospel of Thomas. But the ancient doctrine smouldered on underground. It found its way to the Balkans where the adherents were called Bogomils – friends of God – by the Bulgarians; from there it travelled to Bosnia and the area of the river Po; by the 12th century it had reached France.

In southern France nothing less than a complete Cathar church arose. The heart of that church was formed by a venerated elite, a group of spiritual heroes who had been confirmed as the Pure Ones (Cathars) by the imposition of hands and the touching of the gospel of John. They were rigorists till the tenth degree; they refrained from all sexual contact, they fasted a lot, they ate no meat, they refused to take oaths and they worked hard for their daily bread. The ordinary folk venerated them as saints who preached and practised a doctrine of love and tolerance. Whoever wanted to be a Cathar, but felt that he was not yet able to play in the top division of perfection, could receive the imposition of hands from a pure one on his deathbed and thus earn a second chance in the next reincarnation. Perhaps he would manage then.

The saintly monk Dominic tried to defeat them in public debates and failed. The Cathars were attacking weak spots in the church using the gospel of John and Dominic was defending the good aspects of the church by referring to the gospel of Matthew. They talked at cross purposes. The Cathars were known simply as Good People but they did not care for quite a few parts of the church's doctrine and they refused to swear loyalty to the church and worldly authorities. That was more than a normal person could stomach. In 1209, Pope Innocentius III took up the sword; he proclaimed a crusade against them. One shudders to think what Jesus would have said of that. The crusaders were allowed to grab as booty all the possessions belonging to the noblemen who had given protection to the Cathars or Albigensians (named after the town of Albi). It became an orgy of plundering and a bloodbath without compare. Politically, the conflict was a god-send for the French King, for thus he could extend his power over the independent principalities of the Languedoc. Around the year 1240, the ecclesiastical holy war died down when the leader of the crusaders, Simon de Montfort, was killed during the siege of a town. A ballista on the ramparts was operated by women and they aimed at de Montfort. Their rock hit the crusader on the head, making it explode in all directions. But King Louis VIII was not allowing himself to be robbed of his profitable campaign; he renewed hostilities in the form of a royal crusade. Thus the Province became French; the only part that remained independent was Andorra.

Strange as it may seem, the simple lifestyle of the Cathars became a source of inspiration for the new medieval holy men, the mendicants, who thereby attracted a lot of suspicion. The doctrinal cleansing was done thoroughly by the church department known as the Inquisition. Ironically enough, this was entrusted to one of the new mendicant orders, the preaching friars of Dominic. Soon they, too, were overwhelmed by the demonic traits of the system; and they saw their name blemished by a crime for which the church has not yet asked pardon either from God or from humanity. And the story told above also gives a clue why sodomites got that nasty name of "buggers" or Bulgarians and why the beginning of the gospel of John was formerly read out in connection with the final blessing at the Mass.

I make a small detour to see Montaillou, the village of a famous study about the Cathars. Well, what is there to be seen? Not much. Somewhere higher up on the hill one should be able to find a remnant of a ruin. A tiny fly gets into my eye. Behind a house a number of villagers are observing me with amusement. Carefully I select the most motherly type from among them and she gently removes the speck from my eye. The book was more interesting.

There is very little left of Catharism and the world that belonged to it. Our Western mentality has shifted very far away from that medieval mentality. We are now living in a panoramic moment of time where you can even trace the changes that led to the present Western mentality. Science has played a very important role in this process. In the 19th century, more and more philosophical questions were taken over by the scientists.

Thoughts about how everything had come about were worked out in an evolutionary way by people like Darwin (1860). The astronomers and students of elementary physics reacted to the amazement that we feel in the face of the macrocosm and the microcosm. Analytical linguists reflected on the import, the scope and the range of words. Einstein (1920) offered remarkable insights into the meaning of measurements. Questions about the soul were now the domain of psychologists and psychiatrists. The malleability of human society was the topic of sociologists and economists. New scientific insights determined people's view on life.

Formerly, the common conviction was that all branches of science were somehow interconnected and formed a huge pattern all together. The ideal Renaissance man was the Uomo Universale, like Leonardo da Vinci, somebody who could assimilate all sciences in a harmonious unity. Science became an important rival to the Bible. Ask Galileo. Later on, science replaced the Bible. The awe-filled adoration of scientific empiricism is still popular. "Scientific investigations have shown…" is the beginning of an infallible statement, firmly to be believed. "Scientific investigations have proved that it makes no difference to the children's development whether their parents love them or not" I once read in Libelle, the Dutch family magazine, in the 'eighties.

Einstein has pointed out the naiveté of so called objective scientific empiricism by reminding us that objectivity is by itself an impossible requirement, because the subject always influences the outcome of the experiment, even if it is only by his presence. Neo-Kantians say that by our scientific questions we give nature a certain arrangement. Such an arrangement can have the character of a cross-section under a certain angle. It could also be an arrangement that translates the data of nature into the order of certain terminologies: historical terms, ethical terms, legal terms, educational terms, religious terms, etc. Thus, you can translate Romeo and Juliet into a number of media: you can make a play of it, or a ballet, or a symphonic poem, or a painting. Phenomenology adds another consideration, and says: How did you ask the question? Do you really give nature a chance or are you putting her on the rack of the laboratory to vivisect her?

Whatever the case may be, the more you learn from science, the more you will be able to enjoy nature. And the more you enjoy it, the more questions will pop up. Every landscape has its own character and appeal, and can be looked at in a hundred different ways. Every early morning I gaze with amazement at the dark firmament that slowly becomes light.

From the earliest times, non-understandable irregularities of things in heaven and on earth have challenged man's mind to find an explanation. The funny thing is that the inexplicable events in the world of nature became smaller and smaller in size and the smaller they were, the bigger the discoveries they led to. At first people wracked their brains over the strange fact that every evening the sun set in the west and rose again in the east. Later on they looked for an explanation of the much rarer phenomena of eclipses. Again, some time later they discovered the hardly noticeable fact that some stars stood still and others moved. Later again, scientists invested all their time and energy studying some patches of mist in the universe, more so when they turned out to be patches of stars, invisible to the naked eye. And now the whole world stands on its head when they discover a tiny black spot in a far away corner of the heavens. Our forefathers would have dismissed this as excessive attention to futilities. But that is how it is: the more you know about something the more revelations appear to be hidden behind futilities. That is not only so with science. I notice exactly the same with my knowledge of Scripture: the more you know about it, the more intriguing the smallest nuances become.

At last I arrive in Carcassonne, the famous medieval gem; it cannot fail to impress me.

In the late 19th century, the Catholic Church was satisfied that it had survived the turmoil of the Reformation; the moment appeared to be favourable for a renewed interest in philosophy. Some great minds in the church began to reach back to the last purely Catholic philosophy: glorious Scholasticism of the Middle Ages; Neo-Thomism started its triumphal re-entry. This event coincided with the rebirth of neo-gothic architecture. On that account, the ancient city of Carcassonne can offer us a lesson.

During the 19th century, Viollet-le-Duc took pity on the woeful medieval ruins of this fortified city, in turn the pride of the Gauls, the Romans, the Visigoths, the Moors, the Franks, the indigenous population, the crusaders of Simon de Montfort and finally the French king. After he had done with it, the place was a true gem; even if it looks a bit like castles in comic strips. People started living there again and there are crowds of visitors. All the same, Carcassonne is more a living monument than a living city. The same could be said of the Neo-Thomist renaissance of the 19th century. It called up a tidal wave of spiritual energy that swept though the Catholic Church; but at the hour of philosophical truth, its life appeared inadequate. Our spiritual Carcassonne did not respond to the demands of the time. The old Scholastic spirit which they emulated so much had coincided with the building of the dazzling gothic churches – a recommendation indeed – but it had also coincided with the horrifying crusade against the Cathars and had not been able to point out its pagan character – a fatal shortcoming.

There is quite a lot to be seen at Carcassonne, like in an open-air museum. The most living item is the church of Saint-Nazaire where I concelebrate in a normal Eucharistic liturgy; and in the afternoon I attend a normal organ concert.

Formerly at school, we were taught the distinguishing characteristics of the gothic style in a rough and ready fashion: pointed arches, vertical lines and cross vaults. Romanic style, on the other hand, was characterised by round arches and barrel vaults. We learned to determine them the way you distinguish the great titmouse from the wren. It is remarkable of course that the people of that time never knew they were building in a gothic style. The Lord may know what name later generations will give to us. The term Gothic was not only used for churches, it was used for many other things, like shoes – the long pointed shoes. Their tips were so long that they had to be supported by wires. The length of the tip related to your importance. The longest gothic shoes were for princes: they were allowed to be two and a half times the size of the foot.

After Carcassonne, I want to reach the Mediterranean Sea as soon as possible. To get there reasonably quickly you have to take one of the major roads. Faced with such a situation there is only one thing you can do: start really very early, "before day and dew" as they say in Dutch, and beat the heavy traffic. Quite a few times I hit the road before 5.00. An added advantage is that you keep ahead of the greatest heat. I have learnt how to remain ahead of thirst: drink as much as possible before you are thirsty. Thanks to this practice, I have never been really thirsty on this journey, just pleasantly thirsty. Not everybody is so fortunate. In the Lezignan supermarket I come across two Dutch cyclists at the hottest time of the day. "Thirst!" they groan. "Thirst!!! We have had nothing to drink yet this whole day, except water."

The Provence is an ancient Christian region. Already in the first century, many people joined the ranks of the new religion. As I walk here, my thoughts automatically turn to the ancient tenets of the Christian faith that were new then; like the doctrine of the Blessed Trinity. They must have tickled people's fancy. To many of today's Christians, the Holy Trinity is in danger of becoming a dogmatic fossil. I wonder how many young Christians would still be able to formulate that doctrine: There is only One God but His divinity consists of three persons: the Father, the Son and the Holy Spirit; each of them is fully God, and yet together they are not three gods, but One God only. As I walk along, I try to find ways of making this meaningful. I think you could say the following. The ancient God of the Israelites and probably of all peoples, the Creator, responsible for the existence of the universe, the God of unimaginable power, that God is called by the Christians God the Father. Jesus taught us about Him and invited us to imagine Him as a father, concerned and worried. God saw with a worried eye how His creation went to rack and ruin to the desperation of all good-willing people. He realised that, in order to get things right again, what was required was such a huge injection of wisdom and understanding that this would mean that He Himself should start living among His children. That God, who feels at home among people, Emmanuel, is God the Son, who appeared in Jesus Christ. Divine Wisdom so strong that in human terms we have to describe Him as a person. Not only does God live in our midst, however, He even lives inside each one of us, as God's love for us, a love so strong that this also should be called a person again: the Holy Spirit. Through this Holy Spirit, divine wisdom in us is raised to the level necessary for replacing the old failed world with a better one: God's new kingdom on earth. And all this has to be taken in a poetic sense, for logic will not get you very far.

There are not many poets that try their hand, or rather their heart, at finding new images of God. The German poet Rilke, "the witness to the spiritual" in the words of Gabriel Marcel, is one of them, giving a number of fascinating suggestions, even though they remain far removed from the Blessed Trinity. In one place, he describes God as an old-fashioned blacksmith.

You are the old man and your hairs
are soiled by soot and singed by sparks,
you are elusive, great but hidden,
you hold your hammer in your hand.
You, ancient blacksmith, myth of ages,
your anvil is your only haunt.

You do not know how Sundays feel,
You'd think of what you want to forge;
you'd die over a new-made sword
that did not shine like polished steel.
When all our saw-mills have gone quiet,
and all are snoozing, drunk or tired,
one hears your hammer banging down
on all the church-bells in the town.

You are an expert and a teacher,
no one has ever seen you learn;
an unknown stranger, foreign creature,
an ever more mysterious feature
of whispers and of daring yarns.

(Rainer Maria Rilke, *Das Stundenbuch*: 'Du bist der Alte, dem die Haare')

Now I am quickly approaching the next apotheosis of my journey: the Mediterranean. And, to be sure, the frivolous southern shore of France is bound to be an endless chain of nudist beaches packed with seductive nymphs, a complete contrast with the devout pilgrims' world in which I have lived over the last half year. I am very curious. On 31ˢᵗ July, two months after I left Santiago, I get my first view of the magnificent blue expanse of water near Narbonne Plage.

Solemnly, I descend to join the figures cavorting in the surf. The comparatively few bathers look at me with puzzlement: a grey-haired old man carrying a rucksack and struggling through the loose sand with two ski-sticks and heavy walking boots. If it comes to the point, I really don't like swimming at all and I hate the loose sand that creeps in everywhere. With a mixture of aversion and solemn pathos, I put down my things, pull off my shoes and tread gingerly into the Mediterranean. I have walked from the North Sea to the Mediterranean Sea! Hip, hip, hooray! The water is much too cold. After a brief dabble, I return to the shore. Now comes my walk along the frivolous beach. First I put my big walking shoes back on, for it is too awkward to carry them in my hand along with all the other things I have. And I don't want all that sand between my toes. Really, what I should do now is find a nice and cosy spot and lie down, lazy and relaxed; I have half a day available for that. But I really fear to let the sun hit my exposed skin. I get sunburnt in less than no time, even if it is just my feet. I once burnt them so intensely in a few hours that I could not walk any more for days. I try to use my raincoat as a shade but there is too much wind for that. To lie down in the sun with my full walking gear on is too hot, apart from being ridiculous. The upshot is that I undress but cover myself with my bathrobe. I have to curl up as much as possible so as not to let any burn-prone skin protrude from under the robe. Besides, there are no seductive nymphs anywhere near, just solid moms with their kiddies who are having a nice day out on the beach. It is much the same as any beach anywhere; in fact all beaches resemble each other like two buckets of sand. After a sitting session of two hours my feeling of "What am I doing here really?" gets the better of me; I amble on. I have telescoped my sticks to minimum size but still my appearance gives rise to a lot of hilarious comment. The girl from Tourist Information tells me that all hotels are full. I don't belong here. I take a road inland to find a congenial little hotel in a friendly farming village. I am starting on my way home: from here my way goes steadily northwards again.

THE SEVENTH MONTH

AUGUST

During the month of August, I walk through the simmering Provence, from the Mediterranean Sea to the frosty Alpine mountain passes. This stretch of the road shows clearly that Europe is a collection of divergent and ancient cultural areas.

Up to the 18th century, Europe was a crazy quilt of closed-minded regions. When the time of the nation states had come, these regions were flattened out by the steamroller of patriotism. Now that the national borders are being stretched so far that they begin to coincide with those of Europe itself, these old regions reassert themselves: Aragon, Catalonia, Occitania, Piedmonte, Valdoste. The only future our old-fashioned national chauvinism can count on, is to be found in the world of international sports, the museum of warlike prowess of days gone by.

I do not want to say goodbye straightaway to the Mediterranean; I visit some delightful places. The old ports of Agde and Sète were Phoenician and Greek bridgeheads in the Gaul of yore, tiny fermenting metropolises, points of contagion, where continents touched each other. Now they are picturesque towns with extensive tourist folders. Until very recently, Cap d'Agde was the pinnacle of provocative beach life. Now the nearby nudist town is a carefully closed-off bastion where the reinforced barriers will open only to electronic passes: it does not radiate any recruiting zeal, it has its fixed clientele.

Nudism pretends to strike a blow for the innocent beauty of the human body. That sounds quite fair and aesthetically right. But on close examination it becomes clear that nudity among people is exciting, especially on account of the clothes you have put off.

Through clothes we give added emphasis to what is male or female in our bodies, first of all by dressing in them and then by taking them off.

It is normal to explain all male and female aspects of the human body by referring to the urge to copulate. I would not be surprised if we would discover that originally several of the secondary sexual characteristics have little to do with the profound copulation urge. Do we really have to believe that women have a softer body so that they might seduce men to intercourse? I don't believe it for one moment. I can think of quite a different reason. The little baby inside the womb has been wobbling gently in the soft fluids for nine months without ever feeling anything hard or sharp. So it is best if the child can continue to wobble gently after birth on the soft body of the mother without feeling anything hard or sharp. A man has nothing comparably to offer. Even now, I can remember the feel of the hard bodies of male family members: their rough and prickly costumes, the knobbly waistcoats with the sharp buttons, the lapels stinking of tobacco ash; and then the aunts, how they were much softer and smelled much more sweetly.

I want to spend a few more hours walking along the beach but at an early hour when (almost) nobody is there. I meet two men, each of them having a dog. One dog vomits in the sand where soon the children will be playing, the other one shits.

Philosophically speaking, the second half of the 19th century is like the doldrums. Maybe science had sucked all the life out of philosophy. The only big names I can think of are those of Nietzsche and Newman. There is plenty of fierce action, probably too much. Marx published his Manifesto and everywhere the ominous tornado clouds of revolution were gathering. The industrial revolution burst open, spreading promises of unparalleled prosperity and creating a new slave caste of exploited labourers. Politics and trade became worldwide networks, creating the new phenomena of imperialism and colonialism. Scientists went from victory to victory and entrenched themselves inside their sacred laboratories from where they sallied forth with irresistible aggressiveness. Darwin completed his evolutionary theory, which fitted snugly into the omnipresent optimism of progress. And all this was cemented together by the smug bourgeois mentality. They were sowing wind without restraint, never believing that they were going to harvest storms galore.

When I am on my way to my pension at Montpellier, my walking sticks telescoped under my arm, I overtake a strolling family. "Look, boys," the father says in loud Dutch, "there is a man with super-tiny ski-sticks!" I cannot resist a little revenge. I slowly turn to him and say in equally hard Dutch: "Well, sir, I can see that you know precious little about skiing; otherwise you would have noticed that these sticks are not for skiing at all." The woman is cut to the quick and shouts after me:"But we go on winter sports holidays every year, mind you!" Ha, ha.

*The town of Montpellier is full of classical architecture and loves it. When the architect Ricardo Bofil was given the task of building a new section of the town he designed something extraordinary: the Antigone project in ultra-classical style. The quarter is reached via the back entrance of a shopping mall. As you descend a broad flight of stairs you see before you a high convex wall with pillars, friezes and square windows, a gigantic commonplace of classic tinkering. You even see plants at the top, put there no doubt to suggest a mossy ruin. And you say to yourself: did they **pay** for this? You enter via wings and you imagine yourself to be inside the Baths of Caracalla, the sky-high ruins in Rome, although here they are new and flawlessly masoned. And there are trees; children play with skeelers and skateboard and senior citizens walk with their little dogs. As you go on, you enter a panorama in the style of Magic Realists: pillars and cypresses and white square buildings under a threatening sky. Every hundred metres the style becomes a little more playful but the symmetry remains, monumental, fascistic almost. The buildings are all being used, as offices, hotels, shops and bars. One more kilometre and you have the gothic trick: replace the walls between the pillars with glass. By way of conclusion there is a colossus, half triumphal arch half rubicube, made entirely of glass and standing on the edge of a big pond. It is flanked by buildings that remind you of warehouses along the Amsterdam canals.*

I visit the new museum of Arles; whatever may be new, they stick to the old derogatory custom of referring to the Germanic tribes as "barbarians". And when France has conquered a new piece of land, it is always called a "reunion".

Barbaroi was a Greek word of contempt meaning jabberers, people who could not speak Latin or Greek, who could not speak therefore, nor even think. It is a truly colonialist term.

Let it be that the Germanic people made a mess of the beautiful Roman Empire and that they were not very efficient in imperial government, the antagonism between those peoples also had something to do with the fight between townspeople and farmers. The classical culture was a town culture and the Germans were farmers. Tacitus wrote his book 'Germania' to put the decadent Romans to shame. Invective among nations can follow unpredictable paths. 'Vandals' toppled over to the bad side and 'gothic', initially a term of contempt, toppled over to the good side.

In Spain, the pilgrim saves money by sleeping in the cheap or even free refugios; he will need this money when he gets to the south of France where he has to stay in hotels. I have a rule: I go to the Tourist Information office and take the cheapest lodging in town. That does bring surprises. In one place I got an attic room without windows; the heat was total. Next to me, in a similar room, a man was staying with his dog; the only sound I kept hearing all the time was the shluck-shluck-shluck of the drinking dog. In another place, the heavy stench of sewage hung in the room; every time somebody flushed the toilet in the corridor, the drain of my washing table began to gurgle. In another hotel, I counted 60 staircase steps between my room and the door outside. They had told me that I could leave very early all right but would I please leave my keys on the table in my room. But when I wanted to depart, "before day and dew", I found the outer door locked, so I had to make a safari back to my room to fetch the keys. When I had unlocked the door, I had to go up and down once again to leave the keys on the table: 300 steps at 5.30 in the morning.

At Saint-Gilles, I finally meet some pilgrims again, on their way to Compostella: two Belgian lads, Jean-Philip Akkels and Sam Keersemaker. Bravo. The people of the local Tourist Information office are so delighted at being swamped with pilgrims that they make the firm resolution there and then to give Saint-Gilles once again the true status of pilgrims' station, with printed matter and a place to sleep. For a start they offer us floor space in the hut of the sea scouts.

One of the curious things in Saint-Gilles is a medieval spiral staircase, put together with carved blocks in such a way that they did not need any mortar or cement. The ancient pilgrims' church carries scars of religious violence.

To murder people for the sake of pure faith is an Old Testament attitude that remained rampant for a very long time. It is probably right to say that it disappeared in Europe, as a mentality, in the 19th century, though the practice continued here and there. But the pugnacity remained. The campaigns were sublimated to the spiritual level of polemics. For that you require a certain professionalism, as developed by Thomas Aquinas and other great medieval polemicists.

The 19th century effort of the Catholic Church to get her philosophy going was a brave effort. Science and church were at loggerheads with each other: science was "atheistic" and the church "sabotaged". The church felt supported by countless millions of unsophisticated followers and a glorious past. Would it not be possible to take the incontestable excellence of ancient Scholasticism as a new starting point for a world vision that would expose the erroneous ways of the Enlightenment? Scholasticism was launched again in grand style by Pope Leo XIII and the Louvain philosophers of the Mercier-circle. The seminal treatise of the latter had the significant name of 'Point de Départ de la Métaphysique'. In seminaries, religious institutes and Catholic universities, a whole new generation of self-assured young people were trained in hope and fidelity and the handling of Neo-Scholastic armaments. This movement set a breeze going through the church like a new spring, a new sound, too, as Gregorian chant and classic Polyphonic church music were being restored, accompanied by an intrepid neo-gothic style of architecture. The whole church arose in triumph. But where philosophy was concerned, it remained a "point de départ": not much new was being added, no protection against the contemporary bad climate. The new philosophical church building remained without a roof, let alone a lightning conductor.

I have to tread carefully here; my whole philosophical training has taken place within the confines of Neo-Scholasticism. I owe everything to it. I must not spit into the well from which I have drunk. I owe a great debt of gratitude to my Neo-Scholastic masters. In particular, I am very grateful for the configuration of the 'Transcendentalia' that has become the lodestar of my philosophical reflections in the course of time.

This is the scheme. Everything that is, is true (verum); everything that is, is one (unum); everything that is, is good (bonum). Just as the very act of being, these qualities of being transcend the borders of the particular beings as such; and that is why they are called Transcendentalia. Their mutual relationship is noteworthy: they penetrate one another completely and they are interchangeable; in as far as something is true, it is one and also good. If you mix them all together you get the quality known as beautiful (pulchrum).

This vision suddenly got a remarkable and challenging relevance for me when I changed these qualities from the passive sense to the active sense. I felt this was the proper thing to do, for we experience "being" in an active, subjective way above all, rather than a passive or objective way. So, for "true" I began to say "knowing"; for "one" I began to say "making"; for "good" I began to say "loving". Then you get: all beings are aware (even if it is only to the extent that they offer themselves as knowable, as the phenomenologists say); all beings do something (even if it is only to maintain themselves); and all beings love to be (even if it is only in as far as they resist their own destruction). Thus all beings display the three dimensions of existence, especially human beings. We human beings experience "being" on the inside: knowing it, maintaining it, loving it.

These dimensions of knowledge, work and love are three communicating vessels to one another. If you want to know somebody, you have to work at it; and if you hate a person you are bound to misunderstand him or her.

The three dimensions are represented by three parts of the body. Knowledge is represented by the head; Making is represented by the hand; Loving is represented by the heart. From here, you can take the next step: the head makes new knowledge from questions; the hand creates new unity out of multiplicity; and the heart makes new satisfaction out of desires. That is why questions, multiplicity and desires are such precious ingredients of our existence; perhaps even more important than answers, unity and satisfaction.

The next point will be: how then do we get questions, how do we get multiplicity, how do we get desires? Now we come to something that may seem macabre. The only way to get new questions is by doubting old answers. The only way to get new multiplicity is by breaking up old units. The only way to get new desires is by becoming discontent with old satisfaction.

From here we have to proceed with great caution and respect. If we have to destroy something for the sake of our own profit, we have to do it very carefully. At Kisumu, I know a group of Muslims who insist that the fish they buy in the market should be alive: for that makes it possible for them to ask pardon from the fish before they kill it in order to eat it; you cannot ask pardon from a dead fish. It is here also that ecological concern has to find a place.

If we want to be sure to arrive at a new answer, we have to take care that the question is put in the right way. If the question is really proper, it will contain the answer: the answer is made up of the same words but in a different order. Question: "Is the cow sick?" Answer: "The cow is sick". If we want to arrive at a new product we want to make sure that the multiplicity is promising. If we want to reach new satisfaction we have to take care that our old dissatisfaction is genuine.

This philosophical approach allows me to fight myself free from the clutches of enlightened Western rationalism. That rationalism invests all its energy in only one of the transcendentals; in knowing, verum. I hear the rationalists say that only through genuine knowledge do you get a sure grip on the world; once your knowledge falters, you feel the ground give way under your feet, they say. Is that really so? Do these rationalists really believe that all former unenlightened generations had no grip on their world because of their defective knowledge?

The doctrine of the transcendentals shows that there are big holes in Rationalism. For apart from the world of knowledge, verum, there is still another world, the unum-world of doing and making and skilfulness and coping. Somebody who feels confident, who is aware that he can manage the situation, that person has an excellent grip on his world, even though his knowledge concerning fundamental questions is minimal. And you can turn that round: if a person has refined and unshakeable knowledge but feels he cannot cope, he will collapse.

And then in the third place there is the whole world of bonum, the world of love, of appreciation, of dedication, of irresistible urges. If somebody is excited about something, if he tackles something with great enthusiasm, if he feels attracted to another person, then solid and well-founded knowledge begins to play a very secondary role.

At Arles, Vincent van Gogh is everywhere. Wherever he put his easel, the place is marked with a stand on which the painting in question can be seen; the visitor is led from one place to the other by means of an indicated path. I get particular satisfaction from drinking an absinthe on the famous yellow terrace under a dark blue starry sky. I have not been able to find the bridge with the boats. Many objects shown in his paintings are still there; but all the people are gone. The names of many of the young people in his paintings will be found on the war monuments of the Great War.

The towns of the interior of the Provence are Roman through and through, with their forum, their theatre, their amphitheatre, coagulated in their nostalgic classical dreams and largely buried under their own rubble. In the course of time, the Coliseum of Arles became a fortress with 212 dwellings and two churches. The theatre of Arles and the temples of Orange became quarries. Many of the mortal remains have been re-erected, if not resurrected. My hotel Gallia in Arles lies in the ancient main street of the Roman city. Just before midnight, there is a fight deep below me on the sidewalk: a drunken customer is thrown out into the street and keeps on attacking the bouncer with resounding rage. It is a remarkable spectacle to observe all this from above: we never look at events that way. Details escape your attention and you cannot ask anybody for an explanation. Bang, there he goes down again; people keep him pinned down and shout: "Stop it!" He keeps himself motionless, so they let go. Then he jumps up again for another attack, raging like a bull. What would his wife be doing at this moment? Is she walking around with rollers in her hair ready to go to bed and wondering where her Raymond is hanging out this time? There he shuffles off, growling, disappearing into one of the old Roman alleys just as a police car enters the scene like a deus ex machina.

Arles is full of things that refer to a great past; but often they are scars.

Large parts of France were Reformed at one stage in history. The present situation is the result of well-directed decisive violence. One sees the fingerprints of hatred: raped churches, defaced statues of saints, nasty texts on memorial slabs. When William the Silent and Prince Maurice were in charge of Orange they tried to give the Reformed a chance to live in peace, something very progressive in those days. Normally both sides would offer their vicious cruelties like bloody bouquets at the feet of Jesus who must have found it all utterly loathsome.

And now? There is religious peace in our lands, mainly because people think that religion is not worth a fight any more. Where Christianity has true character it should in principle reject all violence and thus become a lever for peace. To what extent have we assimilated the Good News?

The 7th September 1912 was a black day for Alain Joubert because on that day his wife Jeanne and his brothers Joseph and Jules were killed in a motorcar accident. That is what you can read on a porphyry monument, he erected at the fatal crossroads. On the side they have added a post-scriptum: Alain himself was killed 55 years later, on the 12th June 1967, also in a motorcar accident.

Call the French Revolution a milepost on the road of human progress; it was also at the same time an explosion of inhumanity. Sometimes the savagery was bloody, sometimes it was just nasty. The monumental abbey of Montmajour was sold as a stone quarry.

The supporters of the French Revolution were cock-sure of themselves, people for whom everything was clear and obvious. Just imagine what they did. They started counting the years from zero again. They abolished all classes; something like Pol Pot did in Cambodia. They suppressed religions despite desperate protests of the citizens. They murdered their opponents with industrial efficiency. And all this with the slogan of "Liberté, Egalité, Fraternité". That happens when you reckon yourself to be infallible. Give me people that hesitate and doubt.

Near Les Beaux de Provence it looks as if a gigantic lump of chalk has burst upwards through the surface: a meteorite from the centre of the earth. The imposing beauty of the area attracts many landscape-lovers. They come out of their vehicles in gaudy tight outfits; bicycles appear from the boot; maps are consulted; beaming with ecological elation they go on their way. Others struggle up small paths to reach panoramic viewpoints. Again others disappear in cool grottoes that have been transformed magically into a "Cathédrale d'Images"; I have a vague idea what that might be, something with music by Moussorgski and Debussy. I am tempted but walk on. In the garden of a nice house, a man is working and I ask him about the route. He is English and soon I find myself seated at table with a very friendly family, tucking in for a second breakfast. It is almost a year since I spoke English; that is probably why I choose my words with earnest care; my host does the same in return, and as a result, the meeting rises to the level of a literary interview. By way of fee, I am shown a shorter pathway along a rippling rivulet, over grass and by the backs of pretty residences.

It sometimes happens that a town is disappointing, like Saint-Rémy. I think I had been predisposed to find something wonderful by the very fact that the town figured in the life of Vincent van Gogh. But there is nothing, really. A central square, an ordinary church (but with a most friendly priest), a couple of small but pricey hotels away from the centre and something that looks like an ancient factory.

McDonald's of Avignon, near the entrance of the town, is a bridgehead of stress. The customers stumble out of their cars and have to rest quickly. Plastic chairs, plastic tables, plastic plates, plastic straws, the people have a plastic look in their eyes; for the children there are bunches of plastic balloons. I treat myself to a plastic little bucket with french fries; a printed text supplies me with the important information that I should realise that I have been given an extra large helping and that a number of other attractive bargains are awaiting me.

Yesterday's friendly priest had advised me to go and try hotel Formula I. It takes me ages to find it; in the process I criss-cross through various industrial areas on the outskirts of Avignon. When I get there, it appears to open at 5.00 p.m.. only. I am lucky in a way, for it would not have been a handy place for me. It takes me quite a long time before I have returned to the world of pedestrians, via Algerian quarters. I am rewarded with a place in a delightful old-fashioned little railway hotel, Montclar, smack in the middle of the town.

The years when the popes stayed at Avignon, between 1305 and 1375, were not really a "Babylonian Exile" for them. They chose Avignon as their permanent outer residence in order to have their hands free. Rome was riven with fights between noble families and the political scene had changed in such a way that the Holy City was now situated more or less at the edge of the Christian world. Pope Boniface VIII had managed to subject all Christian kings to the papacy so that they had to pay tribute. The popes rewarded themselves with the three-tiered super-crown, the tiara. As super-monarchs they needed room for their growing departments. Clement V took up his abode at Avignon where the Holy See had many plots of land. Avignon was situated on the river Rhône, which at that time formed the border between France and the German Empire, so it was conveniently placed. The popes installed their international offices there and the department of finance; in 1348, they decided to buy the whole town, from the Kingdom of Naples. The papal court attracted many artists and tradesmen, and thus it became the cradle of Renaissance culture, not bathing in luxury but run in an efficient way. That was the beginning of the modern Holy See with its huge departments.

Rome, however, had its own treasures: above all the graves of Peter and Paul, and of course its history. Young Catherine of Siena put the seventh Avignon pope Gregory XI under so much pressure that he returned to Rome. Three years later the Western Schism occurred, lasting from 1378 till 1417, with popes both in Rome and at Avignon. Unimaginable confusion reigned. One cannot escape the suspicion that this chaos was the immediate result of claiming ever more power. The schism was done away with; but the bad conscience has remained. Surely it was not right for the leaders of the church to amass so much worldly power? The uneasiness about the immense power of the pope is still growing in our days, together with that power itself that shows no signs of diminishing. So much majesty, surely that does not tally with the words of Jesus: "Amongst the pagans the leaders lord it over their subjects, and the rulers make their authority felt. But amongst you this is not to happen" (Mark 10: 42-43)? It has given the Church, the Body of Christ, serious and long-lasting infection. The Second Vatican Council has been courageous in tackling many major problems but not this one. "Among you this is not to happen." I have not been able to find that text in any of the Council documents; if it is written somewhere, I have missed it. The tiara has gone back into the box but a lot more is needed.

In Avignon, it is fashion for young beggars to have a small dog; there are many musical beggars too. Right in front of the papal palace there is a spot where the acoustics are so perfect that a microphone is superfluous. People are lining up to give a performance: a young girl sings a professional aria impeccably; a man with a beard cannot get his Russian macho-song to vibrate properly; a South American combo are larding their tunes with squeaks and rattles and shouts. In a short flash I imagine myself singing something there. Why shouldn't I? Every morning as I walk I go through quite a repertoire of medieval music. A nice item would also be the Our Father in our Luo-language (Wuonwa mae polo, nyingi mondo oluor). Against this medieval castle an old hymn for Our Lady would be fitting: "Virgo Dei Genitrix/ quem totus non capit orbis/ in tua se clausit/ viscera factus homo". But I don't dare. Silly really, for nobody knows me here.

In the smaller palace there is an exhibition of 14th century paintings from Siena. They fascinate me to such an extent that I am unable to move on and leave them. Those colours! It is as if all the images have been painted on glass with gold shining through. The colours of later periods are thoroughly banal in comparison.

Long ago Avignon and everything lying to the east of it was part of the German Holy Roman Empire. Nations as such did not exist, only groups of people with a distinct language and distinct customs. Loyalty was directed not so much to a national head of state but rather to tribal groups with the same language and the same culture. They would fight for power but when nationalism became the deciding factor borders became important; they gave rise to wars.

In the ancient town of Orange I take up my abode in Hotel Arcatel, situated on the old Roman forum. The old theatre is quite nearby; what a marvellous creation, with the ascending rows of stone sitting places. It is without frills; there is an enormous stage, a backdrop and plenty of benches, that is all. No walls, no roof, no other knickknacks or superfluous luxuries. But the seating space is so generous that you will not disturb anybody by walking away from

HANS BURGMAN

your place; and the acoustics are phenomenal. I am told that that is due to the angle under which the stands ascend and also because the backdrop is not smooth but roughed up with niches and statues. Tourists test the acoustics with shouts. Somebody shouts: "Odd fellows, those Romans!" a quote from the strip hero Obelix. Indeed, microphones are not needed.

In the 16th century Orange became the property of the house of Nassau; that was quite in order, since it was under the German Empire. In 1672, with the Treaty of Utrecht it was ceded to France; "reunited" with France therefore.

After Avignon and Orange I definitely say farewell to mundane Mediterranean life.

But what is mundane. It used to denote frivolity in dress. Is it still used in that context? Did it not mean that the ladies did not wear enough clothes? Does anyone in the West still worry about that? Now that everything is mundane, nothing is mundane any more.

A thing that strikes me is that very many holidaymakers visit churches with fitting reverence and interest, oblivious of their, let us say, light clothing. In one church at Avignon they tried to do something about this. At the back of the church big drawings with red diagonal crosses over them illustrated which eight kinds of bareness were scandalous and therefore not admissible. They had moved with the times: also the bare navel had been included in the condemnation. Still, I think they had not gone far enough: what to think of a transparent skirt? Or a tight T-shirt without bra? And what system of screening could winkle out wobbling backsides in time, or tempting eye-shade? No, there is only one fool-proof solution: no more women to be allowed in. Don't say that this is impossible. The Muslims do it, don't they?

From now on I begin to glimpse mighty mountains looming in the far distance: the first storeys of the Alpine range. The Alps! A different world. Everything is going to be different now. There will be a different struggle: not with the heat and the distances but with the height, with the mountain tops. A great excitement takes possession of me: soon I will have to go over Mount Cenis! Over the Small Saint-Bernard! Over the Big Saint-Bernard! Surely, that cannot be done! But I accept the challenge: to cross the Alps lengthwise. I will have age-old snow on my left and on my right; I will see the birth-canal of the River Rhône, the birth-canal of the River Rhine; there will be effervescent thin air and alpine meadows perpetually washed clean. I see it all before me right now.

215

I should calm down; first I must close the French chapter in a worthy fashion. I must salute the vineyards of the Côtes du Rhône and Gigondas on the horizon. I pay a courtesy visit to a surly aristocratic wine-grower who allows me to peek at his gold-leaf-splattered bottles without letting me sample a cool half litre. At the end of the afternoon I find hospitality with a most friendly family living in an old silkworm farm; they open for me a bottle of the renowned local wine – and I do not have the heart to tell them that I find it tart and harsh. I am still used to the more mellow Spanish wine. Meeting these type of people makes the journey worthwhile. They say something all the time; they leave out the small talk and proceed to hit the nail on the head forthwith. They say they would love to keep contact with me. During the precious conversation the household matters go on unabated; little children splutter for attention, a young girl has an attack of allergic chest pain. They have an open house and welcome people who want to reflect on their lives. In my case they will not hear of any payment: they give me the feeling that I have done them a great favour by coming. Their view on life makes them rich; their children are lucky.

For quite some time now it has been fashionable not to educate children in any kind of religious conviction. "They will have to choose one for themselves once they are adult," was the policy of the parents. Did these parents really understand the function of a composite view on life? It seems to me that a comprehensive view on life, which includes a stance on religious values, is very much akin to a language, is in fact like a language of the spirit. Very few parents will say: "We will not force any particular language on our children; let them chose one when they are adults". If they were to do that, they would create psychological cripples. A view on life grows, starting from very simple beginnings; it grows by the exchange of old views for better ones. Who is made to grow up without any definite view on life, is sent on his way with an empty purse, without change. For such a person it will be almost impossible to overcome spiritual illiteracy.

Offering a child a well-tested view on life is a risky task demanding honesty. If you give children one that is too irritating or too unfair, then they will not use those views as change but just throw the whole lot away.

I am extremely grateful for my solidly Catholic education. Very early on I was given an education with quite a lot of enthusiastic certainty but without fanaticism and with a large measure of openness, much adventure, many special attractions and strong emotions. I have exchanged most of the single items of that education for better ones, I think. But I have been able to do it in such a way that I managed to keep the major outlines intact and even reinforce them.

One of the most pleasant offers that I accepted is the one of making pilgrimages on foot. That has brought delightful experiences and inspiring encounters into my life. The manifold marches have also shaken loose many fruitful thoughts. That is a wholesome operation, not unlike the one of the winnower who tosses the flail-threshed harvest rhythmically up into the breeze to separate the chaff from the grain.

Now we are on climbing roads, in rocky ravines and on farmland tracks. The first yellow leaves appear on the lime trees. Morning mist brings cold with a new and pungent fragrance. The birds have seen their chickens grow big and now they are bored: they do not sow, they do not mow, they have nothing to do. Honey has disappeared from the flowers; the bees are well organised and stay at home; bumblebees and wasps, a more disorderly rabble, rummage around at random , looking for something sweet: some test my yellow roll of foam plastic, others try my face. A dead ferret on the tarmac is not rigid yet; carefully I shove it off the road into the grass, wishing it a worthy decomposition. The Alpine landscape presents itself with horizons made of high blue mountains, with gorges and with a new province named Hautes-Alpes. In one of the narrow ravines a small monument keeps reminding everybody how the underground fighters of the Maquis ambushed a German column here in June 1944. Twenty-three guerrilla-fighters died in the skirmish and another dozen were killed later on. On the slab, the word Wehrmacht is spelled wrongly twice, as Werhmacht.

Fifty years have passed since then; that feat of arms has already become an anachronism. A war between France and Germany sounds as much out of date as a war between Yorkshire and Lancashire or between Vermont and Quebec. The modulation to much bigger continental units has brought about some good effects. But many of the cultural attitudes of present-day continents are so narcissistic that one can doubt very seriously if they still contain possibilities of progress. The Western world, at least, seems to have reached a deadlock: some new impulse from other continents will be necessary before it can gather speed again. And that is indeed what we see around us.

Nevertheless, the progress euphoria continues unabated in large sections of the population. There is a very widespread conviction that people are becoming ever more intelligent; that children become brighter and brighter; that the healthcare is improving steadily; that education reaches ever more glorious heights; that marriages are a lot more satisfactory than formerly ("Just imagine the incredible things married people were subjected to formerly"); youth is able to carry an ever greater burden of responsibility; freedom has taken on ever more perfect dimensions ("Promiscuity is one of the most precious blessings gained by the sexual revolution", a psychologist wrote a few years ago in the Dutch Weekly Elseviers Weekblad). An easy and popular way of proving all these points is by distorting the past into a caricature of itself. But I do remember that some years ago I read a study proving that in reality, today's children take longer and longer to become intellectually mature: the subject matter which 12-year-old children could cope with a hundred years ago can be handled by the present generation only when they are 18 years old. I have never noticed that today's youngsters are so much better at geography or history than we were at their age; or at arithmetic; or language.

Painted large on the roads are the names of the cycling heroes of the Tour de France: the battle is on right now. The contestants will have little chance of absorbing the breathtaking views as they lean forward over their racing bicycles: other people's rear wheels is what they see and dancing tricots and miles of tarmac with – lo and behold – their names written on it here and there. A week or so ago, I saw a small monument somewhere along the road, displaying a photograph of a crying Tour de France cyclist: there on that very spot it had happened in the 1930s. I think, that this young racer had built up a decisive lead, enough to win the days' distance, but then he had been forced to give his front wheel to a team-mate. It was his sad lot to have to wait for three quarters of an hour for the coming of the van with the spares, in tears. Here he had been sitting, right on this low wall!

I pass by pretty mountain lakes, backgrounds for fairy tales, and small lodging places run by fairy godmothers; I even have some fairy tale encounters. When I enter the Tourist Information Office of Embrun, all the charming ladies beam at me as if they have a vision of Charlton Heston. They want to know everything about me. Am I looking for a hotel? But no! They know of something much better. The prettiest of them takes me to the house of the parish priest, just in time for lunch, snooze and the offer of staying in his country house outside the town. But the sweetest of the Tourist Office ladies has a better plan still: "Why should you not stay in my own house? My husband would love it." Of course, after interviews with the newspaper and the radio. Her husband is blind. Apart from French, he speaks both English and German faultlessly. It is an exquisite experience to spend the afternoon in lively conversation with my blind host. You can leave out all gestures and facial expressions; you are left with the voice and pure words. Within an hour we are friends. He stands up to feel my hair, my size and my hands. His wife is busy in the kitchen and pours out a glass of port for both of us. When we have emptied it I say: "Can I pour you out another?" He says: "Sssst", puts one finger on his lips and points the other to the kitchen. Like sworn conspirators, we secretly drink another couple of glasses; it is as if we have known each other for years. The next morning he is up at 5.00 to bid me goodbye. I promise him that when I have returned home I will send him a Braille copy of Rilke's poem we have been discussing:

Es gibt im Grunde nur Gebete:
so sind die Haende uns geweiht
dass sie nichts schufen, was nicht flehte,
ob einer malte oder maehte.
Schon aus dem Ringen der Geraete
entfaltete sich Frommigkeit.

Deep, quite deep down we just adore:
our hands have been ordained this way
that all the things they make, implore;
whether one plants, whether one gleans.
The very clanking of machines
turns into ringing piety.

When you walk on mountain roads in the deep darkness before dawn you may expect amusing surprises. The headlights of the rare cars produce entertaining light effects. First you see the lamps as very distant sharp spots of light moving quite fast; then light-beams like those of searchlights swing through the far off valleys; a little later again you see illumined houses and trees; at last a growling monster explodes in a blast of blinding light; and inside that monster there must be human life. From these light effects you can also detect where the road is going. In the pitch dark, I prefer to walk on a road like this, rather than stumble over an invisible footpath. I pass through Gap, Briançon, resounding names; till now I only knew them from newspaper reports about the Tour de France and from history books.

The fascinating character of movement is seen so clearly in the mountains. Because you yourself move, all the mountains and the valleys move along with you. Movement itself is food for satisfaction. Movement is an ingredient of so many forms of basic joy. Pleasant experiences are almost always activities: eating, drinking, looking, activities that make you move. If you see contemporary people kissing in modern films they are not any longer glued together in congealed ecstasy; no, they go on grazing. Even sitting together quietly and motionlessly is enjoyable owing to the barely audible sounds and minimal movements and short glances and open ears that register all this.

People who attribute primacy of importance to standing still have never managed to make eternal life in heaven attractive; they describe it as "beatific vision", something reminiscent of perpetual adoration. The ordinary folk understood it much better; the old Dutch song has it: "There is a big dance in heaven, alleluia; And all the sweet virgins are dancing, alleluia, Benedicamus Domino, alleluia!"

The real mountains are starting now. The varying thermal air currents make adventurous aviation possible. Birds make use of them and humans too. Gliders, emaciated little airships, suffering from anorexia, try to flit as closely as possible past the sheer mountain cliffs; they will be eyeing each other sharply to see if anybody has found an upward air current. After a couple of hours I pass by an airdrome, the nest of these birds. On the ground, gliders are still more helpless than swallows: they are lying down pathetically, one wing on the ground, the other wing held rigidly in the air. When they have to move they need the helping hand of a sympathetic terrestrian who will cautiously and tenderly hold their wing. Tiny super-lights are whirring to and fro. Whirring? An awful racket, that is what they are making. In pictures, they look so endearing: Icarusses that want to ascend into the sun and the clouds on a lawnmower and end up dangling in a pear tree. But their raucous din turns them into brash rascals. Taking everything into consideration humans have overcome their evolutionary handicap of not being able to fly in an utterly convincing way.

When Mother Nature designs new models she often goes back to old solutions. When she was testing the advantages of walking on two feet, she had several earlier experiments at her disposal. She had gained a lot of experience with the tyrannosauruses; with them the front limbs had withered away pitifully. In the case of kangaroos and some birds she had found out that bipeds could propel themselves by two-footed leaps. I think we should be grateful to Mother Nature that she did not integrate kangaroo-jumping into the human scheme of moving; and that could easily have happened. That would have been a sight to behold.

Rain will not easily stop me from walking. At Briançon the rain varnishes all the fortifications to a shining black. The fortresses have been laid out in such a way that they cover one another with their fire. They are impregnable as long as nobody comes around with more powerful guns.

And look, there is the first really high mountain! In the lukewarm rain, I stare up breathlessly at the four levels of traffic. I climb rhythmically, calmly, purposefully. I encourage myself by pointing out to myself that I am doing very well. Steadily on I go, not forcing myself. Cars are labouring around me in an endless procession but their snarling noise does not affect me:

> "The very clanking of machines
> turns into ringing piety."

My tempo is unhurried and regular – and never mind the splashes of the cars. A very slow English car sports a paper in the rear window saying: "Sorry, this is as fast as I can go". On reaching the top I reward my steaming self with a huge plate of spaghetti; I have arrived at Montgenèvre, the town on the frontier with Italy.

The doctor is sitting in her office waiting for me: the assistant priest of Briançon has alerted her. "Of course you can stay with me. I happen to be an atheist but you are welcome to stay for the whole weekend. And I shall make sure that the parish priest on the other side of the border will help you on." She gives me a whole storey of her house. Together we make a preliminary crossing of the border to see people of the Automobile Association of Clavière, who generously book a hotel room for me in my next place and add 400 francs for pocket money; and the parish priest will send a telephone message to the abbey further on.

After the weekend, I officially enter Italy near Clavière in the early morning. The first person I meet I greet in my most elegant Italian. It is an old lady; she studies me intently, and asks: "Are you looking for mushrooms, sir?" The abbey of Novalesa, two days later, is a lot less helpful than the atheist lady. Here, too, the front door has been equipped with one of those cursed little grids containing a tin robot set in such a way that it chases people away. "Yes, we know that that parish priest has phoned but we made it quite clear to him that we had no room here." At long last they relent and give me a room. On the table lies a booklet with the Rules of Saint-Benedict. One of the rules states that visitors are such important persons that they have to eat in the refectory next to the abbot. A special guest-master should be appointed for them, an older man who knows how to deal with people; only in cases of emergency should they give this task to a younger man. That old enthusiasm has cooled down. Next to the booklet, I find a piece of paper, leaving special space for remarks. With phrases of stern eloquence I take revenge on the nasty little grill of the front door. It will be very difficult to make this stagnant abbey flow again.

Walking in the mountains makes you experience space in a new way: it gives the movement the added dimension of high and low. In the abbey, life has come to a standstill; a landscape with high and low areas enlivens movement. These phenomena are invitations to reflect more on the question of standing still and moving. This old question, starting in antiquity with Parmenides and Heraclitus, regains momentum with Bergson, in combination with the modern idea of evolution and – surprise, surprise – renewed interest in the divine (is He coming back?).

Bergson suggests we see reality as drive, as vital force; what we call matter is a sediment, a coagulation of this life stream. Life is future, matter is past. Life implies: relations; matter implies: structures. Instinct and intuition are our hot line with impetuous life; reason and memory give us a grip on the world of things. Whoever lives in the world of life, lives in an open-ended community; whoever lives in the world of things, lives in a closed world.

The human person is being pulled this way and that. By natural descent he comes from the closed world of (animals and) things; but by destiny he moves into the limitless world of humanity. As for his religion, there too a twofold position is possible: he can settle for a vital, open religion; or he settles for a static closed religion. An authentic human person is not static; he all the time breaks his mould, he tries to transgress his limits, he reaches out to a point lying outside his borders. He wants to transcend his limits. His centre of gravity lies outside himself but even when he reflects seriously on any other topic he finds himself transcending the factual borderlines of that object as he assesses the possibilities it contains. Thus, transcendence is a vital part of his constitution. When you think really deeply you feel that you want to cross the borderlines of your own reason even.

Bergson is pretty sure that a static religion is a defence organisation of the powerful to keep the human person safely under control within the enclosure of his reason.

Bergson had Jewish blood; he felt strongly attracted to the Catholic Church. But in a gesture of solidarity during the Second World War, he decided to stay with his people and share their fate.

Novalesa is an old abbey; it goes back to the year 700 AD and was founded by the Franks on what was then the route across the Alps. In the days of

222

Charlemain (768-814), monks were under imperial authority to such an extent that every man who wanted to be a monk could only do so with permission from the authorities. Around the year 850 there were some 500 monks at Novalesa; a garrison? It was in any case a safe harbour for pilgrims on their way to Rome. There are still a handful of monks left, and their future is uncertain.

The day of Mount Cenis has dawned! Just when I leave the abbey the clock strikes 6.00 and a few minutes later it does so again. There is something very special about the clock striking the same hour twice: it suggests that time is standing still for a moment. In the twilight of dawn my eye scans the mountain wall in front of me and my hearts begins to throb faster: do I have to get up there? A cloud plays at being an artificial moon; the sun, still below the horizon, is already shining on the cloud above me and lays mauve and ruby hues over the landscape. Slowly, the winding path climbs higher and higher; it is the path over which the potentates of this world used to pass in ages long ago with their people, their animals and their carts; how on earth did they manage! In some places the old pavement can still be seen: flat stones put together on their side. In order that the pilgrim may reconcile himself to his slow progress, God has made an abundance of raspberries grow by the wayside. Higher, ever higher, till well over the 2,000-metre mark, where the air is cold and effervescent. After the sauna-like heat of the coast, I now taste a crisp chill and feel the air entering my mouth like liquid ice. Right at the top I enter France once again.

Bergson likes to tease us with some of his wisdom. He suggests that thanks to the intellect we are in fact able to forget knowledge. It happens this way. With our senses, we constantly gather immense amounts of information. If all those perceptions would enter into our mind, they would drown us. A few of them only have to be selected to be passed on to our minds drop by drop for further assimilation. All other data are refused entry by the intellect and relegated to the refuse bin of subliminal memory.

In this, the intellect resembles the carburettor of a car: the carburettor makes sure that the mass of petrol contained in the tank is kept out of the combustion chamber and admitted only in tiny drops. If the carburettor does not work well the engine gets flooded.

Titanic mountains surround me on all sides; it is a shame to ignore them and walk on.

Majestic vista and gigantic masses easily give a cosmic dimension to one's thoughts. I am not surprised that in days of yore people thought they would be able to reach God via mountain tops: El Shaddai, the God of heights. Our God was one storey higher still: in heaven. Eventually that appeared to be an uninhabitable place for Him and so He was told to clear out. That posed a problem for people rather than for God. For God's habitat was supposed to be their final home. Thus many Western people felt they had become displaced persons, spiritually speaking.

Teilhard de Chardin supplied those Christians with what they were sorely in need of: a world of new religious images. As a child, he was already a religious eccentric. To him, iron was the best symbol of God: unshakeably firm, unassailable. His first crisis of faith erupted when he discovered that iron could rust and that you could make scratches in it. Since then he constructed ever more awe-inspiring and complicated images. He could clearly see that all things were connected coherently; and that in the course of time an evolution took place in the direction of personality in the perspective of some divine dimension. He did not propose the fruits of his thoughts as a theory or a doctrine but as a synthesis of images. In this synthesis, the data of evolutionary science could be reconciled to the mysteries of religion. In this way, philosophical notions of God could be brought in alignment with Christianity. His cosmos is a prodigious organism granulating into small particles on the inside that form ever more surprising combinations and surrounding itself with spheres: a biosphere of life and a noosphere of awareness; in the end it will be taken up into a megasynthesis with a suprapersonal character.

Teilhard was an astonishing gift from God to His church; but church leaders were not happy with it. They forbade Teilhard to propagate his ideas.

High on Mont Cenis there is a big reservoir; at a vantage point, they have built a neat glass veranda. On the floor I find a pair of dirty underpants, next to them a torn map of the Benelux countries lying in such a way that one expects a heap of faeces under it; on a glass showcase there are lumps of cheese and a soiled shirt. Those that do such things, what kind of people are they? And why do they do it? It beats me completely. The contrast with unspoiled nature is all the bigger. Above me, the freshly fallen feathery snow lies on the mountainous rocks, like powdered sugar on a dish of doughnuts. Under me, the clouds cast large violet shadows on the lake, turning the rest of the water emerald green. Marmots shuffle over the rocks like junior sea lions or stand on their hind legs like small bears, giving out a loud squeak. Shivering in their anoraks, tourists take photographs and wonder how long they will be able to survive outside the warm cocoons of their cars; within minutes, they break off their space walk and tumble back into their crafts.

My path goes down to 1,400 metres and then up again to 1,700. I arrive after a 12-hour walk. Tomorrow I will have to face the Col d'Iseran, 2,770 metres high. I am surprised at not being tired really but what worries me is that I am quite dizzy, even as I am lying in bed. Am I asking too much from myself? Is my blood pressure too high? There is nobody to consult.

This is indeed not a landscape to tire you out; its openness fills you with deep awe and emotions; it has as many shapes as a Beethoven symphony. The loneliness on the other hand is intense. It can happen that I do not talk with anybody for days on end, except for the occasional "bonjour". And the only person to consult is me myself.

During my march I have developed a new feeling: body time. This implies that I feel my own personal speed when I walk and the awareness that I pass through amazingly vast tracts of space. I also feel my journey to be something quite different from the big organised long distance marches like the Four Days' March of Nijmegen. Twice I took part in those, in the days that we still had to walk 55 kilometres per day. As a challenge it was quite good fun. But it did not do justice to the deep joy of walking. Often you allowed yourself to float along with the crowd, a little brain-dead, and to kill the time you sang the same senseless texts a hundred times over and more – for instance, the Dutch popular ditty "En dattewe toffe jongens zijn". It translated into something like: "Tough lads we are, we know it jolly well; and so we come everywhere, everywhere, everywhere, and where the girls are we have a ball". I wonder if it is still sung these days. In the minor seminary, in 1943, we sang it in cripple Greek. Even now I can remember the text: *Hèmas neaniai boulometha gignooskein, ara hèkomen, pantachou, hou hai philai eisin estin ball* (we could not find the Greek word for 'ball'). We once sang it in the presence of the rector; he listened to it with his head cocked sideways and one eye closed; and when it was finished, he did not praise us for our proficiency in Greek but sternly forbade us ever to sing it again because it mentioned something as vain as girls. And that was not fitting for future priests. I was 14 then.

The next morning I start off at 5.00, with unsteady feet and a shade of apprehension in my heart. The slow climb of a thousand metres has a bracing effect on me. In our geography classes about high mountains, we used to learn about the foliage tree line, the pine tree line and the snow line. I have discovered that there is also a tourist line; it lies at 2,000 metres: below that line you find ordinary people, above it all turn into tourists. I pass it today as I walk from Bessance (1,720 m) over the Col d'Iseran (2,770 m) to Val d'Isère (1,840 m). At the height of 1,990 metres, some workmen repair the tarmac. They are getting uncertain and begin to show tourist traits: one of them is taking a snapshot of a white gazelle standing on a rock just above the tourists' line. At exactly 2,000 metres there is a half-hearted farm; a number of cows wander around aimlessly; a confused farmer in his jeep is looking undecidedly for work in the savagely cold fields full of rough tough grass. A little higher, platoons of gaudy motorcyclists are haring round excitedly. Again a little higher and I plough through the snow. Fathers and mothers take snapshots of shivering toddlers with snowballs. A lightly clad walker in short sleeves is like a spectacular optical illusion in these surroundings. A little farther down I get the opportunity of observing paragliders at very close range. After they have put their flying gear on the ground with meticulous care and after they have strapped on their helmets and their instruments and after they themselves have become part of their own outfit, they rise up holding their delta-shaped wing when they feel a promising draught of air, and they wait till the wind is strong enough. As soon as that appears to be the case they break into a trot not very different from that of a pole vaulter, approaching the abyss with long steps; and then they lift themselves on to their seat the way a child gets into the seat of a swing. Some remain airborne for just a few minutes; it seems rather a waste of trouble and of expensive goods. But they do have an unusual topic to talk about. I am surprised not to see any women at it. Would it not be in their line?

The separation of humans into men and women is bound to lead to specific male behaviour and specific female behaviour. It is not at all surprising really. After sexual intercourse has taken place and fertilisation is achieved, the male will not be bothered by the limitations that pregnancy puts on a person. That is why he can afford to behave much more recklessly and even irresponsibly in sexual activities. It is the female that gets overwhelmed by pregnancy. So it is advisable for her to be a little more circumspect and careful. These two different attitudes can make the game of sex all the more thrilling. Modern anticonceptiva have thoroughly disturbed these factors, because the female can reduce the risk of pregnancy to almost zero. This allows the woman to be just as reckless and even irresponsible in sexual matters as a man. Now, do we have to call this progress or not? It is not at all clear to me.

My seven-month-long sojourn in nature has bolstered my conviction that it is better to consider creation to be fundamentally female: the basic pattern of reality is female. The male has been derived from the female. The human body supplies evidence for that. The male has breasts simply because these belong to the basic pattern. The ordinary chromosomes are female, and to get a male individual a deviant chromosome has to be added. We feel that it is quite in order to call nature Mother Nature; the same with Mother Earth. Plants become pregnant with fruits. Beauty is a normal and self-evident ingredient of reality, as it is with women.

Violence is derived from inanimate things; seduction belongs to living things. When Mother Nature had tested the possibilities of living seduction, she thought it might be interesting to have some old-fashioned violence available as well and so she designed the male. When Mother Nature had seen the efficacy of curved lines, she thought it might be interesting to have some straight lines available for use and so she designed the male. At that moment logical reason was born and aggressive science. This does not mean that without the male all technique would have been impossible: from the anthill and the beehive we can learn that female technique is quite possible.

I would not mind trying paragliding; but you cannot afford to do everything. Long ago I was offered a chance to make a series of parachute jumps. I would have loved to accept it just to experience it. But I was training for my first pilgrimage to Compostela and I was afraid I might hurt my ankle; so I waived the offer.

If you take reality to be female and the male to be a derivate of the female, then you will arrive at a rather female God sooner or later. Before we can move around in that kind of perspective, we must try to get a better grasp of the essential contours of the divine.

Martin Buber put God into a new focus. He started off by saying that certain fundamental terms belong to the very constitution of humanity. These words do not just "mean" something, they "create a situation". Examples of such fundamental terms are: I-You and I-It. Through these terms, the human person positions himself as facing a "you" or as standing next to a thing. There is a very peculiar difference between a "you" and a thing: as things all beings border on one another; but a "you" has no borderlines. When a human person reacts to the presence of a "you" he does so by being spirit; he reacts to the presence of things with his reason giving rise to structures. The human person really commits a very grave mistake if he hands himself over totally to the supremacy of the things. If, on the other hand, I turn to the "you", structures begin to crack up. Towards other persons, I establish a relation.

Buber was a pious Jewish man. He considered God to be the living heart of the human community. The divine is the mysterious urge stirring us from within.

Buber's ideas come as a breath of fresh air to those that would like to give God a proper place in their lives; especially when they have seen their God die on account of inadequate proof of his existence. Now it does not matter any more that God has an invalid document of legitimation.

My last lap in France is from Val d'Isère to Rosière. In the early morning fog, I pass through innumerable small tunnels alongside a mirror-smooth lake. Then there is a big town in a deep valley in the distance. There are small church towers on high mountains, followed by more church towers on still higher mountains, and above those, a number of tiny high buildings on a far horizon, and that is where I have to be. It is not really a tremendous undertaking provided you are in the right mood, have time and a fair condition. In Le Plein Soleil, I reach out to my last gourmet dinner in France: the chef comes up with lasagne of fish with rice. I find this a deplorable combination of types of food that do not go together.

When things do not link up with each other, we get thoroughly confused. Deep inside us, we cherish the conviction that all things fit on to one another: the Principle of Continuity.

Also in the world of thought, the new has to find a connection with the old. Sometimes that is hard: the new ideas are there but it is very difficult to bring them into alignment with the established patterns of thought. A disturbing example is Simone Weil. She recognises our common world in the way we do: a world of living relations and established structures. She sees how the structures form a far-reaching web of necessities. The relations, on the other hand, are like lines of energy linked to the overwhelming absolute good outside us: they attract us like a magnet to the Divine. We are in fact much bigger than we believe ourselves to be. Buber feels the magnetism of the living centre; Simone Weil is under the spell of the great reality outside: she articulates human desire for full divine goodness. She is utterly on the side of the oppressed and joins them. Her spirituality is through and through religious. But she cannot take the final step towards Christian baptism. She is intimidated by the unbending structures of the church; these structures have blinded even saints in the past to such an extent that they saw nothing wrong in the Crusades and the Inquisition. She has a name for the world of established structures: she calls it the domain of the Prince of Darkness. She thinks that the church does not have the right to restrict the workings of the mind; does not even have the right to provide the mysteries of faith with binding commentaries; does not have the right to resort to intimidation to make people accept these commentaries. She decides to live in solidarity with those who are outside the church and stay outside as well; but at the same time, she wants to work as an under-cover agent in enemy territory. During the war she does not live in her native occupied France, she stays in London. But in solidarity with her suffering compatriots she voluntarily starves herself to death.

On the last day of August in the early morning frostiness I pass by a smoking car wreck left by a drunk driver, cross the Small Saint-Bernard, greet the big statue of the saint, stop for a moment to cast a shivering glance at the garden of Alpine herbs, leave the month of August and enter Italy.

THE EIGHTH MONTH

SEPTEMBER

Whoever is 68 years of age and goes on foot over the Alpine passes knows that he is no small fry: the towering mountains and the unfathomable valleys make you big. Having crossed the Col de Montgenèvre (1,850 m), the Col du Mont Cenis (2,081 m), the Col d'Iseran (2,770 m) and the Small Saint-Bernard (2,188), I now have to get ready for the Great Saint-Bernard (2,469 m), then I will go through the Rhône valley to the Furka pass (2,431 m) and finally reach the Rhine valley via the Oberalp pass (2,064 m); thus I cross Switzerland diagonally. The first day of September finds me in Italy, even though the region does not feel like Italy. It is called Valdoste and the people hardly consider themselves to be Italians. Everything is so dignified; even the light of a radiant Sunday morning has been checked for impurities, I am sure. At Saint-Didier, there is a Concourse d'Élégance of vintage cars, all of them spotlessly polished. At midday, I eat a fine meal of spaghetti in a beautifully-appointed restaurant at La Salle. Next to me a family settles down with a weak old father, clearly terminally ill. His face is like white alabaster; it is touching to observe how they all do their best to give the old man a pleasant Sunday afternoon. You can see that he has pain. He continually searches for the rare body positions and movements that are still free of discomfort.

Pain is something remarkable. Pain occurs in layers. Not long ago somebody had a headache; then she scalded her finger with hot water, which gave her a lot of pain; but the headache was gone. If the pain in the finger would go instantaneously, I am sure the headache would be back. If the headache were to cease suddenly, it is quite possible that stomach ache would appear underneath. We are towers of pain.

Would the same be the case with joy? And with urges and desires? Sometimes I think that when heterosexuality is taken away, homosexuality is to be found underneath; if the latter would be neutralised, then SM could well be found to lie underneath. And so on.

Are we also towers of emotions?

In my small hotel at Arvier I meet a couple of German motorcyclists. I have seen squadrons of them on armour-plated machines screaming through hairpin bends with much bravura, both in the Alps and in the Pyrenees. Even this morning I saw one that had banged into a Mercedes Benz; not very serious, just enough to make you say aloud: You see? Inside the hotel, they turn out to be most delightful persons. Aosta is a self-assured aristocratic city; it makes you think of dukes and the kings of Savoy. It is strange that people from such an outlying part of Italy managed to gain possession of the throne and were ardent nationalists. It is an old Roman town; its name was originally Augusta. The lady of the Tourist Office offers me an apartment; this suits me well, for I want to insert an extra day of rest. The place is homely. The neighbours downstairs send me a message: would I please come down and talk with them. That is, in point of fact, even more interesting than viewing another amphitheatre in ruins. My command of Italian is very deficient but the people are so inquisitive and so warm-hearted that understanding comes by shortcuts; and yes, that is Italy all right.

Tarmac roads are often more merciful than footpaths when you have to climb: the incline is not so steep. My longest climb takes place on the 4th September: starting from Aosta at 583 metres, I reach the Great Saint-Bernard at 2,469 metres. I start in the dark and it is raining when I try to select the correct gear for climbing. When I reach the first villages the drizzle stops, leaving me in the mist. Then I very slowly climb up out of the mist: can anybody think of anything more beautiful? The Michelin map promises me a restaurant at Saint-Rhémy but it is closed. I am quite happy with that, for it is only 11.00. Next to me, an autostrada lifts itself up on concrete stilts, passes under a long concrete vault before disappearing completely into the mountainside. I follow the old road, winding its way through dense forests; it is clear that we are approaching the frontier, for in many places you can spy casemates squatting in the foliage. It is a day of many smells: the smell of a rainy town before dawn, of a wet street between mossy walls, of a village waking up, of mist, of sunshine on damp grass, of leafy trees, of fir trees, of icy meadows, of cars, of houses, of people.

It is a shame that we do so little with our noses. Smelling could be such a powerful sense. The memory of odours you once sniffed can be well-nigh ineradicable. Even now I can remember the smell of the warm milk I had to drink in the hospital when I was three years of age. And who can ever forget the cloying sweet smell of English cigarettes at the end of the War: Wild Woodbine, Players and Sweet Caporal? Or the harsher smell of the American Lucky Strikes? Small babies smell their mothers to their deep enjoyment. But very soon after that tender age activities with the nose are discouraged if not disqualified. People that have a smell are said to stink. You are allowed to look at other persons, hear them, even feel them, but you are absolutely not allowed to smell them. In matter of sexuality, like in a last bastion, the sense of smell retains its seductive power. This can even be noted with children between four and ten, who are still somehow sexless: they have a neutral smell, like cats and dogs.

A few kilometres from the top, an enterprising couple has transformed a small fortification into a cafeteria where you can eat an improbably large plateau of sausage and cheese. At 3.00 in the afternoon I cross an ever higher skyline for the last time; and there the day's denouement is revealed: cold souvenir kiosks, the cold Italian frontier post, the cold Swiss frontier post, a cold lake, the cold hospice and a small inn for two bottles of cold beer. To be quite honest, I feel as proud as a peacock at having achieved the impossible.

With some people, achieving is a bad word nowadays. Nevertheless, I firmly believe in it. It makes life momentous. A person's life is more than the sum total of good and bad deeds. I think it is more fitting to measure someone's life by its summits, epic moments that overshadow the dullness of daily routine. Does anybody really care if Rembrandt was sexually very active? Did Beethoven have smelly feet? "Nobody is an emperor for his own servant." Who was the one who said that? You should not want to know trivialities, even if they do have some influence on life. Napoleon had a lot of trouble with haemorrhoids at the Battle of Waterloo. Too bad. For all we know van Gogh made such incredibly beautiful paintings because he had a frustrated love life. Perhaps Judas had been a spoiled child, always getting his way. Adolf Hitler, by the way, was a vegetarian and non-smoker and he loved cream cakes. Irrelevant nullities.

It would be nice if everybody would excel in one or other way: that would be good for a person's ego. True size does not come from trivialities but from inspiration and courage and long-burning passion.

On this mountain, I meet other pilgrims whose path I cross. They are people who pioneer a new route, pregnant with symbolism: a walk from Canterbury to Rome. They invite me to join them next time. Well, I don't want to think of another pilgrimage whilst I am still on this unfinished one. On the pass of the Great Saint-Bernard the Augustinian monks have their famous old hospice with the giant Saint-Bernard dogs. Until quite recently the monks would go out every evening before nightfall to look for straggling travellers. Often this was a risky task; the names of the many monks who perished on these errands are inscribed on the walls of the hospice. Another famous traveller who slept there was Napoleon; his visit is commemorated by a pompous marble tableau. Presently, the hospice is a place where adventurous God-seekers can spend time in mountain meditation. To go from the Great Saint-Bernard down to earth is an exercise in majesty: like a king, you descend from your throne to enter Switzerland. The scenery is so magnificent that one goes to the lower regions with feelings of regret. The people look serious and solemn; they all are Swiss and they all are very different. The jovial parish priest of Orsières is a monk from the hospice on the high pass. At Martigny, Archbishop Lefêbvre died, the cross-grained conservative rebel. Saillon, situated on a hill with an almost vertical ascent, has a Spanish priest: excellent for a Compostela pilgrim. The parish priest of Sierre is so busy that he comes home at two in the night but gives me the freedom of his house nevertheless. And when things are closed on a Sunday, they are well and truly closed. I was excited to go and see all this and I am not disappointed.

Before I started this journey, I acquired detailed maps of this area and stared at them for hours trying to conjure up an image of the region. When you do that, then an imagined representation begins to grow in your mind. This can lead to something odd. When eventually you walk through the region in actual fact, you see what it is really like; but soon you forget it and the old imagined representation comes to the surface again. And after some time you do not know any more which of the two is the real picture.

This area is the heart of Europe and it is riddled with borders. In a matter of days I go from France to Italy, back to France, back to Italy, through Switzerland, through Liechtenstein, through Austria, into Germany. Languages, too, abound within a very small space: Italian, French, Swiss-German, Rhaeto-Romanic and normal German. Even the water has its international borders here. Until the Furka pass watershed, all water flows to the Mediterranean; north of the Furka pass, the water goes to the North Sea. The separation between the two continental water systems is a road of four metres wide. Just north of the Austrian border, there is another watershed, between the North Sea and the Black Sea.

Switzerland is a unique country in several ways. It is small, it has no political clout and yet it is the home of global bodies: the Red Cross, the League of Nations. Everybody finds the funny canton system intriguing but nobody adopts it. It is a country of chocolate, watches and yodelling farmers, and it wallows in money.

Switzerland is an oasis of unreal rest in the heart of a nervous and stressed Europe. It is full of people who must spend their working hours counting money, and making cuckoo clocks for recreation. The upheavals of our century have passed this country by completely. And there have been some upheavals: world wars, revolutions and campaigns of apocalyptic rectifiers of the human world.

The 20th century catastrophes were a sign that Western humanity was not going into the right direction, as the efforts of Marxists and socialists were propagated drastically. These seemed to have an inherent flaw, in that they put some preordained destiny at the root of all development; that meant the death-knell for the sovereign person. Some other rectifiers followed in their wake, like the fascists with their principle of canonised authority; again, this left no living space for the human person. The failure of these systems constituted a warning that it was time to thoroughly reassess the meaning of human existence.

People remembered Kierkegard's warning that our search for meaningful human life had to take place in the realm of actual existence, not in the realm of abstract essences. This is what some new thinkers tried to do and so they were aptly called Existentialists. The Existentialist movement anchors our personal being in the experienced reality of universal concrete being.

Switzerland might well be a big country. When you see it on the map, it is very small but it resembles a ball of crumpled-up paper: if you would flatten out all the mountains you may well get something the size of France. In Switzerland, one is struck by the absence of war memorial monuments. There are memorials, but rather for a film star who has been living somewhere or for the jubilee of a brass band. Blessed is the land that has no history. When

I discover a war monument at long last, it appears to be "for our heroes of AD 1419".

Switzerland is a very unusual country. There is still a lot we can learn from the Swiss. How tolerant they are in respect of differences among people! Take all those languages; it happened to me once when I was travelling though the country by train that I served as an interpreter between German-speaking and Italian-speaking Swiss. Sixteenth century Swiss soldiers, dedicated farmers' lads with pikes and halberds who could not be intimidated or cowed by anybody on earth, were reckoned to be the best soldiers in the world. According to some war historians, they have never been surpassed. Switzerland became a heavily fermenting reformation region centred around the city of Geneva and around the Frenchman Calvin living there. Adoration of potentates has always been very unusual in Switzerland. It is difficult to get to know the ruling president of the country unless you look him up in his farm or in his cheese shop.

At Fiesch tourist centre, I am the odd man out. The normal people there are holidaying youngsters who yell and fill the whole place with hullabaloo. Till 2.00 at night, the licentious squeals of boys and girls clatter from the windows of the building they have apparently taken over. The following morning I gather the fruits of my early start: those pests are not to be seen anywhere before 10.00. It is nippy, misty, wonderful.

It seems to me that we could well have interpreted the Gospel in such a way that the church would have become something like Switzerland. I am willing to believe that there are people who can prove that Switzerland is not possible. But at least it is far removed from the classic forms of statehood like an absolute monarchy or patriarchal aristocracy. I do not think that one is far wrong if one holds that the assembled bishops at the Second Vatican Council were determined to get the ship of the church away from those authoritarian shallows.

Once I get properly worked up about the state of the church, a lot of bile rises within me, especially because of the fact that we have lost so many sheep, and I feel we were forced into policies that made matters worse. The lost sheep themselves did not often get the impression that their departure gave our shepherds sleepless nights; these seemed to feel that the removal of the recalcitrant sheep was necessary to save traditional orthodoxy.

Help! As I walk on all by myself I cannot shake off the grim thoughts.

Orthodoxy seems such a deceptively simple thing. But I don't seem to be able to get it right. Would I be orthodox if I described the Gospel thus?

The Gospel is like a building with several floors and each floor has its own collection of texts. There is a top floor for the leadership; below that there is a special floor for the clergy; below that there is one for the religious; below that there is a floor for the faithful laity; and the bottom floor is for the wayward laity. It does not sound very orthodox to me. But sometimes in the past when I heard orthodoxy explained I got the impression that the full and unabbreviated Gospel texts were meant for the bishops only. For the clergy and the religious there was a limited collection of texts; the faithful laity have to be content with a still more restricted collection; as for the wayward laity, the texts have to be protected against them.

When I carry out little tests I remain in darkness. "This is my body, this is my blood, do this in commemoration of me": is that just for the apostles who were in the upper room? "Receive the Holy Spirit; whose sins you forgive, they are forgiven": is that only for the 12 apostles and their successors, the bishops? (Too bad for Thomas: he was not present, so was he from then on an invalid forgiver of sins?) "Whoever hears you, hears me": for the 12 only? "As the Father sent me so I am sending you": for the 12 only? "Go and proclaim the Gospel to all nations, teaching them to do everything I have taught you": for the apostles only and for the bishops therefore?

Reading the Gospel like that produces an awful caricature: the only truly completely genuine disciples of Jesus were the apostles and so the only truly complete Christians to whom the whole Gospel is applicable are the bishops. (Too bad for Paul: he missed all those ordinations by Jesus and so he was really an invalid bishop, together with all the bishops he himself ordained.) And thus all the lower Christians are diminished copies of the bishops. If some people propose this on the one hand whilst on the other hand it is so strongly at variance with the spirit of the Gospel, what is it that gives this interpretation its rather widespread respectability?

It is in fact an old philosophical scheme, known as a construction of reduced monads or modalities. At the top you find the perfect being, the Principal Monad. And below that you get a succession of ever more reduced editions of the highest being, built along the same lines with the same properties but made smaller and smaller. Thus the human being is a reduced God; an animal is a reduced human; a plant is a reduced animal. In the Middle Ages, they applied it to the gradation of the sexes, and hence the statement that a woman was a reduced male, "mas conditionatus".

According to that way of thinking, the bishop has and is everything in the church but shares some of his plenipotential properties with his subjects. The priests get a considerable dose; on that account they become rather complete and competent assistants of the bishop. Lay people get something from the bishop, too, but that comes to very little and so they can be no more than errand boys for the bishops. Lay people are important, especially outside the church "in the world"; inside the church they only have a token role to play. Who leaves the lay state was said to leave "the world"; when a priest is "reduced" to the lay state he returns to "the world", is "secularised".

This theory has been disqualified by the Second Vatican Council. But one comes across remnants of it all the time, in the form of customs, phrases in ancient prayers and rituals, overtones to disciplinary rules. These give many ordinary faithful the feeling that this is indeed the underlying scheme of things ecclesiastical.

The irony is that many leaders that smart under this evangelical caricature are themselves dedicated, zealous, competent and pious persons who worry very much about the state the church is in. But they have become immovably jammed in the centuries' old sedimental crusts and are at a loss how to get out of them.

Having said all that, I feel much relieved.

The Swiss do not feel that their country is small, for their next-door neighbour is Liechtenstein; and that truly is a small country, needing the help of the Swiss. I do get the impression that the Swiss are very much preoccupied with themselves; the result is that they turn their land into a Disneyland. Here we can still add a nice little tunnel, there we can have a small train, there we can have another mountain stream. The whole thing is never finished. And they have everything under perfect control, also inside the families. You still

see a lot of children going to church on Sunday with their parents. I attend a
yodelling Mass but even there the music is in proper four-four time, not just a
free and easy yudeldihee!!

Long ago, when the impregnable mountains were not yet
beautiful, say in the days of Erasmus, Switzerland was full
of ferment concentrated around Fribourg, Basle and Geneva.
Since the 17th century, the frightening Alpine colossuses
have become majestic and awe-inspiring. Ever since then the
Swiss have been utterly mesmerised by their exciting Alpine
summits, a landscape fixated in a permanent state of erection.
This gave them so much satisfaction that they felt no further
need to take part in cultural excesses; they were content with a
better type of mediocrity and with money. When I try to think
of a great Swiss artist, I cannot find any name, except for Paul
Klee. Until recently, people went to Switzerland in order to get
cured from pneumonia or to be one up over the neighbours,
not for intellectual adventures.

The Swiss I meet are invariably genial persons, helpful and showing a lot of
interest. They do not have the wilted sense of grandeur you may well find with
the English or the French; and they try to learn another person's language;
and they dislike fanaticism.

Did the words of the 20th century philosophical giants reach
here? There was Jaspers (1930 AD). He advised us to re-
orientate ourselves painstakingly in the midst of the myriad
beings all around us and thus gain a better insight into the
character of our life's journey. We have to wake up and rise
up from the numbing certainty of the obvious. One of the
things we will see then is the fact that our centre of gravity lies
outside ourselves. (That is also why we are said to ex-sist.) We
can only make progress by escaping from ourselves. When we
try to break away from a lower level and reach a higher level,
it is as if we have to go through a process of shipwreck. By
and by we discover that our religious representations are but
codes referring to something superior to ourselves, something
that may be found on a higher level but still belongs to our
philosophical world.

Heidegger (1930 AD) underlined the important role that
not-being plays in our lives. This negation distinguishes me
form other entities; it is the frame of my existence: I come

out of nothing, I go into nothing. I experience the edge of my nothingness in suffering and death. In the human person reality becomes incandescent; the human person lives inside the house of his language; in language existence becomes articulate.

Gabriel Marcel (1930 AD) stresses that human existence should be authentic. Once it is that, then our relationships will be authentic: full of availability, engagement, fidelity and love. Homo Viator, the human person on the way, tries to fight himself free from the bonds of "quantitative existence", a type of life where he wants to "have" everything, where he sees "problems" on many sides and where he forms "opinions" about other people. Once he reaches the level of "qualitative existence", he wants to "be" with everything, to fathom the "mysteries" of things and to have "Faith" in other people. We reach true authenticity when we begin to believe in a loving God.

At Gletsch, I take up my abode in a hotel where remnants of old-fashioned luxury reveal that this used to be an upper class gathering place. You could not call Gletsch a village: it is just an echo of the past. There is not much more than the hotel and a surrealistic small railway museum. Flashy cyclists in flamboyant costumes smooth as oil come falling out of the Grimsel pass like coloured signal flares; they drink a glass of lemonade on our veranda and shiver with cold. Right in front of our door the steep climb to the Rhône gletscher and the Furka pass begins.

Gloomy thoughts about the exercise of authority in the church keep bubbling up inside me like gas in a swamp. Is it the pure and towering mountain range, that brooks no compromise, that provokes these thoughts in me? The form of our present church government is the outcome of numerous practical compromises, made to get the best out of perplexing historical situations rather than the fulfilment of Gospel dreams. Step by step, these compromises have turned apostles into aristocrats, servants into princes. Today, not many people in the church feel happy about this; but how do you tackle the embarrassment efficiently and charitably?

Spurred on by the spirit of Vatican II, many people in the church nowadays think critically about the evolution of the bishops' and the priests' offices, to spot damaging excesses that may have found their way into the structures of these offices. In the beginning, bishops and priests were elected from the ranks of the leaders of the local church community and the faithful would choose persons who had shown themselves to be capable of good leadership by long service to the church community and good governance of their own families. The community invited them to accept the leadership charism and the whole of the universal church community would accept that choice, often through the approval of the bishop of Rome.

This sacred process has gone through major modulations until a procedure was reached that I myself have experienced with misgivings. In my day, an appeal went out to boys, usually mere children (we used to call teenagers "late vocations"), to opt for the priesthood. When our education had reached a sufficiently high intellectual and moral level, we were separated from our fellow faithful in order to be trained as an elite corps: sacred, cclibatc and obedient. When this training was complete, we were ordained to be elders (presbyteroi); few of us were 30 years of age by then. I myself was 24 (having started my training in effective isolation at the age of 12). Once ordained, we were put into a position of leadership by the bishop, mostly in a parish community where we were virtual strangers. From the beginning, the superiors kept an eye on us to see which of us would be candidates for higher, even Episcopal, dignity because of dedication, good behaviour, leadership capacities, devotion, reliability, orthodoxy and a good brain. Pretty soon, the episcopal candidates were taken out of their pastoral jobs to be trained in ecclesiastical sciences and put in a place where things have to be organised properly: a major seminary, a diocesan organisation, the bishop's office. Up till today, it is not rare that a young cleric is promoted to become a bishop even before he is 40 years of age. It is the pope himself who is supposed to choose all the bishops personally in secrecy, guided by the advice of the papal nuncio and also of the national college of bishops. This advice has no binding character and can be disregarded, as happens. The new bishop is put in any of the dioceses of his ecclesiastical province and can be shifted around after a number of years.

The good result of this comparatively novel method is that the church leaders form a body of superbly trained and objective officials; the involvement of the community, however, is next to nothing. Can one be surprised then that many people view the church now as a gigantic administrative body, a worldwide institution? They find it rather hard to recognise the family of Jesus in it still; consequently they leave the church in huge numbers.

Does it really have to be like that? Is there no alternative?

The weather is splendid and corresponds closely to the postcards available. I am not tempted to buy many of those but I want some of the Rhône gletscher I am passing now to be able to talk about it when I am back in Kenya. There is a very interesting photograph of a corridor they have excavated right inside that gletscher: mysterious emerald light filters through the many metres of ice. Andermatt is the established sanctuary of those that adore winter sports; it is teeming with moneychangers and traders, even outside the season. At this moment it is too late for summer holidays and too early for winter tourists. In many places in Switzerland the mountain sides are so steep that one becomes aware of the presence of space.

Usually we do not notice space at all; which is a pity because space can be a source of enjoyment. I can remember how strongly I was hit by the presence of space when I came home from the seminary long ago and noticed the big difference between the restricted room in our home and the cavernous spaces of the boarding institute to which I had grown used.

In architecture we are invited to appreciate space but that is almost the only example. Outdoors in nature you hardly notice space, unless a very distinct cloud cover hangs like a ceiling above the landscape. Once I had a wonderful experience of that in the Scottish valley of Glencoe, an oblong valley with a rounded floor. Heavy clouds covered it like a lid and to make it more impressive, a helicopter flew under the closed lid like a prehistoric dragonfly. Inside a forest, too, one may feel the space. In ordinary landscapes it does not happen often, except for the fascinating countryside of the eastern Netherlands where trees and farms are arranged like side-scenes or wings of a stage.

Inside a car you are bound to miss the feel of space. And, strangely enough, you miss the feel of speed as well. When you walk on foot you will one moment see a tree on the far-away horizon, and you say to yourself: "That is so far, I will never get there". Then, half an hour later you stand at the foot of the very tree; another half hour and you see it again very small on the horizon, this time behind you. And you wonder by yourself: did I walk that huge distance in this short time? There is also this: when you walk, the whole panorama shifts with every step you take. All these wonderful experiences are offered to those that dare to go on foot.

Many people cannot imagine that I prefer not to use mountain paths. That is first of all because as a pedestrian I want to go from A to B, and winding mountain paths are normally not the shortest distance between A and B. Besides, I have to be able to travel in all kinds of weather: Alpine paths can be dangerous in bad weather. Just these days, two Belgian walkers are killed because a snow squall caught them on a small path. And finally I have to remember that I am all by myself and that increases the risk.

In many spots you can see that the Ministry of Defence wants to hide something behind fences, under concrete covers, and on mountain tops where helicopters buzz to and fro. The military have the situation under perfect control: soldiers are sitting everywhere on terraces sipping lemonade. It reminds me of the Dutch army in 1939; Piet Lustenhouwer of the KRO-Boys' band used to honour them with songs of praise: "True, they are reasonable and kind / but you had better keep in mind / that they will fight the pirates' way / for our sweet Je Maintiendrai." Je Maintiendrai is the device of the Dutch royal standard.

1939: almost 60 years ago. The world has changed in so many ways and yet these immense mountains are the same today as then. Am I still the same person I was then?

Surely. My identity has remained the same and my character too; and even my internal landscape has remained the same broadly speaking. It has been mapped out better; it has been reconnoitred fairly fearlessly; it has been given more internal coherence; and it has linked up with the Gospel words in many more varied ways.

I am thoroughly convinced now that all Gospel texts are valid for everyone. The Holy Spirit has been given by God "as the first gift to all who believe, to complete Christ's work on earth" in the words of the IVth Eucharistic Prayer. Jesus was a prophet who brought the Good News, a shepherd who helped those that were in trouble and a high priest who prayed and sacrificed. And so all of us who are baptised and anointed with His Holy Spirit are appointed to be prophets, shepherds and high priests. We have to be prophets who turn their own lives into a parable of good news; shepherds who turn their own lives into a miracle of good news; priests who make their lives into a sacrifice of good news. And we do all that because in our baptism we have made an agreement with God. And this is the agreement: we take it upon ourselves to drive away the evil spirit wherever we can; and God from His side takes it upon Himself to fill everything with His good Spirit. That is the New Covenant. It is up to the bishops to assist us in these efforts.

Are there still serious people living in Switzerland? Or are they all mountain guides, ski instructors, yodellers and other folks trained to flatter foreigners? Or actors whose duty it is to supply folklore entertainment to tourists? Are there farmers? Don't make me laugh. Several times I saw groups of people dressed up as farmers slaving away on a piece of land the size of a quarter of a football field with a small potato cart; but surely they are not serious?

I have been walking now for ages. Autumn has come; a whole summer has passed me by on the road; I was already on the way when it was still winter. I can still see myself somewhere near Verdun sitting on a bench in the frozen sunlight and taking a bite out of a handful of snow to see how that tasted with a piece of bread.

After all these months my walking movement has become automatic.

If you consider it properly, you have to admit that walking is a wonderful invention. It took nature a long time to discover it. The most simple form of movement is to float along with the wind and the water. The art of walking required a very ingenious construction: limbs had to be fixed to the body and at the same time be loose from it. Nature's solution was: the joint. There was looseness in that two surfaces were merely sliding over one another, and these were fixed through bands. The next big improvement in movement was the wheel; the improvement lay in the fact that the gliding of the wheel over the surface of the axle continued endlessly, not with short jerks as with legs. An extremely beautiful refinement was ball-bearings: these eliminated practically all the friction inside the joint. Even though Mother Nature did not manage to provide our bodies with wheels and ball-bearings, still walking as such ought to be a source of profound satisfaction. I walk, therefore I am.

Saint James continues to provide me with good suggestions. On my last day in the high mountains it seemed a good idea to gain one day on my scheme by making a double distance. True enough, I crossed the last summit, the Oberalp pass, in golden everlasting sunshine on 12th September, and a day later the curtain of autumn came down there with snow and ice; cars overtook me with mattresses of snow covering them. In a small place called Sedrun I eat lunch in a rural inn. They have guests; their young daughters are allowed to help in the kitchen. We all eat together, the same meal, the only one available; excellent food. And when it is finished, it is finished. I find it most enjoyable.

Movement, as we perceive it, always has structure, measure. We experience this as rhythm. Surely our rhythm has been conditioned by what we experience in the very first phase of our lives. For nine months, our mother's heart was throbbing next to us continuously, as if we were living in a disco: a sweetly warm, rose-coloured soft and swinging disco. When our moment of birth arrived, and we were being squeezed through the narrow chute, we probably thought that we were being killed. Our overriding question was: is there life after birth?

That question was not answered in the affirmative straight away in my country of birth, for there we were stored away in a deathly cold and silent and motionless little room, and the bell of the front door was disconnected and the radio put on very softly. And when, in our despair, we thought we could hear some faint human voices in the distance and we started crying for help, our parents said: "Hush-hush! now you have woken up the baby!"

Is it a surprise, then, that we have nourished deep inside us a gnawing yearning for the ancient dancing rhythms of our early life? But in my childhood days we were not supposed to like that: it was something for primitive and uncultured children of nature who allowed sensual rhythms to carry them away into unbecoming states of ecstasy. All responsible people sternly disapproved of it. The rector of our minor seminary said in an unguarded moment that any boy who liked jazz was not a fitting candidate for the priesthood. The dignity and the power of the priesthood could not be reconciled with the levity of dancing. Nobody had ever heard of the ancient Celtic proverb "Never give a sword to one who cannot dance". (Had people taken that word to heart, there might not have been any Nazi concentration camps: who has ever seen Hitler dance, except for those ridiculous prancing goose-steps in front of the railway carriage at Compiègne when France surrendered.)

Counting the measure of movement leads to time; sharing measured movement leads to joining the rhythms, dancing. Measure, rhythm, harmony, that is where you have to look for the secret of good living and health according to the ancient thinker Pythagoras. In our days he is being listened to again and I feel in my very bones that he is right.

At Disentis, I find a small pension, a spotless room with a kindly old lady who likes a little chat but prefers sitting in front of the television above all other things.

In the early morning hours I walk through the dizzily falling spirals of "wet snow"; in Dutch we call falling snow "wet" when it melts on impact with the ground. The feathery flakes are dancing along with me.

I feel sure that dancing precedes walking. Even lifeless things dance: flames, dead leaves. I have often seen babies lying in the arms of their mothers and moving rhythmically along with sound. It is quite common in Kenya that a child, as yet unable to walk, dances standing, encouraged by the rhythmic clapping of smiling grown-ups.

In my memory I carry a striking picture I once saw from the altar of our church at Kisumu: in the doorway, far down the centre, I saw a little girl as a black silhouette, dancing to and fro, in very long clothes, shoes that were far too big, and on her head she had an artificial ponytail. At such a long distance, she looked like a miniature witch. Behind the back of the praying multitude she moved her hands and feet, dancing to the left and to the right to the music of the Gloria in Excelsis Deo and the Sanctus. I had a feeling that we all were singing it for her, or rather for the God who was dancing in her.

The wintry weather does not bother me: my outfit is adequate. I pause a little less and extend my stay in small restaurants to dry out, have a good meal and drink coffee with brandy. What does touch me is the attitude of people: are they friendly or morose? At Ilanz, all the hotels are closed for reconstruction and in the Tourist Office a surly girl spoils my humour. At Laax, one hour further, there is by way of contrast a completely different girl, full of charm and interest. Curiosity is really something very nice in people: it leads to questions and invitations to tell your story. Even the hotel she recommends to me shares her charm. Everything has been made from polished wood, everywhere little lights are burning; in the room next to mine a child is singing.

Dancing relates to walking the way singing relates to speaking. Dancing precedes walking, singing precedes speaking. Dancing does not mean that you are going anywhere; singing is no communication. When people are singing they do not know what to do with their eyes; they often do not know how to look at each other, they look vague or they keep their eyes closed. Even if they sing to somebody, it does not matter all that much whether he is there or not. And so you can sing to obscure things: an ode to freedom; an ode to the fatherland; an ode to a pickled herring. And so, in religious gatherings, singing is a very effective means of addressing the divine. As a form of human communication singing is negligible but it engenders a precious amount of euphoria. Singing is clearly pre-verbal, like sex and eating and drinking and love. And hatred. Language is something comparatively recent.

A holiday feeling overwhelms me; this is hardly avoidable in Switzerland. But it is there also because I have practically completed my pilgrim's programme. The last items were Avignon and the pass of the Great Saint-Bernard. The only holy place left is the grave of Saint Boniface at Fulda. Since I crossed the North Sea watershed on the Furka pass I feel I am flowing home swiftly.

The landscapes and the houses are, I notice, a feast of colours and space and smells; but hardly any music is to be heard on any particular walking day. We have not yet discovered many connections between the sounds in nature and music. The French composer Olivier Messiaen could be an interesting guide there.

You always have to be on your guard when making sounds: they can easily be rude. In a church it is rude to whistle; in the street you cannot sing loud. Sounds and music provoke comment instantaneously. Not so with colours: people do not bother much about those. Nobody is indicted for colour pollution. You can adorn your house with any kind of loud colour; but woe to you if you enhance it with music.

Colours can be objectionable, all the same. Say you go to a museum, to relish masterly paintings with delicately balanced colour compositions; and as you stand in ecstasy in front of one, behold, somebody in fatty yellow or poisonous violet clothes comes and stands next to it, completely ruining the masterpiece. How can they allow such a thing! Truly stern measures should be taken. Either they should make the visitors leave all their clothes at the entrance or they all should be made to put some neutral grey sackcloth over their attire.

The valleys are growing wider, the mountains are growing lower. Long-lasting showers of powdery snow reveal that autumn has definitely started. The evergreen pine forests are boring: they harbour no flowers, hardly any birds, no butterflies, and only two shades of green: young and old. The floor of a pine forest has no shrubs and bushes, just rubbishy dead brown branches. Friends of mine live near Chur; I am going to spend a weekend with them. And in Austria, too, friends are waiting for me: I will stay there for a whole week; the same will be the case at Fulda.

When I hear the names of Chur and Austria and Fulda I am reminded of church dramas caused by the appointments of bishops. I think that the root of the problems lay only partly in the particular persons that were made to do their Episcopal duty. What causes a lot of friction concerning bishops is the relationship the bishop is meant to have with the ordinary faithful: is he a ruler appointed by the pope? Should he be accepted by the faithful? Should he perhaps be selected by the faithful? Should he be chosen from the members of the diocese? Is he the top boss and the owner of the diocese? Is he the embodiment of the fullness of the Gospel? Is he just one of the members of the Mystical Body?

The pope has recently asked everybody to join in thinking about a renewed form of the Petrine office. I think a similar reassessment should be made of the Episcopal office, to see how the successors of the Galilean fishermen can be helped to shed their monarchical dignity, that hereditary handicap with which history has encumbered them.

Let us draw adventurous conclusions from the doctrine of the Mystical Body, in which each organ has its specific function rather than be a reduced reproduction of the head.

For adventurous thinking, one should dare to send one's thoughts into improbable directions; so let us try out some daunting propositions.

In theory, everybody professes to hold the doctrine of the Mystical Body but below the surface the theory of the Reduced Modalities still carries much weight.

Well now, is it not so that a bishop is normally supposed to consider himself as the Prophet of the diocese, as the Shepherd, as the Priest, from whom all other prophets, shepherds and priests receive their assignments? To me, this statement sounds like an echo of that awful doctrine of "reduced modalities". I speak as one less wise but I think even I can give an argument showing that it is impossible for a bishop to be a prophet. A prophet provokes, rocks the boat, and because he does that he makes it necessary for a bishop to be there to try and keep everybody together as a pontifex or bridge-builder. The situation becomes dangerous if a bishop sees himself as the big prophet and as the reconciler at the same time. For the one who has to keep the ship on an even keel is then supposed to rock the boat. Will he not be sorely tempted to use his authority to impose his vision? By doing so he seems to invalidate his prophecy. Is that not happening in our church today: have several prophets not been eliminated by force from above? And does St. Paul not presume that the functions of prophets and bishops better be separate and distinct parts of the Body?

Similarly, you can consider the extent to which the bishop should be seen as the shepherd par excellence. The good shepherd has to leave the 99 good sheep behind to go after the one lost sheep. There is no bishop who can afford to do this: the good sheep would never allow this. I have even known cases where bishops would not allow others to do this in their place. One has to concede that the shepherd function in the church is bigger than what a bishop can make of it.

This line of thought is even relevant to the priestly function. The priest is mediator between God and people through (Christ's) prayers and sacrifice. To be a proper go-between he has to be a familiar person to both parties, so that both parties, God and the ordinary people, can entrust their affairs to him in full confidence. But how many persons does a bishop know? When he exercises the priestly function he will unavoidably get stuck in the ritualistic and the impersonal. This would show that even the priestly function in the church is bigger than what a bishop can make of it.

The minimum I would conclude from these theological acrobatics is that the functions of the Prophet, the Shepherd and the Priest need the active involvement of all the church members in order that they may reach their full stature.

At Chur, my Swiss friends are waiting for me; I am ready for a nice weekend. It presents me with a minor culture shock: I have to adjust to the family programme and let go of my freebooter's agenda. I make my acquaintance with the local dish called Raklet: melted cheese and potatoes and sausages. They have arranged another treat for me: a car-trip to Appenzell. The Swiss make jokes about the Appenzellers the way the Dutch joke about the Belgians, the Americans about the Poles, the Germans about the East Friesians, the

English about the Irish, the Irish about the Kerry-men. To my surprise, I find two war memorials at Appenzell with names of those that fell in the two wars of 1914-1918 and 1939-1935. I cannot quite understand that, for Switzerland was not at war on those occasions. "At war" is a good expression, or "in war" as they say in other languages. In the south of France they likewise talk about a place being "in feast". I saw it announced somewhere: "Tomorrow this village will be in feast". In English we talk about being "in love"; that is very nice too.

In many European towns the Second World War has brought about a caesura in the architecture: many pre-war buildings have been destroyed by bombardments and only the ancient ones have been restored. Here in Switzerland nothing has been destroyed that way. (You can notice the same in Sweden.) This country has not known the dislocation and the despair that created the fertile environment for the post-war existentialist cult in other countries.

In neighbouring France, the intellectuals celebrated the futility of life. Sartre (1943) tried to make the absurd and the fundamental futility of human life acceptable by seeing them as part and parcel of the package of life we get thrown into our lap and by not objecting to them. This approach gave rise to stunning aphorisms. Man is condemned to freedom! Man dies into the bargain! Man is a useless passion! Hell, that is the others! Even if God existed, it would make no difference! Man has not invented himself yet! Man is a failed God! Terrific stuff to toss about but when everything is said and done you are not really much wiser. Today, there are not that many people talking about Sartre; remarkable, for in his own days he was all the rage.

Just before the Liechtenstein border the road passes through a bastion, manned by a small garrison. In the woods next to the road you hear thunderous bangs of exploding grenades, mixed with the rattle of machine guns; it strikes me as the sound equivalent of meatballs and peas. However, let the foes be warned: Switzerland is ready for them.

From the number plates of the cars parked next to the houses I can see that I have arrived in Liechtenstein, a country so small that everything is civilised. All the way through Liechtenstein I march on a sidewalk. Twenty kilometres, in and out, that is all.

And now Austria. That is a different piece of cake. Elections are on the way and all along the route the cold face of the suave but arrogant neo-Nazi is staring at me. I see a woman being interviewed on the television; she says: "It cannot possibly become worse than we have it now in this country". On an advertising pillar I read: "Anal sex by telephone: ring number 539-5203". We have left Lilliput land behind, we are back in the big wicked world. All the same, this land, too, is not without its fairy tales: there she stands on the village square, my black fairy Anjelina. She was one of our Team members at Kisumu; she fell in love with an Austrian stage student and went to Vorarlberg with him. It is a reunion which I have been anticipating for weeks with mounting excitement. African ladies rarely embrace you with abandon, for that is not part of their education, and they find it a bit embarrassing on a village square. But she looks so wonderful, so slender. Small wonder, for her husband is a marathon runner and in athletic solidarity she trains everyday to run ten kilometres; she has gathered several medals already. She is popular and that is what she deserves, for she is amiability itself. Otherwise she would probably have found it very difficult to secure her place here. According to African tradition they have adopted the young son of her late sister. There he is, a dark young boy, eight years of age, who has to learn German with leaden reluctance and who is being taught how to ski by his new father. The boy is lucky to have a new father who has the habit of reflecting seriously about everything and who has an answer to most questions. I make use of the occasion to find out from him why so many youngsters wear their cap backward-forwards nowadays. "Because," he says slowly, "having the peak to the back is 'cool' but having the peak to the front is 'shit'."

Six days later, my friends give me a smoked ham for the journey, weighing all of two kilos. Soon I appreciate it very much; right up till the end of the journey it supplies me with a daily handful of thin slices to be eaten during my short pauses. It rains as I depart and Anjelina walks with me for two hours. The rain is beautiful.

We have to re-learn that rain can be a source of enjoyment. We enjoyed it when we were small children. There is so much to see in the rain: the drops on the tip of each leaf; the string of liquid pearls on a clothes line; the silvery indoor-type of light outside; the shining surface of all things as if they had been newly varnished; the tarmac becoming brilliant black, with a yellow leaf here and there and a mirror here and there. We should recover the fun of feeling wet and not be afraid of it: as long as you keep warm nothing bad can happen to you.

Having arrived at the Bodensee I cross the German border – an empty customs office in the middle of a forest. Vegetatively, I have arrived home. I greet the birch trees by the roadside, the elderberry bushes, the nettles; the air is pregnant with the smell of manure and silo grass; and everywhere one sees farms that are married to the fields. The German landscape is tidy indeed,

250

clear-cut, vast and controlled, nowhere shabby. We Dutch people have a touch of that as well: when somebody is good-humoured we say that he is "tidy"; similarly in English we often use the word "neat" for agreeable. The war monuments start again; here they are for the lads who had to murder the lads on the French monuments, and vice versa. In many villages you even find monuments for soldiers fallen in the Franco-German war of 1871-1872. The modern monuments are painstakingly artistic and the depicted dead bodies are always aesthetically pleasing. Near Illertissen, I pass by a tree planted to commemorate the fact that peace had celebrated her 50th anniversary. Would the misery of war be reaching its end?

In all those horrifying years, religious faith has clearly been a significant support for families torn apart and for tormented individuals. Still, there is a nagging feeling of disappointment. In days gone by the church had so much more influence on human society; it is regrettable that the church, face to face with the cultural poison that led to these barbaric wars, did not manage to produce more antidotes to neutralise that poison and so limit the disaster.

What a pity, verily and truly, that the church did not manage to assimilate the works of Teilhard de Chardin, Newman, Marcel, Bergson, Buber and Simone Weil in time. These were trumps that God put at our disposal but the church was afraid to pick them up. They were vaccines of which the church did not dare to profit, scared rigid in a Neo-Scholastic cramp. Church people had been conditioned to have a blind spot for such novelties. These thinkers were the possible lifeboats for the passengers of the ecclesiastical Titanic, passengers that felt safe in their loyal conviction that their ship was unsinkable and that it would have been modernistic treason to make use of these boats. And that is why the majority of them ended up in the freezing cold waters.

The deciding factor was, I think, fear – fear of the unknown, fear of modernism. It makes people cling to accustomed certainty, even if all their sheep will perish. It makes them try and shackle that untidy Holy Spirit and control Him, otherwise you will never know where you will end up.

Fear is the perennial bane of conscientious people. Jesus had to admonish his friends all the time: Don't be so afraid, fear ye not. Being courageous means: facing up to your fear and staring it down; and then your healthy mind and your warm heart and your eager hands should take the initiative. It is our gospel duty to recognise our fear without giving in to it. God has decided to work with people who cannot boast of much power, who are vulnerable therefore.

An additional thought comes to mind, proposed by Hegel: fear of error is an error and on further inspection will prove to be fear of truth.

There is much consolation in the fact that many of the visions of the above-mentioned prophets have been incorporated into the texts of the Second Vatican Council; but they all have not yet been unpacked . They have seeped through into the works of the theologians and in attitudes of the laity, and they cause considerable consternation in the ranks of the authorities.

Just before reaching Leutkirch, I am given the benefit of eating a new recipe: fried maize with fried bacon. It is tasty but extremely heavy and, as we are in Germany, there is an awful lot of it on your plate.

Sometimes I apply a newly–learnt trick in my dealing with parish priests. I begin by taking a room in a hotel. Then I pay a visit to the parish priest and explain that I am a parish priest myself, in Africa of all places, and that I am making a pilgrimage on foot. I see him think: "Oh my, oh my, he is going to ask for a place for the night." (I know that reaction, for I feel it myself when strange priests come to my door.) Then I add that I have already booked a room in a hotel. Then he says (as I would have done): "What a pity, you could have spent the night here." And then at a later stage I pick up the thread again: "If you want to help me, could you then send a telephone message to the parish priests of the next three places to ask them if they can put me up." It almost always works.

I arrive at Memmingen, a town on the Romantic Route: doll-house architecture all through the town and folklore-filled prettiness and the matching Christmas card feeling.

The period of Romanticism of almost two centuries ago was a surprising phase of our culture. When during the Enlightenment the power of reason had been fully explored, the will and the emotions also had to be given a respectable place in the order of things; so people allowed their emotions to influence their approach to the world. The access roads to nature and history were not any longer lines of objective rational classic ideas; people were now touched on the inside. This constituted the basis for the romantic feeling that spread through the Western world at the end of the 18th century. People were overcome by "Weltschmerz", Cosmic Grief. They were profoundly touched by everything that is loveable and tragic in nature and in human intercourse, and they combined it with nostalgic and blissful memories.

There was merit in this. Traditionally, emotions were an embarrassment: to be moved, to cry, to give in to feelings; all this was childish stuff, unworthy of a seriously thinking person. It was said to belong to the fickle and unstable female world, to be considered gravely dangerous even. It brought you near to sexuality. When being trained in virtue and ascetics, we were warned that we should avoid bodily touching. Jesus had said to Mary Magdalene: "Noli me tangere" (do not touch me). This anti-touch phobia must have been damaging for the child inside us, for children love nothing better than being touched. Fortunately, the imbalance can be redressed now by a good dose of modern haptonomic treatment or caressing therapy.

My romantic euphoria cannot keep me away from a good Turkish restaurant. The boss is very happy to welcome a Dutch customer, for the Dutch are much superior to the Germans. The Dutch take proper delight in Turkish cuisine; all the Germans do is whinge and moan about the food: I don't like this, I don't like that. And so, what should he prepare now for "Seine Herrschaft"? I rise to the occasion: "Effendi, make for me the most delicious meal that you are capable of". I must admit, the meal is excellent; and nicely cheap all the same. After that, the boss takes great pride in showing me a perfect and inexpensive hotel. A Turkish hotel, of course. It's good. The two beds stand head to head in an oblong room; for the toilet you have to descend a creaky staircase to the floor below; and in the cupboard you find some cheap and tattered pornographic magazines.

I can keep abreast of the daily news by means of newspapers and television programmes in the cafes. There is something wrong with the pope's health but it is difficult to know what exactly.

Have we returned to the time of Pius XII? When that poor pope was mortally ill, there was nothing wrong with him officially; all his troubles were inventions of the sensation-seeking media. It was a veritable miracle that he died at all eventually. Because nobody in the Vatican was willing to tell the truth, the media had to do with guesswork. In the end it became a disrespectful bungle indeed, with secret signs via the opening and closing of windows in the papal palace. After the events, professor Galeazzi-Lisi, the papal physician, published an account of what had happened in actual fact; this was quite unethical of course but understandable all the same.

During the Second Vatican Council, the disgusted Council fathers swore that this would never ever happen again. But we are there again. Just like with all immortal potentates – a Franco, a Mobutu, a Roman Emperor – the praetorian guard closes ranks round the sickbed in order that suspected rivals may not get the chance of abusing the ruler's weakness. A very sick pope, on the other hand, should be like a very sick brother: because of our deep affection we want to know the true state of affairs. Lord, let our sick pope be a sick member of the family.

Autumn is upon us and what a splendid season it is! I wander through a world of gold and red and dark brown and fluorescent green and a mighty apotheosis of floral brilliance.

If and when I am going to paint a landscape in the future I want to do it first in autumn colours, then paint the summer colours over those, and on top of those perhaps even the spring colours.

The striking thing is that all this blinding beauty serves no particular purpose. The flowers of summertime are meant to attract bees; fruits and berries are there to attract useful thieves; but the abundant colours of autumn merely signify that everything is finished; not with a whimper but with a multicoloured bang.

Should life not really be like that? Should life's autumn not really be an explosion of tingling experiences (like this journey on foot) that do not have to serve any ulterior purpose? I wish that would happen to everybody.

Talking about happy wishes, in the neighbourhood of Ulm I note a nice legend on the façade of a house. It says: O Herr, gib denen die mich kennen, zehn mal mehr als sie mir goennen. (Oh Lord, grant to my acquaintances ten times the amount of what they wish to happen to me.)

Ulm is right in the heart of what used to be Roman Germania, a region protected by a defensive wall, called the Limes, running from the Rhine to the Danube. For centuries, the Romans were the masters here but they left hardly any cultural traces behind. History might have taken quite a different course; they might have been speaking a Latin dialect here now.

Ulm has the highest church tower of Germany: 161 metres. Inside the Dom I find a remarkable group of Americans: the men are all dressed in black and have ring-beards, and the women wear bonnets like women in fairy tale books. They belong to a Protestant church community, probably Mennists. Long ago they departed from these regions and these faithful are searching for their roots. They feel attracted to me because I look unusual too, and I speak English. They are hungry for information about the church and its past. To be correct, the church is not a Dom but a Munster, because originally the church was not built by a bishop but by the municipality.

They have hung up big shields in the church to display the names of about 25 Wuerttemberg regiments whose young men were slaughtered in epic mass killings. I meet a pilgrim on his way to Compostela, a rare figure here.

I stay as guest in a religious house. One of the priests living here is an admirer of the ultra-conservative Lefèbvrists; he deposits their abrasive literature at the back of his church. In one of the pamphlets, Richard Williamson, a bishop of the schismatic group, writes an in memoriam for the deceased Lefèbvre: "We have lost a giant of a bishop, whose intercessions have shielded us from God's anger. In 1968 Padre Pio died, in 1969 the new Mass came. What new disaster will befall us this time?"

You don't have to be a professional prophet of doom to discern that mankind is threatened by apocalyptic disasters. But these are not punishments of God; they are crises brought about by the fact that Western man has been very arrogant in his dialogue with creation. One could put some blame on the churches for not having joined this dialogue in time, probably for fear of sullying their orthodoxy and also for dislike of that arrogance. In the field of social justice our church raised her voice indeed. But in the overall context of things the church's offensive remained a modest campaign.

One of the most decisive underlying issues was the question: can you remake human society; can you remake nature? Society's leaders said Yes; and that is where their arrogance had its origin. In that same company you found Communists, Anarchists, Fascists, reckless Scientists dreaming of Frankensteins and Eugenic magicians in the tradition of the sorcerer's apprentice. Should they be allowed to do their thing? How can you stop them? I can think of two ways only: you either kill them or you join them somehow or other. So we have to think along with them; let us see where that gets us.

Let us realise that technique has taken over from nature with a *coup d'état.* Let us concentrate for a while on the role of the male in society. You can see that in the course of history the human male works with preference in the area of science and technique, whereas the human female shows a preference for the area of human relationships. Recently, these latter have been in the spotlight but now they are being labelled "wet" and "soft" and abandoned again. The males have regained the saddle; they are going for a brave new world again by technological means. Look at the global economy. Poverty and hunger are on the increase. Why? The experts say that there is enough available for everyone but it is not divided fairly. This is a question of human relations, therefore. But what do the economic captains say? No, we need more food, more of everything; we need a green revolution by using more artificial manure, super-reproductive plants created by patented manipulation of their genes, and a razor-sharp finely honed industry. So, no redistribution of arable land, no reduction of the abominable imbalance between the monopolising opulent few and the squirming poor. The rich do not have to let go of anything and yet the hunger of the poor shall be stilled. That is what the men are going to fix with their technique.

But let us be practical: the way the men are going about it now is a waste of time: it is all far too patchy and piecemeal and higgledy-piggledy, too sweety-sweety, too timorous ; in one word, we are on the wrong track. Within the shortest possible time we will have to resort to stern measures, such as the following.

It is evident that mankind is going to rack and ruin because we are being crushed by an avalanche of aggressive technique. In the last analysis that is because there are far too many males. In order to regain control over technique we will have to reduce the number of males drastically. We cannot indulge in the luxury of half measures. Scientific investigations have revealed that a handful of males are sufficient to fertilise all the available females. It is clear what road we have to follow. Of all the little boys that are born from now on we have to keep the very best only, the Nobel Prize candidates, the possible Olympic champions, the Oscar types; with their spermatozoa we will service all the women of the future. The rest of the male babies that are being born must be "harvested". They have to be kept deeply frozen for future use. All the girls will grow up and human society switches back to the aboriginal and natural system of matriarchy. The store of frozen male babies is a veritable treasure of spare parts. When the females grow old and their organs are getting worn out, brand new replacements can be quarried out of the frozen babies, so that the females will have an endless life to look forward to. Will this not lead to overpopulation? There should be no danger for that. First of all, in the suggested programme we only allow half of the live births to grow up: the females. Secondly, fertilisation will have to take place by artificial implantation; in that way the quota of foetuses can be controlled. Because the world will be controlled totally by females, technique will become nature-friendly and all global catastrophes will be averted.

Another young girl, Natalie, has been murdered in a ghastly way by a sex-murderer. BILD AM SONNTAG of 29th September tells us that the murderer had been jailed before, for raping five women. A psychiatrist, however, had declared that he was not sick so he could not be given therapy. So they had released him prematurely. The idea that a crime deserves punishment, as a form of deterrent, has evidently evaporated.

At Ulm I relish a lovely Italian meal; at Herbrechtingen a super Chinese meal. I enjoy outlandish dishes. In the Chinese restaurant I had this conversation with the girl.

"Haben sie noch etwas fuer Dessert, Bitte?"

"Jawohl, eine Affe flambiert mit Eis."

"Eine Affe?! Aber das ist toch ein Tier?"

"Ach nein, eine Affelllll!"

(You might reconstruct it in English this way: "Do you have something for dessert please?" "Surely, a bear, flambée, with ice." "A bear? But that is an animal surely!" "Ah no, a ppppear!")

How fond the Germans are of rough-hewn unpolished pieces of stone, to serve as decorations for their churches and monumental buildings. Going back to primitive forms provokes deep emotions in them; but they do not like to play with them. Evidently the playful, the art of seeing the relative side of things, is not their strongest suit. At times they react to humour in an unusual manner; I have often heard them clap for a joke, as if it were an acrobatic feat. Many of them avoid having too much humour in their conversation; it makes things unnecessarily intricate. When English persons have said a few sentences and the conversation threatens to become boring they conjure up a light-hearted witticism. At that moment Germans would look for another topic about which they can wholeheartedly agree or disagree. The Swiss often come up with humour without laughter; Germans tend to enjoy jokes without humour ("a mouse is bigger than a louse" or so).

To all this there are big exceptions. Like a parish priest at Crailsheim. His opening bid was very promising: "I am not put off by secularisation, I welcome it". He loved lumps of stone but nicely polished. He showed a malachite of about five kilograms, which he used for the exposition and veneration of the Blessed Sacrament. He had a big fossilised ammonite; during Mass he would put the gifts on it to offer the whole of evolving nature to God. Every Easter

Monday he had a special service; instead of giving a sermon he would invite people to come forward and tell jokes about religion and the church and the parish priests and the bishops. On that day he would have even more people in his church than on Easter Sunday, if that were possible. He had also made the pilgrimage to Compostela; there he had picked up a replica of the Botafumeiro, the humungous thurible. From time to time he had it swinging in his own church now. And so there are still prophetic leaders in the church, not just people who cannot stop ringing alarm bells about secularisation.

Scientists have devised a scale to measure the size of earthquakes and tornadoes. A number of years ago theological scientists devised a scale to measure degrees of loyalty to the magisterium of the church. They composed a list of things you have to be against or at least to deplore. One of those items is secularisation. In their eagerness to get the measuring equipment ready, the protectors of the faith overlooked the fact that secularisation can have two meanings at least.

The first meaning is: a vision on life in which there is no room for the transcendental, for something above nature. Earthly matters explain themselves, the earth ("saeculum" in Latin) provides its own support. The sacred, the supernatural, is a superfluous and misleading illusion. So there is no more room for holy places and holy times and holy actions, nothing is holy any more. That is the officially accepted meaning of secularisation. The orthodox reaction to this interpretation is: show that it is wrong, that there is a need of the transcendental, that there are still many unexplored regions on the map of life that can only be given meaning by the presence of the divine.

But there is still another meaning, promoted by the New Testament. You are entitled to say that in the New Covenant there are no more separate holy places or holy times or sacred things or sacred laws, simply because everything has now become holy. There is no need any more to reserve a special place for the transcendental. The transcendental is there but it does not begin where the secular ends: the transcendental has become a dimension built into all earthly things. Everything is holy for the holy; God can be found in all things, adored everywhere.

I am quite ready to accept that the earthly can explain itself. In the same manner, you can describe Leonardo da Vinci's Mona Lisa completely in terms of chemistry and optical reactions; but the beauty of the Mona Lisa does not begin where the paint ends! You are quite right if you say that in the Mona Lisa there is nothing but paint. So also, everything that is transcendent has its completely earthly equivalent. And God has become incarnate completely, as far as we are concerned in everything.

Are we not behaving paternalistically towards God when we reserve special little corners of creation for Him? Surely, God is quite capable of looking after Himself. We cannot demand from Him that He gives us special signs, that He adjusts Himself to our arguments.

All this makes me think of a poem by Rilke:

> Some say that you are there indeed,
> some doubt and think that you are not.
> The slothful and the sleepy lot
> distrust themselves, their shining creed,
> desire that the rocks should bleed
> or else they say they do not know.
>
> You bow your face in silent woe.
>
> The mountains' veins you could cut up
> to prove a very urgent case;
> but for the haughty pagan race
> you do not care that much.
>
> You will not fight with trick and snare
> nor pander to the love of light;
> for for the Christians and their right
> you do not really care.
>
> You do not care for those that cry.
> Your tender eye
> sees those that carry you and try.

(Rainer Maria Rilke, *Das Stundenbuch*: 'Geruchte gehn, die dich vermuten').

THE NINTH MONTH

OCTOBER

This is the last month of my journey. My next big town will be Wuerzburg; from there I will go to Fulda. There I will spend a week with friends; and from there I will start the last lap to the Netherlands via the ancient city of Munster. The part of Germany I am drifting through is new to me: Allgau, Franconia, the Roehn, Hessen.

The roads are strewn with apples. I feel the temptation to pick them up: free food, something happening in fairy tales only. But I do not like to interrupt my walking rhythm, spoil my balance by bending forward with my rucksack on my back, having to select a few good apples with the risk of choosing worm-eaten ones. At last I give in to the temptation and gather half a dozen delicious-looking yellow ones. I keep them in my pocket for an hour to give them the right temperature and then try one. It is so tart and bitter that the poisonous taste stays in my mouth for days.

North of Ulm I pass the limes, the old imperial border of the Roman Empire. There is nothing left of it. Here and there you find a notice leading to reconstructed Roman forts. I cannot be bothered to go and look; I suspect they will be imitations of the Roman fortifications you see in the strip books of Asterix and Obelix.

An astonishing and extraordinary phenomenon, that Roman Empire. And the urge in people to found empires, placing huge territorial areas under a new order and a new language. Is that urge related to the missionary drive?

The Latin language is a monument by itself. Half a century has passed since I had to read it but loose segments of Virgil still float about in my mind. Here on the clay of southern Germany near the limes I hear the Roman equestrian cohorts thunder by in the charming line: *Quadrupedante putrem sonitu quatit ungula campum* (with quadruple rumbling the hoof hits the waterlogged meadow).

In the eyes of the Ancients most of society's development was decay, ever further away from the Golden Age. The medieval dilapidation of the Latin language must have hurt them profoundly. In one part of Europe it became transliterated German; in other countries it was pronounced in a Frankish or Iberian way. When the Renaissance started and the classic authors with their perfect grammar and syntax returned to the limelight the experts thought: Ah, thank God classical Latin is making a comeback. But what happened? Good grief, with Dante, Chaucer and Hadewych, the folksy pseudo-languages actually became respectable; the end of the affair was that even the Bible was translated into that unworthy gibberish. The church reluctantly took part in that dreadful lowering of proper norms and conscientiously stuck to Latin in the liturgy and ecclesiastical studies.

When I studied philosophy at the Gregorian University in Rome in the 1950s, all lectures and all official textbooks were in Latin, normal. My favourite story is that once I had to sit an oral examination in Latin on the relativity theory of Einstein. I can remember one of the questions: "Reverend Sir, can you give me the equation of Lorenz?" Surely: "*Utique; radix quadratus ex minus uno est...* (the square root of minus one is...). At that moment, the professor mercifully gave me a piece of paper to write it down, when he saw I knew it.

In the centre of the town of Aalen they let the brooks simply run right through the pavement. I wonder what they will do when there is high water. Texts by the side of the road are for pedestrians; so I always read them. Somewhere I find the announcement that on that spot two young German soldiers were killed when they tried to stem the American advance in March 1945. Could they not have kept their heroism in check just for a couple of days, for the sake of their parents and their brothers and sisters? Did I say brothers? Perhaps these had fallen already. Still you have to know when it makes sense to lay down your life.

Near Ellwangen, I cross the watershed of the North Sea and the Black Sea. When I was preparing this journey I have been toying with the idea of following this watershed as long as possible. This could be a challenge for setting out an unusual route; but it turned out to be too intricate. I would find it interesting to see a map indicating to what different seas the water of various regions flows.

At one crossroads I find a small wooden post with the name and the age of a young woman, the date on which she was killed here in an accident and a bunch of flowers: a heart-rending family tragedy condensed into a small bouquet, mortal remains of sorrow. A human person stopped here; the children are asking where she has gone now.

What is left of the lump of clay with the spark inside, the old icon of a human person? We know now that we are an infinitesimally small fragment of an immeasurable universe. Following the lines that run away from us to the outside our structure links up with the lines that run to the stars in a dizzyingly unthinkable and infinite panorama. Following the lines that run inwards we enter a web of physical energies that plunge into a depth that appears to be just as infinite as the things outside us. As living bodily creatures we are situated at a point where two infinite distances of the universe are tied together.

It used to be said that you become ever more purely yourself the more deeply you descend inside yourself: the Platonic image of the spark in the clay. But that image has become unstuck, since physics has taught us that you can continue going down ad infinitum, moving ever further away from yourself. Psychology too has ruined this ancient image: at the deepest point in our interior we are all commonplaces, governed by anonymous impulses. Where then is the human being most personal? I would say somewhere between his skin and his clothes, and just for a certain time. Levinas hits the mark when he points at the primary role played by the face. I am no longer hiding behind this mask; I am my own mask; it is the face of my personal clock.

Rothenburg is an unspoiled 16th century town, so popular with the Japanese that many notices have Japanese subtitles. I am there on a Saturday; the weather is nicely autumnal and the town is so full that there are no hotel beds left; the youth hostel sends away all persons older than 27 years of age. But the parish priest allows me to sleep on the floor of the parish hall for two nights. It is quite adequate, and even good fun, for that very evening there is a concert for zither-orchestras in the upper hall and I am given the role of guest of honour. The musicians are the nation's best, their performance is impeccable, and still I keep on finding the instruments odd and even the music odd. Great evening.

262

Towards the end of the war, 50 percent of Rothenburg was destroyed by an aerial bombardment, made by mistake. That day there was a lot of fog and the allied pilots could not find their target, an oil refinery; so as not to waste their precious bombs they dropped them on the first town they came across and that happened to be Rothenburg. Oops.

Mistakes like that were not uncommon. Curious is the case of Hengelo, my own home town. The Allies had two styles of bombing: one for German towns and one for Allied towns. German towns were flattened from very high up; for Allied towns they flew lower and took more careful aim. The pilots who were bombing Hengelo on 6th October 1944 thought they were dealing with a German town and treated it accordingly. When they returned to base it was made clear to them that they had attacked a Dutch town. So next day they went back to bombard it once again, this time in the proper Allied way, by way of reparation.

People here perfume their notices with the word lieblich, love-filled. I walk through "the love-filled valley of the river Tauber"; a funfair booth advertises that the bacon cubes are being put on their pancakes "with love-filled hands".

At Bieberehren I eat a dish called Meerrettichschnitzel (seahorse radish fillet) in a Gasthaus where a notice on the door says that "This place is closed on account of the apple harvest except on Sundays". Two hours after the Meerrettichschnitzel I have to eat again at the insistence of passing friends and another two hours later I have to eat once more with mine host, the kindly parish priest.

Somewhere far away on the horizon I see a church tower, as sharp as a supernatural injection needle.

At Wuerzburg, the North Sea comes within reach: there is a big fish restaurant of a chain named Nord-see. I often remember places by the things I have eaten there. Wuerzburg means: two salt matjes-herring (special offer) and fried plaice, and a Turkish lunch, and a Mexican dinner, and tasting wine in a medieval hoisting apparatus on the river bank.

The giddy Rococo style of Wuerzburg awakens in me two different emotions. First there is aesthetic bewilderment about the artistic audacity: how on earth did they dare to let themselves go haywire in wriggling twists and turns, those painters and stucco-men. Secondly, I fall prey to utter confusion when I think that all this was created at the behest of the prince bishop or the prince abbot. Did they really have nothing better to do than build these snorting palaces? The big worry of the prince bishop, so we are told by a guide, was that the Empress Maria Theresia was going to come for a visit and he had only three months left to finish his palace; but thanks to the merciful Almighty he managed. Never has the spirit of the world penetrated so deeply into the church as it did then; and we hear of few leaders in the church who worried about it.

At the end of the War, 90 percent of Wuerzburg town was devastated, although it was classified as a hospital town.

Towns may perish but their names remain. In the beginning was the word, at the end there is the name. Of many towns the name only is left; of many people the only thing left is the name. A name is a kind of soul. Today I stay in a hotel with the beautiful name of The Golden Cock; tomorrow I stay in The Golden Angel; that is a lot more meaningful that a dry code like XP35.

Names are needed but they can be odd, especially when they are tied up with a concrete context. "North Sea" is only correct when you are near Antwerp; in Norway it makes no sense. In Germany they call the Baltic the Ostsee or East Sea; that makes no sense to the Russians. We used to have a little joke in Holland. The oddest town in the whole country is Arnhem: to the west of it lies Oosterbeek (Eastern brook), to the east you had Westervoort (Western ford), to the north the Zuiderzee (Southern Sea) and to the south, North-Brabant.

The name "Middle Ages" has gone wrong. Originally it was the time between Classic Antiquity and the new Renaissance time. After the Enlightenment came a time when they spoke proudly of The Modern Era: a time of irresistible progress, of exact knowledge, of definitive and undeniable insights, of controllable laws. That time has been past for many decennia already, even if quite a few people do not know that yet. We now live in the Post-Modern Era. We are not at all so sure anymore that we are making progress; our knowledge is far from clear. On the contrary, our mental panorama is a vast grey area with here and there some useful and rather promising fixed points, though not so firmly fixed that it would give us a solid foothold. We know how to switch a TV apparatus on and off but we do not have a mental image of aerial space crowded with television signals. We even have no good image of electricity. Then the trouble started already. Who can picture to himself what is going on inside his computer?

Our Rationalism has been battered badly; new Romanticism has announced its coming on the horizon, there is new faith in old ideas, a faith that has been given the honorary title of *New Age.*

I badly miss my fellow pilgrims of Saint James. We used to give each other a name and an identity. I am now a functionless tramp. But not always. At Hohenberg, a church of Saint James is awaiting me, an old reunion place of pilgrims to Compostela who followed the Swabian route, a route that is coming alive in our days. Its enthusiastic old parish priest forces a second breakfast on me. The church and the other buildings have been covered with murals concerning Saint James. The artist is somebody whose star is rising like a meteor here, called Sieger Koeder. He lets himself go in a colourful idiom that reminds you of Chagall. I like it; there are lots of things to see and he dares. At Arnstein, a lady stops me in the street as she recognises my Jacobine cockle-shell. She is a member of the local society of Saint James. The encounter leads to a pleasant evening in the Golden Angel and a spontaneous bond of friendship. Bad Kissingen is a healing spa for the well-heeled, one of the many in these parts. It is blessed with therapeutic waters in which you can bathe and which you have to drink above all. The town is somewhat elitist, somewhat decadent and the water tastes revolting. Only those people who can switch off their sense of humour completely now and then can get themselves so far that they swallow – with a solemn face – for an awful lot of money – water that smacks of rotten eggs. They are getting very near to the Emperor's new clothes.

Has anybody tried to make a comparative study between the two health spas Bad Kissingen and Lourdes? That would be a delightful challenge. Both are centred around healing waters. Lourdes has heavy religious overtones, Bad Kissingen has financial overtones. Both are making heavy demands on their clients' faith. At Lourdes, the atmosphere is devout and homely; at Bad Kissingen there is no need to display any faith, for you have paid for everything. Would it also be fair to say that Lourdes caters for sicknesses that fell upon people by accident, whereas Bad Kissingen promises relief for those sicknesses that are the result of luxurious living?

Everything at Bad Kissingen is well arranged and manicured. Men in overalls walk on the lawns to remove the fallen leaves and they do this by means of a mutant of a vacuum cleaner giving off the sound of a first generation helicopter and emitting clouds of poisonous smoke. As I leave the place I pass by a contraption made of carefully stowed faggots through which the brackish water seeps; the briny vapours wafting on the wind seem to give relief to people suffering from asthma.

I have been told that most sicknesses in the civilised West are the result of luxury. Eating too much combined with sitting too much gives rise to sicknesses of the heart and the blood circulation system. Drinking too much poisons the liver. Smoking too much invites lung cancer. Undisciplined sex opens the way for AIDS. The abominable consequences of luxurious living are not limited to the bodily area of health. Alcoholism can wreak havoc in personal relationships as well as in the economic balance of families. Uncontrolled sex can easily cause ravages in people's lives and relationships. Abundance of money is a favourite feeding ground for rampant avarice, for a numbed sensitivity to norms and values, for distorted relationships and for insoluble global problems. If we want to keep ourselves healthy, we have to admit restrictions to our lives, our behaviour, our freedom.

This will be almost impossible if we look at limitations with a hostile eye. This hostility has much to do with the way you look at the notion of freedom. If you describe freedom as the absence of limitations you turn limitations into unwanted and hostile factors. Unconsciously, many people do this. Indeed, others limit my movements, so they are nuisances ("Hell is the others"); and so I arrange my little private space in such a way that I am not bothered by anyone.

The image of the hemmed-in person, imprisoned inside his own body, locked in the chains of his surroundings: that is a picture ultimately derived form Platonic philosophy. It retains its popularity: the free person is the one who casts off his chains. Personally, I am not very fond of this unchained platonic individual. I feel much more at home with Aristotle. He reminds us that our limitations contain our possibilities. And vice versa. Other people are not your hell, they are possible relationships; strangers are friends you do not know yet. Your body is not your misery but an invitation to mastery and joy. The Germans say: Limitations provoke mastery. Your difficult surroundings are not your prison in which you are wasting away; they are your arsenal of un-lived things. The true pilgrim refuses to be locked up; he breaks out into his surroundings.

Kreuzberg is a popular and jolly pilgrims' sanctuary, where the children get nicely tired on the 292 steps leading to the crosses, where a brass band and fried sausages and cold beer make piety humane.

Good religion leaves its fingerprints on the landscape; on a different level, good religion will enrich your interior landscape as well. My own preferential philosophical landscape is the one conjured up by Teilhard de Chardin; it enables you to zoom in on the past and the future: the immense and mysterious cosmic evolution of living organisms that have been touched by the divine. My landscape architect is Aristotle; his vision on matter and form fertilises. He has taught me to realise that "to be" is an analogous actuality: when you speak about "to be" and "beings" you should use analogous terms, images, symbols, codes, parables, riddles and poetry in preference to univocal terms: definitions, dogmas, absolutes, cast-iron logic. To come to terms with the religious, and also the irrational, you have to have recourse to analogy. Irrationality has become a fact of life in our post-modern era; you find it in the process of evolution in the role played by mutations that happen purely by accident; you find it in the very core of matter where sub-atomic particles are said to be moving according to the Principle of No Principle. As I survey my interior landscape I am very grateful to the Scholastics, too, for supplying me with the doctrine of the three Transcendentals – One, True and Good – combining to form Beautiful. With these key notions I have been able to open all doors so far; and holding the Gospel in my hand, my head and my heart I feel I am able to work at a more just world.

Fulda is another city worthy of conspicuous display by a Prince Abbot. Boniface, murdered near Dokkum in Frisia – when was it again? 754 AD? – and buried in a tomb made of marble lace. His church above the crypt is a mini-Saint Peter. Boniface was an English missionary tramp. In his day, monks used to swarm out for Christ: peregrinari pro Christo as they called it. Boniface did that on the Episcopal level. The pope had appointed him as "Bishop in Germany" and after some time promoted him to Archbishop with the task of putting bishops everywhere. That is what he did; at the head of each new diocese he placed an English monk. Only at the end did he allow himself to be tied down to a particular place, namely Mainz. But he kept living on the road; he even went back to the Netherlands, outside his jurisdiction. The Frisians were his first love; and near Dokkum they became his executioners. They buried his body at Fulda in his own monastery, not at Mainz. Even in death he remained a vagabond. He was a rugged apostle, not a display-loving prelate.

I have a whole week to wander through Fulda and its surroundings thanks to my friends' hospitality. Among the Catholics I detect a feeling of nostalgia for former times and a worried anxiety about the way the young generation look at religion and church.

I had looked forward to a meeting and a talk with the Archbishop of Fulda. According to what I had read about him and his activities when he was the Apostolic Nuncio in The Hague, he was the great driving force behind the ruinous policy the Roman authorities embarked upon towards the Dutch Church. For months I felt excitement growing inside me as I thought of visiting him, entering the lion's den, not to bicker with him but to chat with him in a friendly manner, giving him the chance of sweeping away my angry prejudices about him. The parish priests on the way had given me a fair chance "for he is like that all right". But however much we tried, his doors remained firmly shut. And so I am stuck with my home-made image of the Hammer of the Dutch.

Next to the Dom of Fulda you find a small church, Saint Michael's. It is very special, not only because it is old but more so because of its construction: when you go down into the crypt you can see that the whole church rests on one central pillar.

My original plan was to continue northwards after Fulda, to reach the Baltic. Having rewritten my itinerary in the month of February, I will now turn to the north-west towards Munster. This will cause me to miss the Wartburg, Luther's hiding place. I really do not want to miss that chance of enriching my ecumenical side and so we visit it by car.

The castle is situated on a high rock; it was the home of Saint Elisabeth of Thuringia (the one who had been forbidden by her husband to take loaves of bread to the poor; when he caught her doing so and jerked her mantle open, the loaves had changed into roses). At some moment in history the Mastersingers are supposed to have held their Euro song festival there. Now it is the great memorial for Luther: when the German Reichstag had declared him to be an outlaw, he found refuge there from the Catholic princes. Swarms of Protestant pilgrims make their way through the venerable apartments. Impressively sober is the room where the great and courageous reformer translated the Bible into German in an orgy of inspiration. But oh dear, the irony of history! It would be an understatement to say that Luther was not fond of sacred relics. The old table you find in the room is not the original one used by Luther to write on: it comes from his parental home. Luther's original writing table has been removed bit by bit in the course of time by devout pilgrims, in the form of sacred relics. Pilgrims are the same wherever you find them. At one moment Luther declared that he had combated the devil with (pen and) ink. That word gave rise to the legend that the devil had appeared to him and that he had

268

thrown a pot of ink at the devil. Visitors to the Wartburg kept asking where the ink blot was on the wall. To satisfy the faithful, the authorities flung a pot of ink against the wall. Now, that ink stain has also been removed bit by tiny bit by devout pilgrims; after that the authorities decided not to use any more ink but to restore the wall to its original state.

After Fulda I make my acquaintance with Protestant Hessia. It is a picturesque land, in a rather solemn way. During the daytime very few pubs are open; and on Sundays people stick to the rules. No, this Protestant spirit is not the answer today's pilgrim is searching for: it is not playful enough; it lacks the joy of celebration; it suffers from cramp.

Hessians are an ancient and big Germanic people; Tacitus calls them *Chatti*. In my own country we call ancient trading routes Hessian roads. Not very long ago Hessia was an internationally-renowned German state. Hessian mercenary soldiers formed a part of the British Army; they fought for the British in the American War of Independence. They gave their name to footwear, to a kind of textile and to an insect. Hessia is now a romantic part of Germany. Prussia must have overshadowed it as the German heavyweight; even though the name Prussia or Borussia indicates Slav origins. Prussia has ceased to exist, whilst in my youth it was so important that its name was a synonym for Germany.

The relations between nations have changed dramatically. They all now meet in the talking hall or parliament of the United Nations. Europe is no longer the cockpit of the world. European thinking is no longer the guiding star for universal human action. Those that like to think that their European country has a pilot function in the world live three generations behind the time.

In the world of the mind the alterations have been really momentous. All of a sudden, to people's surprise, Western philosophy has become a stagnant pond. Theoretical Socialism, a typical fruit of Western thinking, has lost its relevance. In its place they have reinstated the old-fashioned market dynamics. For contemporary philosophy to be relevant it has to give maximum attention to global economy. The unfair distribution of the resources of this world has become a pressing issue, together with the population explosion and a disturbed ecology; these three are like so many fuses running to the cosmic powder keg.

In the light of all this there is, believe it or not, a re-appreciation of the religious phenomenon taking place, even more than a revaluation of philosophy. The Western scientific establishment is finding itself more and more isolated with its condescending if not arrogant rejection of religion as if it were a form of underdevelopment (*Wissenschaft im Anfang*, the initial stage of science). For good measure, this rejection implies contempt for those cultures that have a high esteem for religion. This contempt provokes a violent reaction among the fundamentalists all over the world, especially in Islam. We should not cheat ourselves with the thought that this fury is nurtured only by Islamic militants. In a more tempered form you will find it in many other cultures.

The caricature of Whites in East Africa says it all: they are self-assured know-alls who are determined to demolish the local culture as being something hopelessly antiquated and who take pride in disturbing the young generation with their roguish immoral behaviour. This caricature is the result of what the people perceive via television, video, radio and newspapers. Many people in the West do not appreciate that through their substandard sexual mores they too share in the culpability for the fundamentalist atrocities in Algeria, Afghanistan, Iraq, Egypt, you name it.

In the Protestant place called Oberaula, the Catholic services are so rare that I have to forego Sunday Mass for the first time on this journey. I feel it as a painful lacuna, thank God. The landscape becomes more and more homely. Blue tits tumble through the shrubs. Two weasels pursue each other and just miss getting run over by a car. Standing on a bridge of a small castle I am being watched from above by an owl, from below by a roe standing in the dry ditch. A nuthatch tries to imitate a woodpecker hammering a tree – upside down . On a ploughed field I count some 25 buzzards sitting motionless in the warm sunshine. In the folds of the land the mighty Saxon farms begin to appear and the local patois begins to resemble more and more the Twente language we speak at home. Autumn is a feast of abundance; many animals are as fat as pigs. The fields are teeming with pheasants and partridges jump up from near my feet with a whirring sound.

The name partridge derives from an old Germanic word *prt* meaning fart; no doubt suggested by the sound a flying partridge makes.

Autumn is considered to be a period of dying; but that is not altogether correct. The earth's movement causes the weather in the winter months to become freezing cold. Certain plant juices cannot stand this and so the tree withdraws them well in time from the leaves; the latter become yellow and superfluous. Once the leaves are gone there is no more food for many insects and consequently little food for birds; and so the birds depart. From this it is clear that autumn is a busy time of preparation for the coming of winter: it is the start of a new yearly cycle. Once the temperature is safe, the plant brings the precious juices out again.

You could ask if the old summer returns after the spring or if a new summer is due to come. There you have two schools in philosophy. Those who consider creation as fully established, a reflection of the eternal immutable truth, will say that summer comes back. Those that see creation as an unfolding process will greet a new summer. These two viewpoints reach out into our day-to-day thinking.

I reach the Edertalsperre; in May 1943, RAF pilots braved murderous gunfire to blow up this dam by means of rotating bombs: these bounced like smooth pebbles over the surface of the water until they hit the dam, sank down and exploded at the foot of the dam, making a gaping hole of 60 by 25 metres through which a nine-metre high wave hurled down, killing 69 people. Most of the aeroplanes' crews were killed as well. The intended destruction did not occur and in June 1944 the dam was closed again. Inscriptions in capital letters adorning the dam proclaim the major facts, like which German emperor had the dam built and who had it enlarged; but its destruction is nowhere mentioned. The only information about it is found on the other side of the dam on a few paper cuttings pinned up under a small roof. I remember it very well and if I am not wrong it was Douglas Bader, the legendary pilot with two artificial legs, who led the attack.

Waldeck is a name that makes me think of Queen Emma, the mother of the old Dutch Queen Wilhelmina. The splendid castle rises aristocratically above the forests once inhabited by poor coal-burners whilst the humble serfs lined the road cap in hand to await the passing of the ducal landau. Little Wilhelmina must have seen lovely childhood years here.

The Netherlands are not far any more: I see the first Dutch motorists out for a daytrip. It makes me realise that the end of my journey is approaching. It is time to draw up balances, also concerning myself. Have I learnt more about myself? Have I made up my mind if I am either conservative or progressive?

Progressive and Conservative: sometimes we have to make do with seriously crippled terms. The expression "progressive" is so nebulous that I would not dare to entrust myself to it. It calls up the image of somebody who is fed up with the past and firmly believes that new things are always better and that he wants the new things at whatever cost. So-called progressives do not hesitate to resort to caricatures: if only you depict the past sufficiently darkly, the present promotes itself automatically. In the American world they like the term "liberal". That is another disagreeable word, conjuring up the image of somebody who judges all limitations to be detestable. If that is so, then I am an arch-conservative.

Who knows, perhaps I *am* conservative. It is true, I like to conserve things. I find it very hard to discard things: I always think that maybe a moment will come when I want to use them. I have the same feeling with ideas. What I really want to toss out is: intimidation, exploitation of people's fears, denigrating others. But I would refer to that with the name "redemption" rather than "progressiveness". Soberly speaking, everybody who is going somewhere is progressive: he is stepping forward.

Often I feel happy about being old and old-fashioned therefore. I know Latin and Greek fairly well, which I often find useful. I have an excellent topographic ready knowledge the way I learnt in school formerly; I would not like to do without it. In my youth we had to learn strings of historic dates by heart; I still have them at my disposal as coat-hangers of past happenings, enabling me to have a three-dimensional panorama of past times. I am good at real Twents, our local dialect that is being eroded quickly. I know my Shakespeare. And the Bible. And the catechism. And how you can fix a paper kite with sticky potato flour. And how you can tease the long hair of a girl with an ear of grass.

There are many things I have refused to discard. Going to confession for instance: admitting one's guilt to somebody else, I think that is quite good for myself. In Africa, many people still want to go to confession. I still like to pray before food: a brief gesture of gratitude for an activity that corresponds to our deepest needs, a privilege denied to many starving children, and a small feast that is so easily taken for granted. In church I love incense, candles, glittering costumes; I find it lovely to play the liturgy. I still like to read the lives of the saints to see how people got themselves to go over the brink of normality and ordinariness and mediocrity. I do not believe in discarding, certainly not in abolishing traditions of faith. We received them from former generations and they are not our property. We are allowed to make use of them to our heart's content and then pass them on again to the people of the next generation for them to use in their turn. If there are broken items among them we ought to repair them. If there are items missing, we should pass on the gaps with suggestions of how they should be filled up. When formerly in our home we had unpacked the gifts brought by Santa Clause we would at the end very carefully inspect the empty boxes and papers to make sure nothing was thrown away undiscovered. That is the kind of conservatism that suits me.

In a big meadow near Korbach two men try to catch two frisky horses with a long rope stretched out between the two of them. They do not manage to drive them into a corner. I follow the tactics with great interest. I wonder if what they are trying to do is possible at all. It is similar to a chess problem: is it possible to catch a horse with two bishops? My walking speed carries me past the field of contest before it is concluded, alas. In the town I stay in an inn with an old-fashioned pillory in front.

In my life I have grown accustomed to a number of different cultures, Western as well as African. Westerners no longer consider their own culture as greatly superior; they would say now that all cultures are good and that therefore African cultures, too, are worthy of respect. This approach is a step in the right direction but I suspect that there is still more to the question of different cultures. It is my strong conviction that each and every culture has some special ingredient that other cultures do not have and that other cultures need. From that it follows that all cultures are unique and necessary. To illustrate my point of view, I can use the example of the jigsaw puzzle. All the ideas of people are like pieces of a huge jigsaw puzzle. People assist one another in putting the pieces together. To do that more effectively they gather together all the pieces that look alike on account of the colour. Say now that the Westerners have collected the blue pieces, and have gone very far in putting them together; they can see already that the blue represents the blue of the sky. There is only one piece left they are still wanting. At last it appears that this missing piece is to be found with the Africans. The Westerners get it and to their utter astonishment they discover that on this last piece a small boat is to be seen. Thus it becomes clear to them that the blue does not stand for the sky but for the blue water. That means that all their pieces, though fitting together, are lying in the wrong place: the whole Western part of the puzzle has to be turned upside down. One could imagine that the Westerners will resist such a discovery tooth and nail.

Near Muehlhausen they have constructed a battery of metal windmills, about 30 of them and each one as high as a four-storey house. I have not made up my mind yet if I find them beautiful or ugly. At Obermarsberg, formerly called Eresberg, the Saxons under Widukind had their big stronghold. In 772 it was captured by Charlemain. It was somewhere in this neighbourhood that the Irminsul was found, the sacred pillar or tree trunk of the Saxons; Boniface cut it down. Aha, now I understand why Saint-Michael's church at Fulda was built on one heavy pillar. In the abbey church of Obermarsberg I meet a married couple from Hawaii. They are Baptist missionaries working in Germany. They talk to me and they cannot stop, delighted to be able to converse in English: they do not seem to have mastered any German.

The name Saxon is interesting. A sax used to be a kind of knife; the word is related to sickle, scythe and saw. Some German tribes united into a federation with the name of the Free or the Frank; other tribes united under the symbol of a sword-knife or sax.

In the supermarket of Marsberg I find a lovely salt herring in vacuum-sealed plastic. I will eat it with my evening meal in my hotel room. Opening this type of package is always a very dicey operation. For it contains a lot of liquid and when you break the vacuum seal with a knife the liquid can squirt in all directions – and liquid from a fish can be most unpleasant. I could do this operation in the sink but if I do that the sink will smell of fish for the rest of the evening and the night. So, I prefer to do it above the toilet. I manage only just: the herring is so slippery that it jumps out of the package together with the liquid and I grab it at the last moment before it disappears into the toilet.

During this walk, did I wake up to the fact that I am old? One would expect that on a journey like this old age would be felt to be a serious handicap since one's bodily condition is so important. Strange enough I have to confess that my old age did not dawn on me, as long as I restricted myself to simple walking. Because walking is so much in agreement with the body, I rather experienced the trip as a rejuvenation. It has been a very long time indeed since I have felt so young.

There is a paradox: due to my old age I get busier. I notice that I prepare things more carefully. I do so not just because I want to avoid unnecessary risks but also because I am better at preparing myself. Because of my old age I have at my disposal a very considerable treasure of experience and insight; I am better at sizing things up. That being so, one can understand that there is a serious danger for an old man of doing too much. Nature sees that and puts a brake on him: she makes him forgetful, not because his brains are getting scrambled but because his worn-out body cannot keep pace with his superbly honed razor-sharp brains. Through the system of forgetting, nature tries to slow him down.

Leaving Marsberg I take the Via Regia, the royal way, a carolingian track.

Another noteworthy thing is that I am in a good mood continually, day in, day out. I am a bit high, I have no doubt about it, for months on end already. I can attribute that only to the walking I do.

A rapport published in DER SPIEGEL tells me that the new generation of teenagers does not make use of the unlimited sexual liberty so courageously secured for them by a preceding generation. They seriously value love and fidelity and a sense of responsibility. Who could have foreseen that?

The tumult about children being abused has accompanied me the whole way. In Belgium, the photographs of Julie and Melissa stared at me from every window; in Germany it was Natalie. Is this popular rage a result of media-fed hysteria, as a German judge suggested to me? To me it seems more likely that it indicates the bankruptcy of the sexual revolution. A few decades ago the apostles of the sexual revolution, convinced that they were doing a commendable thing, broke down all sexual taboos. They did not realise that these taboos have the same functions as the dikes along the rivers. If you destroy the dikes, then God's water will flow over God's fields, as they say in Dutch, unchecked, useless and dangerous. That is what has happened to sex: it has lost its tension, its excitement. Sex has become a triviality and whoever makes problems about sex is an old fogy. Porno is freedom; how could that be bad for children? Friendly educators write booklets for children to teach them the nicest ways of masturbating. And let us be logical, if sex is a triviality, then sexual "transgressions" must also be trivial. But suddenly, good grief, the poor sexual wreckers find themselves face to face with utterly provoked enraged mother-monsters who feel that their young ones are being threatened. Theory crashes into nature. So, dear boys, run for all you are worth.

We have to take another direction; to make sex exciting again and special, we have to give it back its dignity, we have to re-establish its link with love. Sex should be a game that you have to play with much fantasy and resourceful excitement.

Nature supplies me with an endless variety of colour combinations, sometimes very striking ones indeed. I saw a dark wood of alder trees, fallen yellow leaves lit up from the ground with fluorescent sheen and the trunks hid themselves in grey and black.

At Bueren, I treat myself to a simple meal in an Aldi-Imbiss. Simple can be quite tasty; but here it isn't. The fish on my grimy plastic plateau tastes as if it has been fried in engine oil. By way of an antidote, I take a good evening meal in a stylish restaurant: the well-tried combination of matjes-Nelson herring and fried plaice. The helpings are so generous that I cannot finish them. That is saying a lot.

Church renewal is a difficult enterprise. The Neo-Scholastic restoration at the end of the 19th century injected the church membership with a spirituality that was quite alien to their contemporary world. In the prevailing defensive mentality, this alienation from the world was taken to be a form of loyalty. This was most clearly the case with the religious, because this brand of spirituality had become the well-spring of their lives. In the 1950s, a serious crisis manifested itself in many orders and congregations: no more new members offered themselves. They were forced to change course. This led to more difficulties. The religious had never been trained to follow a course that resonated with the modern world. Having been marinated in obedience, docility and submissiveness for decades, they found it very hard to handle freedom and exposure. When clerics cannot stand being called by their first name, it could be a symptom of something seriously bad: of resenting and rejecting personal contacts. That is not good, for love lives only by the grace of personal contact. Where personal contact is lacking, love becomes a phantom. Where there is no love from person to concrete person, the gospel cannot take root. When these religious were being trained for their future community life they had often been told that "particular friendships" were to be shunned; how then could they cope with them now? The very foundation of their spirituality was, so they were told, self-sanctification; but now they were supposed to reach out to God in their brothers and sisters, and that was poorly known territory. Their God had been their private property in many ways; now they had to share Him suddenly with sceptic fellow-parishioners. Tensions ran high and many religious left their communities. And many initiatives of their colleagues who were determined to find ways of helping the wandering sheep were stigmatised as forms of disloyalty.

Lippstadt has been twinned with the Dutch town of Uden. This is the first time during this journey that I see a Dutch town named in that capacity. Twinning of towns became a rage after the Second World War; by now I have forgotten why it was such a wonderful idea.

The end of my journey is near: the names of the towns begin to sound like Dutch names: Buren, Beckum, Liesborn.

Against the background of the Neo-Scholastic restoration, attempts to bring about *aggiornamento* become difficult. Here is one example. To us, Neo-Scholastics, obligatory celibacy for priests is normal. To our contemporaries, not Neo-Scholastics, obligatory celibacy is was it was to Jesus and the apostles and the first Christians: something abnormal. So, should we discard that feeling of normality for the sake of *aggiornamento*? Some would even go as far as saying that obligatory celibacy is like obligatory mutilation. I think it may well be true what psychology suggests: that a celibate person runs a high risk of never developing a true and full *I-Thou* relationship with anybody, thus becoming a stunted and mutilated personality. It reminds one of the words of Jesus that some people will chose to become eunuchs for the new kingdom.

That personal mutilation must have a personal justification, e.g. the likelihood that epic possibilities will present themselves to the person in question. This is how I look at my own celibacy: I have to justify it by trying to do something extraordinary or impossible. At times I think I have not altogether failed in this respect. And I also think the same can be said of many other priests and religious sisters and brothers. But those that fail in this respect will be sorely tempted to find compensation for this mutilation. Thus priests may appear to people as being excessively self-centred, or parasitical, or addicted to honour and glory.

But of one thing I am sure: it will appear increasingly unjust and impossible to make this mutilation a *conditio sine qua non* for receiving the priesthood.

At one of the eucharistic celebrations I find a very special girl acolyte. She is a young woman who suffers from a handicap associated with prenatal Softenon poisoning: she has no arms and very short legs. She carries the ablution cloths on her shoulders; she is so charming, quick-witted and relaxed that everybody manages to deal with her in a normal way. One cannot bear to think of her personal everyday problems; she has hardly any feet to take over the functions of the hands. I find it beautiful that she can join in the celebrations without any fuss; it shows that her parish community is a very good community.

The church of Liesborn smells the same as Saint Lambert's church in my home parish. At the back of the church I find the heart-rending book I saw in many a church: an album containing the photographs and the curriculum vitae et mortis of soldiers killed in the war. I count 40 of them of this one parish. Some of them were killed when the war had hardly started, others moments before it ended. I try to imagine how the messages were delivered to the families. Was there a postman who came with a letter from the authorities, saying: "To our regret we have to inform you that your husband/son/brother has fallen on the field of glory/been listed as missing (delete what is not applicable). The fatherland is proud of its heroes. Heil Hitler"?

If we want to make progress in our thinking and at the same time retain our links with the past, we had better seek the guidance of Bergson, Buber, Teilhard de Chardin, Simone Weil, Jaspers and Marcel than just stick to Neo-Scholasticism. Like the good scribes of the New Testament, we will have to bring from our store new things as well as old. At the beginning of this century these names appeared as stars in the philosophical firmament. They were unable to prevent the virulent germs of the previous century from festering on; within a short space of time these brought catastrophes on the world, the like of which no previous era had seen: two global wars, the Spanish civil war, the Holocaust, the death of God, the sudden collapse of colonialism, the Cold War, the failing experiments of socialism, and the incredible contrast between haves and have-nots. The well-to-do sat in front of their television sets enjoying moon landings, whilst the destitute were dying of dirty water and vermin. After a brief and fashionable flicker of negative and absurdophile Existentialism the philosophical flame all but died in the second half of the 20th century. Who were its philosophical torchbearers? Fukuyama with his essay

The End of History? The world itself looks like a seething cauldron.

But human beings cannot live without a vision. It seems to me that the above-mentioned thinkers form our nearest link with the past and are at the same time firmly rooted in the 20th century. As Western man is trying to recover, there is irony in this that, having made a mess of religion, he now tries to compose himself again with the aid of new religious ideas. They have to be ideas with overtones of peace and justice and the wholeness of creation.

Westphalian church life is quite animated. I come across a church choir of eager boys and girls who surprise us with excellent music of Jean Langlais and continue their harmony over a jolly meal of spaghetti and wine; I meet a group of candidates for the sacrament of Confirmation who join the clergy in doing pastoral work; I stay in presbyteries where crowds of people are coming and going; I marvel at the discussions: there is no rancour.

The memorable date of 28th October the comes round. That day is etched into my memory for ever: on that day in 1944 we were liberated, in Tilburg, the town where our "minor seminary" was situated. On the evening of the 27th we had bedded down in the cellar under the Goirke church, for the infernal upheaval of war was on the point of rolling over us. The floor of the cellar was covered with mattresses; by carefully subdividing the available space it was just possible to fit in some 30 boys, albeit like sardines in a tin. In one corner of the cellar a metal tub was placed for the boys to pee in. In the middle of the night the guns started their ear-splitting bombardment. Later on we heard that it killed the mother of one of the boys in the part of the town called Bokhoven. When the deafening explosions stopped for a little while, boys got up and struggled to the tub in the corner to relieve themselves. But alas, at those moments some of them mumbled or grinned a bit, and that was a major transgression since during the night the heavy rule of the *Silentium Magnum* was in force: the total silence of the medieval monks. At the entrance of the cellar the priest in charge lay; with poignant sorrow he heard how, between the crashing bombs and screaming mortars, the boys were breaking the rule of most holy silence. When the guns fell silent at dawn, everybody crawled out of the cellars and heaved sighs of relief. But for us that was only the beginning of major misery. The priest in charge made us gather in a classroom and there he started a vocal bombardment, lashing us with reproaches. It was made clear to us: if ever there had been a moment when we should have shown our metal by honouring the *silentium*-rule, it would have been that night. Every boy received a piece of paper on which he had to write down exactly what he had done: talked, laughed, with whom, etc. The dossier was collected for further analysis and fitting punishment. Everybody was scared stiff but thank God we were freed from our distress by the advance of the Allied troops. We heard the cry outside: "They are in the Goirkestreet!!" At that, pandemonium broke loose and everybody ran outside. Yes, there they were, the Tommies, compact little green men from a totally different world; they disappeared in a tidal wave of ecstatic citizens. Everybody congratulated them in the Tilburg dialect and patted their shoulders. The first soldier I greeted was called Alan Smith; he was 19 years of age and came from Scotland. One of the soldiers did not feel well; motherly figures in the crowd insisted that he should go and see a general practitioner living just down the street. The soldiers tried to explain to us that the situation was very dangerous; some of them lay down on their stomachs behind a machine gun in a side street leading to the Dongenseweg, a street running parallel to the Goirkestreet. At that very moment long columns of German soldiers were leaving the town via the Dongenseweg. Later on we heard that a boy of the Geboers family, who we knew, had sprinted through the German ranks to go and see the Tommies in the Goirkestreet. When the first excitement died down the priest in charge unfurled the Dutch flag on the playground and gave an impassioned speech at the top of his voice. The *Herrenvolk* had gone for good. Fortunately, the nasty consequences of the broken *Silentium Magnum* were swept away at the same time.

Westphalia (what on earth is Phalia really?) is an old-fashioned land; but it is as if they have been able to keep their composure in church matters a little better by going more slowly. They have been able to keep the game going, attracting at the same time a good number of young people.

There is an odd but profound connection between being young and being old-fashioned. It is not as if young people are by definition progressive. When youthful persons discover something, it is not something new but something old. Young people begin to talk about old commonplaces in a new way. Babies are old-fashioned through and through. Their existence in their mother's womb does not differ from that of babies 20,000 years ago. So is the existence of new-born babies. Every person has to start at the beginning again, recapitulating.

The only way in which people can pass on their interior life's experience is in the objectified form of commonplaces, stereotypes of thinking and acting. The authentic treasure of personal living experience disappears with the death of a person. That is why all cultures, except our own, value the insights of old people. On the other hand, one has to admit that all inherited insights and all second hand experiences are in fact very much like prejudices. But it is with those that the process of cognition begins.

Knowledge does not come out of nothing, it arises out of second hand wisdom we receive from a previous generation (prejudices therefore), from the perceptions we make with the assistance of those prejudices, and from the *a priori* we ourselves are. For surely, everything that is to be found outside us, is to be found inside us, in potentiality, in surpassing vagueness. By readjusting the inherited wisdom slowly with the help of personally acquired perceptions the human person arrives at authentic knowledge.

This takes time. Youth is the home area of prejudice. It is tempting to glorify youthful knowledge, newly polished prejudices, as being identical to progress. But youthful persons have to go through the full learning process; if they do not, they will get stuck in their accumulated prejudices.

Near Munster a man gets off his bicycle just to give me 50 marks. In the city, a lady stops me in mid-stride. "Sir," she says, "I think you look terrific; that is all I wanted to tell you."

Eastern philosophies are in great demand. Many people among us do not care any more for our crude rationalism. It has dawned on many faithful that their spiritual life too had become far too rationalistic. Thomas Merton, the well-known American monk, submerged himself in Buddhism. The English Benedictine Bede Griffith took up his abode in India. I can understand very well why. In Europe itself there is still a lot of unused mysticism lying around: from the time of Hadewych and Juliana of Norwich and Meister Eckhart, from the time of Saint John of the Cross and with contemporary mystics like the Dutch Carmelite Titus Brandsma who perished in a Nazi concentration camp.

After Munster I have reached my home area. Havixbeck, Eggerode, Alstaette: I have explored them all before; the farmers talk the same way as us; the rain is the same and you have the same smell of silage; only the windows are smaller.

My pilgrimage is definitely over. For many months I have confronted myself with my own inside and I managed to keep my balance. *Cursum consummavi, fidem servavi,* to speak with Saint Paul: I have completed my run, I have kept my faith. Not only have I kept my faith, I have been confirmed in it. My conviction that the good news of Jesus can be of decisive importance for people and communities has become stronger than before. If that message of Jesus is understood and accepted in the right spirit it will prove to be a unique means of bringing people together, of making people take notice of each other, of creating solidarity everywhere. The same message is also able to feed that very enigmatic feeling that we are being cared for, that nobody is useless, that we are not handed over to mindless powers, that the good shall be victorious in the end. These are precious values and I would not know where else I could get that type of inspiration. They are worth some inevitable concomitant rubbish.

Searching for the sense of life following the suggestions of the Gospel is not very different from gathering gold. In both cases you start with a lot of mud and a lot of faith. To extract the gold you have to add something, mercury I believe, the quicksilver of your own life. The quicksilver is not the gold. If you are lucky you will see a few grains of gold plus considerable heaps of rubbish.

Going home is so different from going to the place of pilgrimage. Going to a sanctuary means: leaving home for something new, for a future. Going home means: going back to something old, to the past. That causes me to be disoriented: I am going back to the starting point.

At Havixbeck there is market. I see a big kiosk with the myriad types of Dutch liquorice sweets. At Eggerode I stay in hotel Tegeler, well known to me. It is funny to stay in a hotel so near home; it gives me a feeling of being an important dignitary.

Final questions and conclusions begin to assault me. For nine months I have been living outside the fishbowl of my own world, vulnerable. All those days I have been thinking with two feet on the ground, praying with my eyes open. That shakes you up. I feel at home in many forms of atheism. I often felt that by learning Saint Mark's gospel by heart I had put on a lifejacket. Saint Mark's gospel moves me profoundly. It is a short but complete compendium of faith, the faith of Peter, of Mark and of other disciples of Jesus. It is a tightly composed narrative, a true short story with an immense penetration.

I have seen also how many people there are who are looking for authentic values and feel inspired by Jesus, even though they are "not practising" any more. What a horrible expression that is. Is it still being used? Formerly it referred to people who did not go to Sunday Mass. By making "practising the gospel" to be identical with "going to church on Sundays" the church brought upon herself a serious narrowing of the arteries, a calcification even, a high blood pressure that had little relevance to the spirit of the gospel.

How awfully badly the Christian churches are faring! The throngs of runaway sheep are immense. What caused this? Prosperity? On the wall of a respectable German restaurant I found written: ADVERSITY BREEDS HE-MEN; PROSPERITY BREEDS MISFITS. I can't believe that that is true. How the faithful have tried to be good, also in times of prosperity. All along the roads you find the traces of their faith and their loyalty: crucifixes, devout texts, reminders of parish "missions", parish schools, parish hospitals, parish halls. All the ruined churches have been restored; they have never been so splendid – and so empty.

At the same time we must not make things worse than they are. In the past people made a mistake by equating the new kingdom of the gospel to going to church. Jesus has given us a very clear warning not to do that. In the New Covenant the temple – the church building – as God's favourite dwelling place will disappear; instead God will make His abode in the heart of each person. There you find the temple of the New Covenant: the dwelling place of the Father, the dwelling place of the Son, the dwelling place of the Holy Spirit. In the course of the centuries this vision of Jesus was lost sight of to make room again for the restored primacy of the temple in the form of sacred church buildings. It is true, these temples are growing empty; but I have not at all noticed that the gospel was disappearing from the hearts of the people. I would say: on the contrary. Everywhere I met many people in whose hearts the dimensions of the gospel were even more visible than in former times: a readiness to help the weak, to respect the honest opinions of others, to make justice grow on earth, to respect everybody's human dignity, to treat creation with respect.

All this does not take away from the fact that the old familiar church in the West is sinking fast. It is not a surprise. During the Neo-Scholastic restoration they did not stow the cargo of the ship called church in the right way, despite all good intentions: no good balance was reached, too much was stored on the deck, too little deep down in the hold. They reached back too eagerly to the Middle Ages, they invested too little in contemporary reality. It was a restoration, not a renewal.

Pre-Vatican II Catholicism, it was so promising and so genuine on all levels of the faithful. The burning fire of inspiration swept through the ranks of the people, aroused contagious enthusiasm and brought them to great deeds. It had true depth; its depth also appears today from the numbed bewilderment and disillusionment on the part of so many elderly faithful as they see what has happened to their beloved religion. But much of the deep draught of the ship had been caused by the heavy stuff piled up on the deck.

Leaders of the catholic community have not been sufficiently alert to read the writing on the wall: the loss of the industrial proletariat, the rightist predilection of farmers, the support for fascism in Italy, Spain and Germany given by many committed faithful and not rarely by church authorities. Then already the cargo began to shift.

Authentic renewal has started, but only just. It should not be a nostalgic return to safe orthodoxy but rather a sincere dialogue among people: a sympathetic dialogue with all of today's people who are of good will, with the immense multitude of those that have a soft spot for Jesus in their hearts. We should entertain a loving dialogue with all major religions whereby the gospel should not be made to serve as a Procrustus-bed on which those faiths can be cut down or stretched out to reach our familiar size. What we need as well is an honest dialogue with our own religious past, whereby the past should not be put into the place of the living Spirit. Once again the gospel should be sown as seed on new and distant fields. And finally we should dare to start a courageous dialogue with our own selves. We have to find out where we have worn thin. We have to make a careful catalogue of our religious wardrobe.

Faith dresses itself up in images. We used to have an extensive wardrobe: images of a Creator of Heaven and Earth, of Adam and Eve, of the First Sin, of Redemption, of Heaven. Without those images you cannot tell the story of Christianity. But our culture has lost those images. Our culture now has different images: of evolution, of the male being derived from the female rather than the other way round, of science unmasking disease, of psychology discovering the ground plan of the soul, of technique penetrating the macrocosm as well as the microcosm. These new images do not fit into our old wardrobe; so we feel naked. Without images vision becomes blurred, active engagement becomes a pipe dream, committed church membership becomes impossible, and we ourselves become religious nudists. This may be exciting for a short time but it makes it impossible for us to move around. What we need very sorely is a new wardrobe of contemporary religious images.

How do we get new religious images? For that we need prophets: children and drunkards that speak the truth, poets that tease and caress, women that cannot keep their mouths shut, theologians that have to try and systematise the confusion of the Holy Spirit, mystics that balance on the edge of heresy. May there be room for prophets in today's church. May church leaders not monopolise the Holy Spirit may they be ready to give Him free access to the ordinary faithful.

A fundamental theme in the gospel of Mark is that the new Spirit will drive out old depravity; and that this new Spirit is like the spirit of the children and the powerless. He who aims at a spirit of power is bound to miss the mark. When Boniface hacked down the Irmin-trunk of the Saxons, he was really using a missionary method of the wrong spirit. The Crusades belonged to the wrong spirit. The secular power of church principalities belongs to the wrong spirit.

How can we undo all that? The Reformation was a determined effort; but Protestantism moved too far away from the spirit of the child. We should have the courage to entrust the gospel once again to the child inside us. And that should become a magic adventure. At Lippstadt I spent much time in a huge funfair. All the latest technical refinements were there: a dizzying Ferris Wheel of 44 metres high, a spine-chilling roller coaster with built-in infernal pandemonium, a sickening aerial spinner flinging people into space to the accompaniment of flashing and unnerving lights. Can Theology really do nothing with all that? See that festive merry-go-round full of toddlers who wave excitedly to their daddies and moms from a dream world every time they come round: no use at all for catechesis? See how everybody walks at a fair: quietly and almost solemnly, as if they were celebrating a liturgy, with a tiny spark and a hardly perceptible smile in their eyes.

Does that not have the makings of a parable?

Santa Clause or Saint Nicholas belongs to the world of the child. Saint Nicholas is a true parable. There are two Santa Clauses: the one of children that believe in him and the one of those children that have gone through the crisis of faith and do not believe in him any more. The first one is nothing more than a magician. As for the second, when the child loses his faith in the magician, he is upset for a short while but then he becomes a fervid participant of the second Saint Nicholas, and that is the real one. I can see a clear parallel there with our Christian commitment. If we dare to entrust the gospel to the child in us, that child will teach us gently not to leave miracles to chance but to let them happen secretly in the lives of others.

Nietzsche's Zarathustra says that if man is to find salvation, he has to become a poet, a solver of riddles and a liberator of chance: by taking the responsibility for chance happenings upon himself.

This long journey on foot has caused many beautiful thoughts about God to be brought to the surface. Rilke has a poem that celebrates how a growing knowledge of God could mean a strange and adventurous voyage. This is how he addresses God.

Who first detects the marks you leave,
Him hinder neighbours and the clock:
he walks, bent down over your track
like someone burdened or bereaved.
But soon he lifts his searching gaze;
he feels the winds, sees distant paths,
he hears you whispered by the haze,
and serenaded by the stars;
you stay forever in his heart,
all creatures seem your hiding place.

To him you seem a novel dream
about a great and magic trip:
he travels in a silent ship

286

on an expansive scenic stream.
And on the banks he is passing by
he sees the towns rise to the sky;
they come to greet his wanderings
with festive flapping of their wings.

The boat turns sometimes to a beach
where no one lives; some empty strand
lies waiting, at the waters' reach,
for those that have no fatherland.
There stand some chariots they will need
each drawn by three young steeds that chase
the setting sun with breathless speed
by paths that no man can retrace.

(Rainer Maria Rilke, *Das Stundenbuch*: 'Du meinst die Demut')

For cyclists, a special path has been set out from Munster to Holland. It is pretty but in many places the written signs have been destroyed or obliterated. At Altstaette, I sleep in style for the last time, in the Bradeck Bakker hotel. To finish my telephone card I send a last call to Anjelina in Austria to let her know that her smoked ham provided me with a lovely daily snack.

If I were to tie together all the words that passed through my mind during this trip, the body of my thoughts would not fit faultlessly into the traditional ecclesiastical frame. But it is my sincere conviction that the traditional ecclesiastical frame is not always in alignment with the Gospel. An outstanding example of this is the way authority is exercised in the church. Improvement is long overdue there and may take a long time: *ecclesia semper reformanda est*. In all honesty we cannot see that this improvement is taking place yet. At the same time I have to admit that I cannot function properly as a worker in the church if I do not fit into the church frame. Here lies a dilemma. There are some that throw in the towel at this point. A more elegant solution should be possible.

Perhaps we can learn from Simone Weil. She was outside the church and felt a strong pull to join the church. But some aspects of that church upset her so much that she could not stomach them. She took up the following position. She remained outside the church, in enemy territory so to say, but as an undercover agent of the Gospel. That gives me an idea. I will not take up a position outside the church structures; but if I stress some of my convictions too strongly they will land me outside those structures. Most certainly I will not forsake the Gospel the way I understand it in all personal honesty. What if I stay firmly inside the church and at the same time work there as an undercover agent of the Gospel? As peaceful as a dove and as clever as a snake? Words of Jesus Himself.

On 1ˢᵗ November I cross the border of the Netherlands again, the land of the big windows, the land where you have to make appointments for everything: even for appointments. And the land of the salt herrings with onions. Friends and relatives wait for me at the border and give me a treat of this national delicacy. We all foot it to Hengelo to complete the last 15 kilometres of the planned 6,000.

The arrival is eerie; as if it is not happening in actual fact. My feelings of this last day resemble those of the first day: all this is not true, really, it is far too unusual. But true it is. This whole adventure should remain true in the shape of a story: I must write it down properly.

I have walked for nine months on end, 6,000 kilometres without missing a single metre. Nine months of unimaginable luxury, of shameless pig-headedness, of just doing what I wanted to do. Of dwelling endlessly on thoughts, catching words that pass by. Of dream visits to the past. Of intently peering at the future. Of trying to touch the intangible, hearing the footsteps behind the closed door, listening to melodies hummed in the tonality of silence.

The prosthesis has held. I am back in one piece. Although, "back" does not really exist.

The Eighteenth Synod of the Archdiocese of New York:
Perspectives on the Theology of the Local Church and its History
Father Pat F. Rossi

If the definition of papal infallibility at Vatican Council I (1869 – 1870) can be viewed as the culmination of certain ultramontane tendencies within nineteenth century Roman Catholicism, then it might likewise be said that the ecclesiology of Vatican Council II (1962 – 1965) represented an attempt, by that same Church, to balance an earlier centrist ecclesiology with a more distinctively collaborative model.

This collaborative model, which was articulated at Vatican Council II, can be seen as having completed a task largely unfinished, in the previous Council, by more clearly formulating the nature of episcopal ministry within the Church while also reemphasizing the notion of communio as a model for shared ministry in the Church.

An effort to incorporate the ecclesiological insights of Vatican Council II, within the life of the local - diocesan church, was undertaken by the Archdiocese of New York when it convened its Eighteenth Diocesan Synod. This synod, which reflected the conciliar notion of communio, likewise attempted to revitalize the local church, through a collegial expression of shared pastoral renewal. The goal of this proposed "experiment in ecclesiology" continues to challenge all those responsible for the implementation of conciliar ecclesiology at the local-diocesan level.

This work, which represents an integrated study of a unique historical event in the life and mission of a given local - church, may also provide a paradigm by which to contextualize the history of a particular church within the overall mission of the Church Universal.

Size: 234mm x 156mm
Binding: Harback with Dust Jacket

Pages: 183
ISBN: 978-1-906561-31-4

£13.99

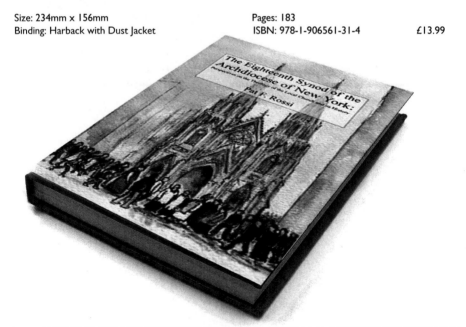

St Thomas' Place, Ely, Cambridgeshire CB7 4GG, UK
www.melrosebooks.com   sales@melrosebooks.com

MELROSE BOOKS

If you enjoyed this book you may also like:

Sleepwalking
Celia De Piro

Sleepwalking is a remarkable collection from a writer of sustained poetic intelligence who has the scholarly knowledge to place her work in its literary and historical context. Faith and Art in the Age of the Image is an analysis of a crisis in our epoch. It challenges the popular science of Richard Dawkins, questioning its deceptive intellectual assumptions about faith and culture. As a Christian she examines the very concept of progress, describing consumer capitalism as a dream-filled sleep endangering the survival of specifically human values.

Size: 198mm x 129mm
Binding: Paperback

Pages: 224
ISBN: 978-1-906561-49-9

£9.99

St Thomas' Place, Ely, Cambridgeshire CB7 4GG, UK
www.melrosebooks.com   sales@melrosebooks.com